# Folk Art of the Andes

# Folk Art of the Andes

By Barbara Mauldin

Photography by Blair Clark

Museum of International Folk Art

Museum of New Mexico Press
Santa Fe

# Contents

7    Foreword

9    Acknowledgments

13    Introduction

## Part I
# Religious Folk Art

25    POPULAR SAINTS

27    POPULAR RELIGIOUS PAINTINGS

33    RELIGIOUS SCULPTURE

46    PORTABLE ALTARS

62    HOLY CROSS AND CRUCIFIX

69    RELIQUARIES

71    SCAPULARS AND RELIGIOUS BADGES

73    MILAGROS

80    STONE AMULETS

86    CONOPAS

90    RITUAL OFFERINGS

93    EKEKO

## Part II
# Textiles and Costumes

98    MEN'S PONCHOS

104    WOMEN'S MANTLES

108    WOMEN'S OVERSKIRTS

110    CARRYING CLOTHS

111    WOVEN BAGS

116    WOMEN'S HEADBANDS

117    BELTS

120    ANIMAL ORNAMENTS

123    WOMEN'S ADAPTATION OF EUROPEAN-STYLE CLOTHING

134    KNITTING

140    LOOPED FIBER BAGS

141    DOUBLE BAGS

142    EMBROIDERED COSTUMES

145    FEATHERWORK

Part III
# A Diversity of Folk Art

150     JEWELRY

161     STAFFS

163     WOODWORK

166     LEATHER AND HIDE TRUNKS

168     MAJOLICA

172     CARVED GOURDS

178     FLASKS AND DRINKING CUPS

180     SILVERWORK

188     MINER'S LAMPS

189     TINWORK

191     CEREMONIAL DRINKING VESSELS

199     HOUSE BLESSING ORNAMENTS

206     FIGURES FROM EVERYDAY LIFE

215     TOYS

222     PAINTED SCENES OF DAILY LIFE

229     PORTABLE BOXES WITH MINIATURE SCENES

Part IV
# Festivals and Masquerade

238     FESTIVALS AND MASQUERADE IN THE CUZCO REGION OF PERU

246     CORPUS CHRISTI FESTIVALS AND MASQUERADE IN THE CENTRAL HIGHLANDS OF ECUADOR

254     CARNIVAL AND MASQUERADE IN ORURO, BOLIVIA

263     FESTIVAL MASKS

269     FESTIVAL SCENES


273     Glossary

279     Notes

289     Bibliography

299     Index

# Foreword

The artistic legacy of the South American Andean region, extending from prehispanic indigenous times through the Spanish Colonial period and into the present, is recognized as being among the leading artistic traditions in the world. Thus it is no surprise that the Museum of International Folk Art has long had a committed interest in the folk arts and their makers from the Andean region. Considered one of the museum's premier collections, it numbers some six thousand objects and textiles, dating mainly from the nineteenth, twentieth, and twenty-first centuries.

But numbers alone do not tell the full story of the museum's involvement with the folk art and people of the Andes. The Museum of International Folk Art is one of only two museums in the United States to have a dedicated Curator of Latin American Folk Art, Barbara Mauldin, who has been traveling to Latin America and actively engaging with its artists for nearly two decades. In addition, it is fortunate that the museum is located in a state where the Hispano language and cultures make it a comfortable place for Andean artists to come and work for months at a time, then return home with the proceeds from their efforts. For example, Bertha Medina, from Cochas Chico Huancayo, a small village high in the Andes of Peru, spends several months each year in Santa Fe carving and selling her gourds, each of which tells a story of daily life in the Peruvian Andes. She is the second generation of her family to do so, as her world-famous father, Evaristo Medina, also traveled to Santa Fe in the last quarter of the twentieth century with his intricately carved gourds. In fact, Bertha has identified work by three generations of her family in the museum's collection.

This book, and its accompanying exhibition, allows the museum, for the first time, to show a sampling of its collection that reflects the full spectrum of the folk arts of this region. However, it is more than a catalog of artworks. Author and curator Barbara Mauldin has tackled a large and complex cultural geography. The folk arts encompass all major media, from ceramics to metal to wood to textiles. Mauldin leads us into this remote and mountainous region through thematic sections that offer comparisons of the objects and illuminate their relationships to the lives of the people who made and used them. Even in the twenty-first century, in many instances these folk arts continue to be integral to the lives of the makers, their families, and their communities. But there have also been successful transitions, whereby traditional folk arts have been retooled for sale to people beyond the mountain villages through such organizations as the Centro de Textiles Tradicionales del Cusco in Peru, a women's weaving cooperative founded in 2005 by Nilda Callañaupa Alvarez. The daughter of a Quechuan master weaver, she began spinning alpaca and sheep's wool at age six and started weaving at age seven. She worried that the weaving was dying out, explaining, "It was something that was practiced by the very traditional elders . . . no more by the young people. The young people were changing so fast. We were realizing how much we were losing from our cultural heritage. So that's when I came up with the idea to create the center." Today the center includes more than 350 weavers and has a shop in Cuzco that sells their textiles, with the proceeds going to the cooperative, the weavers, and their communities. In this way the weaving continues to support the families while sustaining their cultural heritage.

Florence D. Bartlett, the founder of the Museum of International Folk Art, in 1953, expressed the desire to support the traditional folk arts of the world by sharing them with visitors from around the globe. Embedded in her intentions was a vision that the museum would become the catalyst for creating a bond between the peoples of the world through their traditional arts. From the beginning, this museum has understood that the art remains a true gift offered to future generations in the spirit of generosity, hope, and peace.

Marsha C. Bol,
Director
Museum of International Folk Art

# Acknowledgments

My interest in Andean folk art began in the late 1980s when I worked as an assistant curator at the Museum of International Folk Art. After being appointed Curator of Latin American Folk Art in 1991, I was able to focus more attention on the wealth of Andean materials in MOIFA's collection. My first field trips were to Ecuador in the mid-1990s and later I conducted research in Bolivia, Peru, and Venezuela. I became fascinated with the intermixing of Indian and European artistic and cultural traditions in Andean folk art and in 2003 I decided to produce an exhibition and publication of this material. Eventually I focused on textiles and objects from the nineteenth and twentieth centuries, the period after South Americans gained their independence from Spain and Andean folk art flourished in a more open environment. I have not attempted to present an exhaustive study of materials from all ethnic groups in all regions but rather to show the highlights of Andean folk art represented in MOIFA's collection and in other public and private collections in New Mexico and other parts of the United States.

Much appreciation goes to Laurel Seth, executive director of the International Folk Art Foundation, and to the IFAF Board of Trustees, who generously funded my fieldwork for this project and provided financial support for the exhibition and catalog. The Folk Art Committee of the Museum of New Mexico Foundation also contributed valuable funds. I want to thank Connie Thrasher Jaquith, who has been one of my major supporters since I began talking about the Andes project and has donated funds for acquisitions and to help produce the exhibition.

Although the text in the essays and captions for this publication has been intentionally condensed, a great deal of time and research went into compiling the information. I am indebted to a number of scholars whose works are listed in the bibliography. Since some of the categories of folk art included in the book and exhibition have not been well documented in published materials, I interviewed many people who willingly shared their knowledge and helped me conduct my own fieldwork.

Among these are colleagues in the United States who have spent many years working with Andean folk arts, including Martha Egan, Patricia La Farge, Jonathan Williams, Enrique Lamadrid,

Andrea Heckman, Marion Oettinger, Cynthia LeCount Samaké, and Leslie Goodman. In Peru I am indebted to John Alfredo Davis, Mari Solari, María Elena de Solar, Soledad Mujicay Bayly, Jaime and Vivian Lebano, Julío Cuba, Nilda Callañaupa, Pedro and Javier Gonzáles, the Jiménez Quispe family, Julio Urbano Rojas, Bertha Medina, and Pompeyo Berrocal Evanán. In Bolivia I was assisted by Ryan Taylor, Peter McFarren, Gale Hoskins, Mariam Rojas, Freddy Taboada Tellez, Arthur Tracht, Mercedes Ranjel, Elizabeth Rojas, Elizabeth Torres, and Ramiro Molina Rivero. In Ecuador I was helped by María del Pilar de Cevallos, Marcelo Naranjo, Claudio Malo, Ricardo Muratorio, Gloria Anhalzer, Gloria Pesántaz de Moscoso, Amado Ruiz, José Ignacio Criollo, and Juan Antonio Supligüicha. In Venezuela I want to thank William and Marisol Hamilton, Glenda Mendoza, María Teresa López, Gladys Mendoza de Gonzalo, Carol Cañizares, the staff at Fundación Bigott, Mario Calderon, Ramon Antonio Moreno, and Mariano Rangel.

Although limited by space in the book, the field photographs I was able to use add another important level of information. I want to thank the people who provided these outstanding photographs, including Johan Reinhart, Andrea Heckman, Shari Kessler, Peter McFarren, Bruce Takami, A. Tim Wells, Luis González, and Robert Jerome. I am also indebted to the San Antonio Museum of Art, the Museo de Arte de Lima, the Instituto Cultural Peruana Norteamericano, the Banco Central de Bolivia, and the Quipus Foundation for providing images of featured artwork not photographed here in the museum.

We are fortunate to have collectors in the United States who have acquired wonderful examples of Andean folk art and were willing to loan some of their pieces for the Andes project. These include Paul and Elissa Cahn, Jonathan Williams and Kisla Jiménez, Bob and Gay Sinclair, David and Mayi Munsell, Andrea Heckman, Patricia La Farge, Leslie Goodman, Earl and Shari Kessler, and Sue Stevens. The San Antonio Museum of Art also generously loaned one important piece.

The majority of items featured in the exhibition and catalog were drawn from the holdings in the Museum of International Folk Art. Over the past seventy years, the International Folk Art Foundation has purchased hundreds of outstanding examples of Andean folk art for its collection (housed at MOIFA), many of which were selected for the project. An impressive group of nineteenth- and twentieth-century items were donated by the museum's founder, Florence Dibell Bartlett. Additionally, many important mid-twentieth-century items featured in the project were donated by the Girard Foundation, and others came from Lloyd Cotsen and the Neutrogena Corporation. Numerous individuals have also contributed to the collection of Andean folk art at MOIFA. Some of the more recent donations came from Peter Cecere, Connie Thrasher Jaquith, Jonathan Williams and Kisla Jiménez, Laurie Adelson and Bruce Takami, William Siegal, Nancy Reynolds, and Hank Lee and Paul Bonin-Rodriguez.

Many members of MOIFA's staff helped the Folk Art of the Andes project come to fruition. Former director Joyce Ice supported my ideas from the beginning, and current director Marsha Bol continued that support and provided guidance as the project moved forward. Ruth LaNore, MOIFA's assistant curator, has been a major asset in helping me prepare the manuscript and exhibition. Ree Mobley, librarian and archivist, tracked down obscure references and acquired many books through interlibrary loans. The collections staff, registrar, and volunteers assisted with hundreds of acquisitions and in-loans of objects.

I am also indebted to staff members in various departments of the Museum Resources of the New Mexico Department of Cultural Affairs (DCA) who helped with different aspects of the Andes project. The Director for Museum Resources, Barbara Anderson, was very supportive from the beginning and willingly read and commented on an early draft of a few sections of the manuscript. I particularly want to thank Blair Clark, the Museum/DCA photographer, who spent several months in the studio photographing the objects and then additional time processing the digital images that appear in this book. Mary Wachs, editorial director, Museum of New Mexico Press, coordinated the various aspects of bringing the publication to completion. Margaret Moore Booker did a thorough job of copyediting and creating the index, and Deborah Reade designed and produced the intricate maps. David Skolkin, art director for the MNM Press, created the design format for the book, and Mary Sweitzer, graphic designer, did a beautiful job laying out each page.

The conservation staff, Museum/DCA, spent a considerable amount of time stabilizing and restoring a number of pieces I selected for the project. Anya McDavis-Conway did a great job conducting the survey of objects and carrying out many of the conservation treatments. In addition, for several months Larry Humetewa dedicated himself to restoring many pieces with skillful attention to detail. Maureen Russell, Conor McMahon, Beth Rydzewski, and Rebecca Tinkham also assisted with this work.

Nancy Allen, exhibition designer with the Museum/DCA Exhibitions Department, created the complex floor plans with numerous cases and fanciful architectural details, and designed the layout and display for 850 plus objects that were installed in two large galleries at MOIFA. Jay Pearson, exhibition preparator on MOIFA's staff, oversaw the mount making and installation of the pieces, and designed the lighting in the galleries. The fabricators and preparators on the Museum/DCA exhibitions staff also assisted with this work. Tom McCarthy, videographer, edited and produced the short video programs shown in one of the galleries. Monica Meehan, graphic designer with the Museum/DCA Marketing and Outreach Department, oversaw the design, production, and installation of the text, captions, and other graphic elements in the show.

I also thank several close friends for their moral support and patience while I was busy focusing on the Andes project over the past few years. I am particularly indebted to Andrew Mauldin, who carefully read the manuscript for the catalog at various stages in its evolution and provided valuable editorial comments and corrections. He also volunteered to work with the collection and assisted me with other aspects of the project. Finally I want to acknowledge the folk artists who produced the variety of beautiful work illustrated in this publication and the Andean people who adapted to changing circumstances and were able to keep their rich culture and spirit alive.

# Introduction

The Andes is the great mountain range of South America that extends along the western coast of the continent. It is separated into three natural regions, with the north running through Venezuela and Colombia and the south through parts of Argentina and Chile. The central area encompasses the highlands of Bolivia, Peru, and Ecuador.

The central region was the most important for the evolution of prehispanic Andean cultures. Tiahuanacan people built an urban center just south of Lake Titicaca, where they flourished, spreading out over much of the central Andes from AD 500 to AD 1200. After the collapse of that empire, a number of independent rival states emerged. Aymara-speaking groups were in southern Peru and Bolivia, while other tribes were living in the highlands of central and northern Peru and Ecuador. One of these regional groups, the Quechua-speaking Inca, was based in Cuzco. In the early fifteenth century, its ruler used military force to begin expanding his kingdom; by 1528, his heirs had conquered all of the territory from northern Chile and Argentina in the south to the Colombian border with Ecuador in the north.[1]

Spanish conquistadores reached the Andes in 1526, and by the 1530s the Europeans had conquered the Inca and were in control of most of the ethnic groups living throughout the vast territory. They introduced many aspects of their own culture, including the Spanish language and Roman Catholic religion. They also brought new food crops and domesticated animals, along with a variety of sophisticated technologies and tools. The indigenous people were once again forced to submit to a powerful force; some tried to resist. In 1569 Francisco Toledo became the viceroy for Peru and the surrounding region, and he began implementing a series of ordinances aimed at resolving problems with the Indian population. As part of this, many groups were forced to move from their rural homes to Spanish-colonial cities and towns.[2]

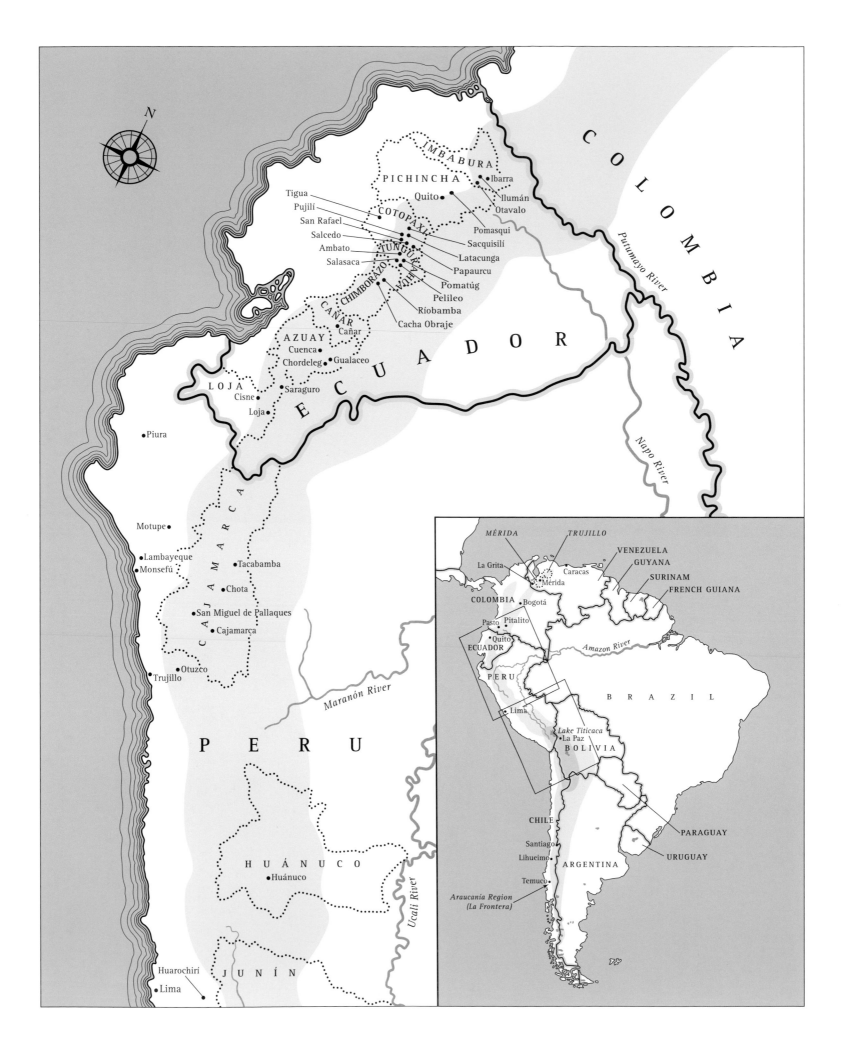

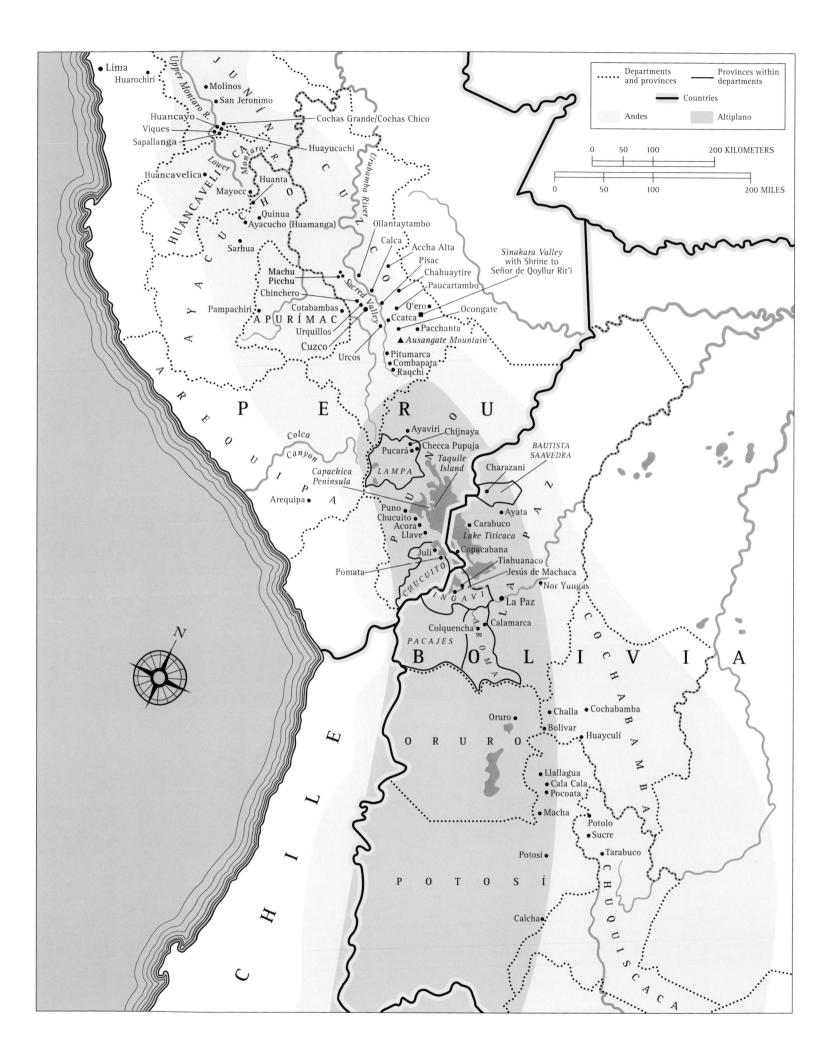

A strict class system was also imposed within the new colonial society. The elite were Europeans who came to the Andes to help form the colony and establish a better life for themselves. The next tier down were *criollos* (creoles) descended from European parents but born in the Americas. Members of the Inca royal families living in Cuzco and other towns were also granted upper-class status and allowed to wear elite European clothing.[3] Below these groups were the Indians, who fell into three categories. The top were the *mestizos/mestizas*. In some cases, they were offspring of Spaniards and Indian women, but most were indigenous people living in colonial cities and towns who had adopted a European lifestyle and clothing of the Spanish middle class. Mestizas generally served as domestics in upper-class homes. The men were skilled workers who served as foremen for building projects, or as assistants in European studios that produced artwork for the Catholic churches. By the late sixteenth and early seventeenth centuries, many mestizos were running their own workshops.

The social classes below mestizos were the Indians who had been forced to resettle in colonial centers, or had moved there for other reasons. Many men were sent to Spanish mining towns, where they worked under stringent conditions to extract and process ore. In other cities, male Indians assisted Europeans and mestizos with a variety of work, such as building, making paintings and sculptures, and other types of crafts. Indian women often functioned as market vendors and developed networks to acquire food and other products from the countryside to sell for profit in town. Indians living in the colonial cities wore clothing modeled after the Spanish lower class, but they still spoke their native languages along with some Castilian. They also retained many of their indigenous cultural practices, including Andean religious beliefs and rituals that were hidden under the guise of Catholicism.

Indians who continued living in small rural communities, herding animals and growing crops, were at the bottom of the social scale. For the most part, these *campesinos* wore their traditional

FIG. 1-1 Melchor María Mercado, *Koya Runas, Mestizos e Indios.* Potosí, Bolivia, 1849. Watercolor, paper. Collection of the Archivo Nacional de Bolivia.

This watercolor portrays different classes of indigenous people in the Spanish city of Potosí, Bolivia. On the left a miner works while a woman and child pass into the background. An inscription below—*Koya* (Colla) *Runas*—refers to their Aymara Indian heritage. In the center is a mestiza in her Spanish-style costume. On the right are an indigenous man and two women dressed in a combination of European and traditional forms of clothing.

FIG. 1-2 Melchor María Mercado, *Cholos y Mestizas*. Cochabamba, Bolivia, 1850. Watercolor, paper. Collection of the Archivo Nacional de Bolivia.

A chola and cholo in the city of Cochabamba, Bolivia, are portrayed on the left side of this watercolor. They are wearing the clothing styles that had evolved for indigenous people of their class. The women in the center and right side of the painting are mestizas wearing slightly more elegant garments, while the woman between them is dressed in a more traditional Indian costume and holds a drop spindle.

clothing until the late eighteenth century, when they were forced to adopt a Spanish peasant-style costume. They spoke their prehispanic languages and continued to live a traditional lifestyle as best they could. This included carrying out a mixture of Catholic and Andean religious practices, as well as producing weaving, pottery, and other forms of arts and crafts. A small percentage of the lower-class population also included *mulatos* or *zambos*—descendants of African slaves, Spaniards, and/or Indians.[4]

In the early nineteenth century, criollos in various parts of the Andes began to organize an independence movement to free themselves of the Spanish Crown that charged heavy taxes and controlled their business enterprises. This led to a series of battles against the Spanish military with troops consisting of criollos, mestizos, Indians, and mulattos. By 1829, they had succeeded in ridding themselves of the European authorities and began to form independent nations.

Campesinos in rural communities were no longer suppressed by the colonial system and began incorporating more of the European material culture into their traditional way of life. Meanwhile, indigenous people still living in the old colonial centers started to develop a stronger identity within that social structure. The Aymara in cities of southern Peru and Bolivia adopted the names *cholo* (for men) and *chola* (for women), and eventually these terms spread to other regions of Peru and Ecuador.[5]

Within this post-Independence environment, folk art began to flourish. Mestizo, cholo, and rural indigenous artists were freer to create things for their own use, or for trade to a broader market.[6] Much of the work produced reflected the impact of European artwork and utilitarian products that had permeated the colonial Andes. A wide variety of folk art was made for use in indige-

Catholic/Andean religious practices; originating in the late seventeenth century, these practices were carried out more openly in the nineteenth. The ritual objects that were made ranged from paintings, sculptures, and portable altars featuring Catholic saints to stone amulets and ceramic figures of domesticated animals.

Weaving had been the most important art form among prehispanic Andean ethnic groups. Production continued under the Spanish, but much of it went to colonial authorities as part of the tribute system. The nineteenth century saw a renaissance in traditional weaving. Quechua women in the Department of Cuzco, as well as Aymara and Quechua weavers of southern Peru and Bolivia, created beautiful ponchos, mantles, belts, bags, and other items. The European-style costumes imposed on cholos and Indians during colonial times were adapted to their sense of fashion and made their own. Knitting, introduced by the Spanish, became an important technique utilized by indigenous men to make caps that they wore as a form of ethnic identity and pride. Embroidery was another innovation adopted from the Europeans that added lively and colorful decoration to clothing and other items. Jewelry worn by mestiza, chola, and indigenous women in some areas also became more elaborate, much of it influenced by adornment used by the Spanish elite. Festivals were carried out with great joy, and the costumes and masquerades of the performers often made fun of the Spanish oppressors.

During the colonial era, workshops produced diverse items for churches and private homes using silver, wood, gourds, leather, clay, and other materials. Mestizos, and some Indians, began running many of these shops in the late sixteenth and seventeenth centuries, passing them down through generations of their families. In the nineteenth century, they were able to broaden their market, fabricating a variety of beautiful and useful objects for mestizos, cholos, and indigenous families living in the rural communities. Folk artists in cities and smaller towns also enjoyed making toys for children based on European models. The nineteenth century saw development of the European interest in *costumbrismo*—learning about the customs, dress, and daily activities of people in cities and rural communities in other parts of the world. This curiosity encouraged artists in different regions of the Andes to create paintings and sculpture that depicted festivals, ceremonies, and scenes of everyday life. Much of this folk art continued to thrive into the twentieth century, and some forms are still made today.

The *Folk Art of the Andes* exhibition and catalog highlights the abundance of folk art made in the Andes in the nineteenth and twentieth centuries. Some pieces from prehispanic and colonial times are included, along with a few examples from the twenty-first century. Most of the material is from the central Andean countries of Bolivia, Peru, and Ecuador, but a few items from Venezuela, Colombia, Chile, and Argentina are also shown. This folk art reflects aspects of the interweaving of Indian and European cultural traditions, while providing windows into the rich spirit and aesthetics shared by the Andean people.

# Folk Art of the Andes

# Religious Folk Art

S oon after the Spanish conquest of Cuzco, in 1533, the Europeans dismantled the political and religious stronghold of the Inca Empire that had spread through much of the central Andean highlands. Underneath the imperial network were a variety of ethnic groups made up of small kinship communities, known in the Quechua language as *ayllu*. Each community's identity was focused on the land that was held in common. They also shared ritual responsibilities connected with the cycle of producing food and other goods, as well as reproduction of families and their herds.

Everyone in the ayllu was descended from a common ancestor and natural formations on the property, called *huaca* or *wak'a*, were thought to possess the life and personality of that person or another important relative from the past. The huaca were regarded as hero-gods who had lived through great exploits and then turned themselves to stone to guard the resources they had created for their people. Representing prosperity and good fortune, the huaca at times would communicate with their kinsmen to solve problems and help the overall well-being of the group.

The regional ethnic groups also worshipped a pantheon of deities generally known as *apu*, who were thought to control various aspects of the natural world around them. The apu resided in special rock formations, mountains, lakes, rivers, and other natural phenomena. The people sought to keep a harmonious relationship with these gods through offerings and special ceremonies. Often a group pilgrimage would visit the apu's site, where religious specialists, or shamans, would carry out the appropriate rituals and the people would pay tribute with drinking, feasting, and dance performances.[1]

Catholic priests arrived from Europe in the first decade after the conquest and spread out into the highland territory to convert the Andean people to Christianity. They were confronted by the existing religious practices, which they viewed as the work of the devil, and began a campaign to replace them with Catholic beliefs and rituals. They sought out shrines to important Andean gods

FIG. 2-1 *Sacred ceremony in which a stone, representing the sacred deity of a quarry, is dressed in a small poncho and coca bags and given ceremonial staffs and offerings.* Colquencha, La Paz, Bolivia, 1988. Photograph by Johan Reinhard.

and substituted the prehispanic idols with images of Catholic saints. Initially, Catholic religious artwork was imported from Spain, but soon studios were established in some larger cities to create paintings and sculptures for Catholic institutions and elite European and criollo colonists. Eventually, other workshops were set up where mestizo and indigenous artists produced less expensive religious imagery to serve the needs of rural communities..

As Christian missionaries moved out into the countryside, they established churches in larger towns and assigned Catholic saints as their patrons. Along with this they brought in small sculptures of the patrons, as well as other Catholic images, to help in their teaching. The priests also introduced the Catholic festival calendar and encouraged the Indians to perform their traditional dances and songs for Catholic feast day observances. However, with all of the changes taking place in the world around them, the Andean people felt the need to hold onto the practices they knew would help to ward off sickness, to bring rain for their fields, and to improve fertility for themselves and their herds. They were willing to add representations of Christian supernatural forces to their collection of huacas, idols, and pantheon of deities but not to rely on them as replacements.[2]

By the late sixteenth century, Church authorities realized that their missionary work had not been entirely successful. A majority of the Andean communities were still carrying on much of their prehispanic religious practices under the guise of Christian rituals, festivals, and devotion to images of Catholic saints. This led to a concerted campaign through much of the seventeenth century to "extirpate idolatry" in all regions of the Andes. The huacas and mummy bundles of revered ancestors were destroyed and images of idols confiscated. The Indians were no longer allowed to perform their traditional dances for Catholic feast day observances but instead were forced to participate in processional dramas that told biblical stories about good and evil. The Church also banned the use of Christian images in any rituals being carried out by Andean religious practitioners.[3] During this period of extirpation, the unorthodox practices directed at both Andean ancestors and gods, and images of Catholic saints, went underground together and a stronger relationship was created between them.[4]

By the late seventeenth century, the Church began to change its approach, and there was more tolerance for the popular, or folk-style, Christian rituals and ceremonies practiced by indigenous communities. This opened the way for an even greater acceptance of Catholic saints in the lives of the Andean people. Because some Christian images gained reputations for performing miracles, their chapels and sanctuaries became important pilgrimage sites. The miraculous figures, along with Catholic images which stood over altars in every local church, came to be viewed as living presences with whom the Andeans could communicate through offerings, song, and dance. With the expulsion of the Jesuits in 1767, and the gradual secularization of the Catholic Church in the late seventeenth and eighteenth centuries, Indian communities took control of local churches and the images housed inside them. Following the Spanish *cofradía* system, religious brotherhoods were formed within communities to take care of the saints, raise funds, and carry out religious festivals and other activities. The brotherhoods paid Catholic *padres* to visit their community and perform required rituals, but the priests no longer had direct jurisdiction over the day-to-day operations of the church.

By the eighteenth century, Christianity had finally taken root in a way that served the needs of the Andeans as communities, families, and individuals. The mestizo and indigenous production of less expensive Catholic images continued, and most people could afford to acquire them. Catholic *santos* proliferated on home altars and were accepted as living personages with whom one could have a familial relationship. Candles were lighted and offerings made to ask for help with the needs of everyday life. During mass, or on special feast days, the small household images were taken to the local church to be blessed and to visit with the community's patron saint. At other times, the personal santo might be carried on a pilgrimage to visit the shrine of a Catholic saint famous for performing miracles. Small images of the miraculous figure could also be purchased at the site and brought back to place on the home altar.[5]

Alongside these folk Catholic practices, the Andean people continued to believe in their traditional gods and make offerings to pay tribute and ask for their help. A majority of the prehispanic huaca and mummy bundles had been destroyed by the Catholic priests, but the larger natural formations, such as mountains, lakes, and rivers, still existed and many people made annual pilgrimages to the special sites where the deities resided.[6] Most Andeans also continued to keep small stone amulets, known as *illas*, *chacras*, and *mesas,* and other stone or ceramic figures, called *conopas,* in their homes to use in ceremonies to assure the fertility and well-being of the family, herds, and crops.[7] Other materials were used to make special offerings to the gods, sometimes with the help of Andean ritual practitioners.[8]

This combination of religious beliefs and rituals endured throughout the remainder of European colonial rule in the Andes and made the transition into the Republican era of the nineteenth century. In many areas the leaders of the new countries disbanded the official Catholic institutions; by the late nineteenth and early twentieth century, the Andeans had even greater freedom to practice their religion more openly.[9] Much of the folk art produced during that time period for their altars, rituals, and public events has survived to this day. These items serve as inspiration for some religious folk art still made and used in the twenty-first century.

## Popular Saints

### VIRGIN MARY

Beginning in the sixteenth century, certain Catholic saints emerged as more important or more popular as they were incorporated into the Andean religious beliefs and ritual practices. The Virgin Mary was at the top of the list due to the fact that she was a woman, loving mother, and someone who could sympathize with pain and suffering. As a female deity she shared the role with the Andean goddess of the earth, Pachamama, in helping to bring fertility and well-being to families and their animals and crops. Following Catholic history and iconography, she appears in various roles such as the Virgin of the Immaculate Conception, of Sorrow, of the Rosary, of Mercy, and many more.[10] Each city and town throughout the Andes has churches and small chapels with images of the Virgin Mary that are lovingly taken care of and prayed to every day by devoted worshippers. Many of these figures are attributed with performing miracles.[11]

One of the most popular avocations in Spain and the Americas is the Virgin of Candlemas, or Virgen de la Candelaría, that portrays Mary undergoing the Jewish rite of purification when she presented herself and the baby Jesus in the temple, forty days after giving birth. She is shown holding her son in her left arm and a candle in her right hand, with a basket hanging from that arm containing two doves to be given as offerings. Forty days after December 25 is February 2 and that is the Catholic feast day for the annual celebration of the Virgen de la Candelaría, also known as the Virgin of Purification.[12] In the northern hemisphere this date coincides with the beginning of the spring planting season, while in the southern hemisphere it marks the beginning of the harvest.

There are many important Andean images of the Virgen de la Candelaría, such as La Virgen del Socavón in Oruro, Bolivia (figs. 2-6, 2-7, 2-61, 2-65), La Virgen de Cocharcas in Apurímac (figs. 2-22, 2-46), La Virgen de Chapi and La Virgen de Caymi in Arequipa, and La Virgen de la Candelaría in Puno, Peru.[13] One of the earliest and most famous Virgen de la Candelaría figures in the central Andes is housed in a sanctuary in the town of Copacabana, located on the southern shores of Lake Titicaca in Bolivia. In Inca times, this had been the last stop on the pilgrimage route to the sacred Island of the Sun. The statue was carved by a local descendent of the Inca rulers who traveled to Potosí and apprenticed under a Spanish sculptor to learn the skills to create the work. After being installed in a chapel in Copacabana in 1583, the Virgin started performing miracles, and soon her reputation spread, drawing pilgrims from all over the Andes. This led to the production of images of La Virgen de Copacabana sold at the site for pilgrims to take home with them (figs. 2-7, 2-21, 2-27, 2-28, 2-29, 2-30).[14]

Another highly revered image of the Virgin Mary is housed in the cathedral of the colonial city of La Plata, now called Sucre, in the Department of Chuquiscaca, in southern Bolivia (fig. 2-2).

FIG. 2-2 Diego de Ocaña, *Virgen de Guadalupe*. San Francisco Cathedral, Sucre, Chuquiscaca, Bolivia, 16th century. Paint on board, silver, and precious stones. Photograph by Barbara Mauldin.

This is a sixteenth-century painting done on board that was cut out in the profile of the front-facing figure. It was created by a priest, Diego de Ocaña, who wanted to promote the devotion to Santa María de Guadalupe housed in a monastery in Extremadura, Spain. Unlike the well-known image of Our Lady of Guadalupe in Mexico, the Spanish figure holds the Child Jesus in her left arm and a scepter in her right hand and both she and the Child are crowned and richly dressed. The original painting in Sucre closely follows that iconography, but the silver plating and hundreds of precious jewels attached to the form were added by local devotees. Like the figure in Copacabana, this image became known for performing miracles for the residents of Sucre and people living in the rural communities of that region.[15]

### ST. JAMES, OR SANTIAGO

The second most popular saint within the folk Catholic devotions in the Andes is St. James, or Santiago. As in Spain and elsewhere in the Americas, he was known as a valiant fighter on horseback who helped the Spaniards conquer the Moors and then the indigenous peoples in the New World. During a fierce battle between the Spanish and Incas in Cuzco in 1533, a thunderstorm moved in and a large lightning bolt hit one of the Inca buildings. The Spanish army saw it as a vision of Santiago and yelled his name in greeting to help their fight. This must have impressed the Andeans, who soon embraced this Catholic saint as a deity who could help them; within a few years after the conquest he began to be identified with the prehispanic god of lightning, known as Illpa. Many villages and districts in the Viceroyalty of Peru were given Santiago as their patron saint by the missionaries, and the indigenous people began conducting ceremonies to Illpa using the new image. Before long the Spanish realized what was happening and tried to stop it, but they were not effective. Mestizo and indigenous folk artists creating images of Santiago in the nineteenth and twentieth century continued to show the saint dressed as a Spanish warrior holding his sword and riding his horse over the bodies of the conquered (figs. 2-9, 2-10, 2-21, 2-32, 2-33, 2-35, 2-41, 2-62, 2-65). Over time Santiago also came to be viewed as the patron of horses and horseback riders, as well as the patron of all animals.[16]

### ST. ANTHONY, ST. MARK, ST. LUKE, ST. JOHN THE BAPTIST, VIRGIN OF CARMEN, AND ST. INEZ

One of the primary livelihoods of the prehispanic Andean people was raising alpaca and llama. After the conquest, European animals—mules, cattle, sheep, and goats—became an important part of their herds. Over time, certain saints were associated with helping the prosperity of specific types of animals, and by the nineteenth century these religious figures had become the dominant images used on home shrines. This tradition continued into the twentieth century and in some areas is still observed today.

Up until the 1940s, mule trains were used to transport goods all over the Andean highlands, and St. Anthony was known as the patron of mules and *arrieros*, traders who traveled with pack animals (figs. 2-1, 2-25, 2-36, 2-37, 2-42). Following the Catholic iconography of the evangelists, St. Mark was the patron of lions. As an extension of this, the Andeans saw him as the patron of all wild animals. St. Mark also came to represent the mountain spirits, or apu. St. Luke was the patron of cattle and bulls, however, in some regions Mark was also associated with the ownership and breeding of bovine animals (figs. 1-10, 1-14, 1-43, 2-44, 2-45). St. John the Baptist, who is always shown holding a lamb, was the patron of sheep (figs. 2-9, 2-10, 2-20, 2-22, 2-36, 2-43, 2-44, 2-45). The Virgin of Carmen also oversaw sheep as well as other animals, while St. Inez was generally recognized as the patron of goats (figs. 2-88). Slight variations to all of these assignments were found in different regions of the Andes.[17]

### ST. ISIDORE, OR SAN YSIDRO

Agriculture was the other important livelihood of the Andean people, and the Catholic saint of farmers, St. Isidore, or San Ysidro, was adopted as the patron of planting, care, and the harvest of crops. Images of him usually include two oxen used to plow the fields and sometimes an angel is also there to help (figs. 2-13, 2-14, 2-19, 2-25, 2-46).[18]

## Popular Religious Paintings

Workshops for producing religious paintings were established in Spanish colonial cities such as Lima, Quito, and Potosí, but Cuzco became one of the most prolific areas for the creation of these pieces. Initially, the studios were set up by European masters using local artists to carry out the work, but by the early eighteenth century mestizo and indigenous painters were operating their own workshops. Rather than follow the naturalistic features of the European models, they developed a distinctive style of painting that featured a flattened background and great attention to decorative detailing.[19] At first, the work was commissioned by Spanish and wealthy native patrons, but by the nineteenth century the clientele broadened to include members of the lower class, who wanted images for their own devotional practices. These paintings were usually smaller in size and often included portraits of the people who commissioned them. Artists in Bolivia also responded to the broadening market and began producing small religious paintings done in a simple style. Some of these were painted on boards, but in the mid-1800s sheets of tin or zinc became more common.[20]

During this time, artists in Cuzco and Bolivia began to incorporate scenes of everyday life, or costumbrismo, into their religious paintings. Some portrayed patriotic emblems of the new secular republics, while others showed masked dancers and festivals that were part of popular religious practices. Images of rural Andean life were portrayed alongside specific Catholic saints who had become important protectors for the farmers and animal herders.[21]

### PAINTINGS OF THE VIRGIN MARY

The Virgin Mary was one of the most popular subjects portrayed in small, nineteenth-century paintings produced in Cuzco and Bolivia. As stated earlier, the immense devotion to Mary by the Indian population was due to her association with Pachamama, the Andean goddess of the earth and fertility. The mountain form was one of the symbols for Pachamama; artists came to adopt a bell-shaped gown for the Virgin Mary that had the same shape. The fabrics of the cape and dress in these paintings were almost always painted with ornate decoration, accented by elaborate lace.[22]

FIG. 2-3 *Our Lady of the Angels of Urquillos.* Cuzco, Peru, 1855. Paint on metal, 7" x 5½" (17.8 x 14 cm). Gift of Florence Dibell Bartlett, MOIFA.

This image is a copy of a painting of the Virgin of the Angels that hangs in a chapel located on the grounds of an old hacienda called Urquillos, near Chinchero in the Department of Cuzco, Peru. By the eighteenth century, this Virgin had become known for performing miracles, and many devotees prayed to her for help in times of crisis. Some commissioned paintings from local artists and had themselves put in the picture as part of the *demanda*, or request. Here the petitioner is shown in the lower left corner dressed in festival masquerade and his name, Cipriano Talas, is inscribed across the bottom. As in the original painting, both sides of this panel depict scenes narrating some of the miracles the Virgin had performed, such as bringing a man back to life after being hit by lightning (upper left) and saving a woman from being stabbed to death by a man (upper right).[23]

FIG. 2-4 *Adoration of the Virgin in Death.* Cuzco, Peru, 19th century. Paint on wood, 6 ¾" x 11" (17.2 x 27.9 cm). Gift of Florence Dibell Bartlett, MOIFA.

This painting portrays the Adoration of the Virgin in Death with God the Father and the archangels San Miguel and San Gabriel looking down from heaven. The Virgin is lying on an awkwardly composed bed/altar placed in a local landscape with two devotees dressed in festival masquerades dancing around her.

FIG. 2-5 *Virgin.* Cuzco, Peru, 19th century. Paint on wood, 11½" x 8" (29.2 x 30.3 cm). Collection of Kisla Jiménez and Jonathan Williams.

Here the Virgin Mary is shown in a simple setting with the clouds of the Andean skies overhead. The devotees who commissioned the work are shown at her feet wearing festival costumes of *Ch'unchos*, a popular masquerade in the Cuzco region. The tunics, feathered headdresses, and bows and arrows characterize Indians from tropical forests of the Amazon, who once threatened indigenous people living in the Andes.

**FIG. 2-6** Attributed to Maestro de Arani, *Virgen del Socavón* and *Nuestra Señora de los Amparos*. Potosí or Cochabamba, Bolivia, mid-19th century. Paint on metal. Largest: 12" x 8 3/4" (30.5 x 22.2 cm). International Folk Art Foundation Collection, MOIFA.

By the early to mid-nineteenth century, small devotional paintings produced in Bolivia were generally done on sheets of tin or zinc and referred to as *laminas*, or plates. These portrayed the Virgin Mary as a flattened image with ornate detailing around her crown and gown.[24] The piece on the left portrays an image of the Virgen de la Candelaría holding a candle and the Child Jesus. However, this figure's name was changed to the Virgen del Socavón (Virgin of the Mineshaft) in 1789, after she was reported to have performed a

miracle in a cave near one of the mines in the Bolivian town of Oruro. She became the patron of that city and protector of the mine workers. In the nineteenth century, she also became the patron of soldiers.[25] Devotees of the Virgin commissioned paintings that included images of themselves.

The painting on the right depicts Nuestra Señora de los Amparos (Our Lady of the Protected or Sheltered). The two nude figures on her gown probably represent sinners asking for her help. Bolivian flags proudly flank the Virgin, reflecting the patriotism of the newly established Republic.

FIG. 2-7 *Virgen del Socavón* and *Virgen de la Copacabana.* Potosí, Bolivia, late 19th century. Oil on silver, glass. Largest: 6" x 5½" (15.2 x 10.2 cm). Private Collection.

Since the early colonial period, miniature religious paintings framed in silver, known as *relicarios*, or *medallones*, were used by nuns in the convents and upper-class citizens of the society. However, after Independence in the nineteenth century, they became popular with mestizo and indigenous populations throughout the Andes. Painting workshops in Potosí produced a great number of these pieces painted on small elliptical sheets of silver. Depictions of the Virgin Mary were common, particularly those portraying La Virgen del Socavón and La Virgen de la Copacabana, as shown in these two examples.[26] The Virgen del Socavón is shown in the center of parades of troops from both Peru and Bolivia, representing soldiers who fought Chile in the War of the Pacific (1879–1884).[27] In the scene around La Virgen de la Copacabana we see a line of cholas standing in front of the Virgin's sanctuary and a Peruvian soldier on his knees asking for her help while his comrades stand on the hill behind.

FIG. 2-8 *Virgen de Guadalupe.* Tarabuco region, Chuquiscaca, Bolivia, mid-20th century. Paint on rock. Left: Gift of Nancy Reynolds, MOIFA. Right: 8" x 7½" (20.3 x 19 cm). Collection of Bob and Gay Sinclair.

In the nineteenth century, artists in Bolivia and the Cuzco area began painting images of saints on large rock formations, as well as on smaller portable stones. Scholars who have studied these works believe they relate to the Andean belief in huaca—rocks that embody ancestor spirits and represent prosperity and good fortune. Painting Christian images on huaca was a way to combine two religious systems.[28]

By the mid-twentieth century, in Sucre and the Tarabuco region of southern Bolivia, rocks were being painted with the image of the Virgen de Guadalupe, copies of the one housed in the San Francisco Church in Sucre (fig. 2-2). As stated earlier, the sixteenth-century painting in Sucre follows the iconography of Our Lady of Guadalupe in Extremadura, Spain, rather than the Virgin of Guadalupe in Mexico. She is highly revered throughout this region of Bolivia; many people visit her sanctuary to ask for her help.[29] Mestizo and indigenous artists living in rural villages of the area, such as Tarabuco, painted these rocks for the worshippers to have in their homes or carry into the fields.[30] As in the nineteenth-century paintings, the Virgin is flanked by Bolivian flags and she floats over a local landscape complete with bulls that symbolize bullfighting, a popular activity during religious festivals.

## RELIGIOUS PAINTINGS WITH RURAL ANDEAN SCENES

Another type of religious painting that evolved in the Cuzco region of Peru, in the late eighteenth and early nineteenth centuries, arose from the desire to show costumbrismo, or scenes from everyday life in combination with religious figures. In these paintings the celestial world with Catholic saints was portrayed in the upper part of the work, while the pastoral world of the Andean campesinos, or rural people, was shown below. The saints were generally Santiago, St. John the Baptist, St. Anthony, St. Luke, and St. Mark, who had become the patrons and protectors of the campesinos' animals. Placing the saints above scenes of rural life was a petition for their help. Initially, these works were painted in oil on canvas in mestizo and indigenous workshops of Cuzco, but by the mid- to late-nineteenth century the campesinos were creating them for themselves, using tempera paints on rectangles of serge-type fabric that was coated with plaster or gesso.[31]

FIG. 2-9 *Saints and Rural Scene.* Cuzco, Peru, ca. 1810. Oil on canvas, 12½" x 19¾" (31.8 x 50.2 cm). Collection of Kisla Jiménez and Jonathan Williams.

This is an early nineteenth-century example of the paintings produced in Cuzco workshops for campesinos to use in their devotional practices. The image of Santiago on his horse trampling the Moors fills up a large part of the right side of the painting, with St. John the Baptist and a flock of sheep floating in the background. In the upper left are other patron saints: St. Mark and St. Luke on left and St. Anthony and St. Luke on right. Below are rural Andeans milking their cows while other animals graze nearby.

FIG. 2-10 *St. Luke, St. John the Baptist, and Santiago with Rural Scene* and *St. John the Baptist and St. Luke with Rural Scene.* Cuzco region, Peru, mid- to late-19th century. Paint on gessoed fabric. Largest: 17" x 12½" (43.2 x 31.8 cm). Private Collection.

These two paintings are typical of the work produced by campesinos in the rural highlands outside of Cuzco during the mid- to late-nineteenth century. The patron saints are shown above the Andean people and their animals, but the line of demarcation is not always defined. We see this in the painting at right, where the larger figure of St. John the Baptist is shown walking among the sheep he protects. The crude materials making up the pieces, combined with the primitive style of drawing and painting, create a wonderful form of popular art.

## Religious Sculpture

In the late sixteenth and early seventeenth centuries, a large quantity of religious sculpture was imported from Spain and delivered to Lima, the coastal capital of the Viceroyalty of Peru. Spanish and Italian artists also came to work in the region and take advantage of the lucrative opportunities created by the wealth and prosperity of the rich silver mines in the Andes. They helped establish workshops in colonial cities such as Lima, Quito, Cuzco, Huamanga, and Potosí to create artwork for the religious institutions and elite European and criollo citizens of those regions.

Priests working in indigenous communities also wanted Christian imagery to place in the rural churches to help foster the devotion of the local people. This led to the creation of workshops run by Spanish artists and/or Catholic priests who supervised numerous mestizos and Indians in the production of inexpensive sculptures that had wide distribution throughout the Andes. In some areas, the workshops utilized sculpting materials and techniques introduced by the Europeans, while elsewhere they relied on prehispanic methods, or a combination of the two. Eventually the mestizo and Indian artists took over full operation of these workshops, and they continued producing Catholic images into the nineteenth and twentieth centuries, with iconography that followed the European models but expressed in a more popular, folk style. This work continues to be made today in some areas.

## QUITO, ECUADOR

Ecuador was initially administered from Lima under the Viceroyalty of Peru; in 1563, it became a Royal Audience with the highland city of Quito as the capital. Later, in 1717, the territory was separated from Peru and incorporated into the Viceroyalty of New Granada. The earliest sixteenth-century religious sculpture produced in Quito was the work of Spaniards who set up workshops there, but soon the leading artists in this field were mestizos and Indians who worked within the guild system established by Spain. By the early eighteenth century, they had developed a very sophisticated and unique Quitenian style that continued into the early nineteenth century.[32]

FIG. 2-11 *Archangel San Raphael* and *Archangel San Gabriel*. Quito, Ecuador, last quarter 18th century. Wood, paint, metal. Largest: 20 7/8" x 9 1/4" (53 x 23.5 cm). International Folk Art Foundation Collection, MOIFA.

Using hardwoods from forests in the Quito region, the mestizo and Indian artists became very skilled in the European technique of carving exquisite figures and their clothing in wood. They finished the skin areas in *encarnación*, a technique in which several layers of paint and polish created shiny, life-like skin tones. The heads of the statues were carved in two pieces and glass eyes were inserted into hollowed-out sockets. Then the two pieces were carefully joined, so that the seam was invisible. This pair of archangels was made in the late eighteenth century, when the rococo style—characterized by a sweet and ephemeral expression in the figures—was at its height in Quito.[33]

FIG. 2-12 *San Jacinto* and *San Antonio*. Quito, Ecuador, late 18th–early 19th century. Wood, paint, glass. Largest: 14" x 6 1/4" (35.6 x 15.9 cm). Gifts of Mr. and Mrs. Harry P. Lapham, MOIFA.

The sophistication of the Quito school of sculpture continued into the late eighteenth and early nineteenth centuries, as seen in these beautiful rococo examples of San Jacinto and San Antonio. Glass eyes were inserted into their heads and the skin on the faces and hands was finished in the encarnación technique. Another characteristic of Quitenian sculpture was the detailed carving of the garments. These were finished in the e*stofado* technique in which gold leaf was painted on the surface of the wood and then covered with a layer of oil paint. This was then incised with very fine lines to reveal the underlying gold ground, to simulate the gold thread seen in European brocade fabrics.[34]

## CUENCA REGION, ECUADOR

Cuenca is the capital of the Azuay Province located at the southern end of the high mountainous region of Ecuador. It was an important colonial center and many workshops were established there and in surrounding villages, to produce goods for the European colonists. They utilized mestizo and indigenous workers; some were sent to Quito to be trained. Upon returning to Cuenca, however, they were not required to be members or follow the strict rules of the guild system. This region had some hardwood forests that provided materials for artisans in the small towns of Gualaceo and Sigsig to produce carpentry for churches and other buildings in the area.[35]

FIG. 2-13 *San Ysidro* and *Virgin of the Immaculate Conception.* Cuenca region, Azuay, Ecuador. Left: Early 20th century. Wood, gesso, paint. Gift of Peter P. Cecere, MOIFA. Right: late 19th century. Wood, paint, 11" x 3¾" (27.9 x 9.5 cm). International Folk Art Foundation Collection, MOIFA.

FIG. 2-14 Juan Antonio Supliguichi, *San Lucas* and *San Ysidro.* Gualaceo, Azuay, Ecuador, ca. 1990. Wood, paint. Largest: 10" x 4½" (25.4 x 11.4 cm). International Folk Art Foundation Collection, MOIFA.

By the eighteenth century, woodworkers in the Cuenca area were also producing some religious sculpture for local use, but in a more popular style than those being created in Quito. The clothing was simply carved and painted to look like that done with the estofado technique. This work continued into the nineteenth and twentieth century, as seen in these examples.[36] The two images in figure 2-14 were made by one of the last *santeros* working in Gualaceo, Juan Antonio Supliguichi, who carried on the tradition handed down by his father and grandfather, until his own death in the late 1990s.[37]

FIG. 2-15 *Virgin Mary.* Cajamarca region, Peru, late 19th century. Wood, paint, metal, glass, 20" x 9" (50.8 x 22.9 cm). Collection of Kisla Jiménez and Jonathan Williams.

This nineteenth-century example of the Virgin Mary is undressed, showing the basic torso and articulated elbows to allow for dressing the figure in fabric clothing made by her devotees. Her face has glass eyes and she probably once wore a wig. One of the hallmarks of Cajamarca woodwork is the use of reverse-glass painting to decorate architectural elements, as seen on the pedestal for this sculpture.

## CAJAMARCA REGION, PERU

The colonial city of Cajamarca is the capital of the Cajamarca Department of northern Peru, bordering the Loja Province of southern Ecuador. As elsewhere, workshops were set up by Spanish settlers to produce a variety of goods, and by the eighteenth century some of them were devoted to woodworking and carving of religious sculptures using hardwoods from the nearby forests.[38] Artists were taught to create separate hands, and heads with glass eyes inserted into the back of the faces. The skin on these pieces was finished in the encarnación technique. The hands and heads were later attached to simply carved bodies intended to be covered in fabric clothing.

## LOJA PROVINCE, ECUADOR.

The Virgen de Cisne is an important religious figure in the Loja Province of southern Ecuador. She miraculously appeared in the sixteenth century to help the indigenous people in Cisne to survive a plague of rats, and she has continued to perform miracles ever since. Today, she is housed in a large sanctuary in Cisne designated as a National Shrine of Ecuador; for six months of the year she is taken to the cathedral in the larger city of Loja, some 45 miles away, to be more accessible to the thousands of pilgrims who come seeking her help. Her feast day is August 15, when a multitude of people from Ecuador and Peru travel to pay their respects.[39] Many of these pilgrims want to buy images of the figure to take home with them.

FIG. 2-16 Maestro Guzman, *Virgen de Cisne*. Loja Province, Ecuador, ca. 1990. Wood, paint, cloth, woven straw, hair, 12¾" x 5½" (32.4 x 14 cm). International Folk Art Foundation Collection, MOIFA.

This sculpture of the Virgen de Cisne was made by an itinerant folk artist named Maestro Guzman, who traveled from Cuenca to Loja and probably into northern Peru, in the mid- to late-twentieth century, to sell his work.[40] It is not known where he learned his craft, but the style of this piece is similar to the image from Cajamarca discussed above (see fig. 2-15), rather than the wood sculptures produced in Cuenca (see figs. 2-13, 2-14). Both the Virgin and Child have glass eyes and their faces and hands were created separately, finished in the encarnación technique, and then attached to simple wooden bodies covered in fabric clothing. The Virgin is wearing a long wig and rests on a box-like pedestal.

### CUZCO, PERU

Although Cuzco is well known for painting workshops established there in the colonial period, sculpture was also an important aspect of the artistic production in the city. European artists came in the sixteenth and seventeenth centuries to help create altar screens and sculptures for the churches. Initially, they worked in hardwoods brought from the coast, as forests did not exist in the high-altitude landscape of the Andes. This was an added expense, however, and some workshops began using the prehispanic technique of carving the images in dried stalks of the maguey plant.[41]

FIG. 2-17 Left: *Nuestra Señora de Dolores.* Cuzco, Peru, late 19th century. Maguey, glass, paint, hair, fabric, 12¼" x 12" (31.2 x 30.5 cm). International Folk Art Foundation Collection, MOIFA. Right: *San Juan de Dios.* Cuzco, Peru, late 19th–early 20th century. Maguey, glass, gesso, paint, fabric. Gift of James F. Adams, MOIFA.

The face and hands of the Cuzco sculptures carved in maguey were made to look as natural as possible using the encarnación technique; glass eyes were inserted in the face; and the simply carved bodies were painted and then dressed in elaborate fabric clothing. In some maguey sculptures, the figures' bodies were dressed in *tela encolada*, a European technique where fabric is soaked in gesso and then draped around the figure. Once dried it is painted to look like actual clothing. In either case, the head of the image was covered in a wig, or detailing of the hair was done in gesso and then painted. By the nineteenth century, almost all of the mestizo and Indian sculpture workshops were using maguey, and yet the finished products were still quite sophisticated, as seen in these figures of Nuestra Señora de Dolores and San Juan de Dios. It is interesting to note that San Juan's body was covered in tela encolada and then dressed in layers of clothing.

FIG. 2-18 *Child Jesus with Thorn in Foot* (Niño de la Espina). Cuzco, Peru, 2008. Maguey, glass, paint, fabric, 8½" x 4½" (21.6 x 11.4 cm). International Folk Art Foundation Collection, MOIFA.

It is said that a small figure of the Child Jesus made in Naples, Italy, was brought to Cuzco by a priest in the seventeenth century, and shortly thereafter Niño Dios became the patron of the Indians.[42] The Italian figure had the posture that originated in Naples with one bent knee and arms extended out, so the Holy Child could be put in a reclining or seated position during the Christmas season.[43] Cuzco sculpture workshops began making similar figures of the Child Jesus using maguey and other techniques described above and then widely exported them to other regions of the viceroyalty.[44]

Many sculpture workshops in Cuzco continue to produce these figures today, but the Niño Dios is usually displayed in the seated position, rather than lying down. Some of the artists even sculpt the Child with an exaggerated bent ankle that shows the sole of the left foot with a thorn wound in the heel. Catholic priests would view this as a symbol of his future passion with the crown of thorns,[45] but local Andeans tell stories of the mischievous Child leaving his home altars at night and going out to play in the countryside where the thorn wound occurred. As a symbol of affection and adoration, most of these seated figures are richly dressed in the type of festival clothing worn by young Andean boys.[46]

FIG. 2-19 Hilario Mendívil, *San Ysidro* and *Flight into Egypt with the Virgen de Leche*. Cuzco, Peru. Left: ca. 1965. Maguey, pasta, fabric, gesso, paint. Gift of the Girard Foundation Collection, MOIFA. Right: ca. 1975. Maguey, pasta, fabric, gesso, paint. 16¼" x 13" (41.3 x 33 cm). International Folk Art Foundation Collection, MOIFA.

By the late eighteenth century, some mestizo and indigenous workshops were producing small secular figures from everyday life to place in nativity scenes. They were made of maguey and dressed in tela enclolada, with additional detailing done in *pasta*—a malleable prehispanic material made of dried potato, gesso, and various forms of liquid. A few of these artists also produced small, Catholic religious images for use by the lower-income residents of the area and beyond.[47]

Some workshops carried this tradition into the twentieth century, including that of Hilario Mendívil and his family, who live in the San Blas district of Cuzco. These examples show San Ysidro with his oxen and the Holy Family in the Flight into Egypt with the Virgen de Leche nursing her baby. Mendívil intentionally elongated the necks of Joseph and Mary to honor the llama, a sacred animal in the Andes.[48]

### LA PAZ REGION, BOLIVIA

When the Spanish arrived in the Andes, they discovered that the region on the south end of Lake Titicaca was particularly important to the culture and religion of the indigenous people. As a result, Dominican and Augustinian missionaries began establishing churches in rural villages to spread Christian teachings. By the late sixteenth century, Catholic priests had set up indigenous workshops in the area around Jesús de Machaca and Tiahuanaco, now part of the Department of La Paz in Bolivia. Artists were brought to train them to produce Catholic religious sculptures and, as in some of the workshops in Cuzco, they utilized the prehispanic technique of carving the images in maguey. They used European methods to create realistic skin tones, insert glass eyes, cover the heads in wigs, and dress them in elaborate fabric clothing. By the seventeenth and eighteenth centuries, these workshops were sending sculptures to various regions of Bolivia and brought high praise from the Spaniards.[49]

FIG. 2-20 *St. Michael, Virgin Mary,* and *St. John the Baptist.* La Paz, Bolivia, late 19th–early 20th century. Left: maguey, paint, fabric, metal. Gift of Tom Wilson, MOIFA. Center: maguey, glass, paint, fabric, metal, 19½" x 11¾" (49.5 x 29.8 cm). Private Collection. Right: wood, paint, fabric, metal. Gift of Tom Wilson, MOIFA.

When the economic and cultural life of the region south of Lake Titicaca declined, in the late nineteenth century, many people moved to the capital city of La Paz. Some sculpture workshops were reestablished there, and the work became more popular in style. Examples of this are seen in the figure of the Virgin Mary, who has glass eyes, and the images of St. Michael and St. John the Baptist, whose makers simply painted eyes into the sockets on the face.

FIG. 2-21 Charcas Family Workshop, *Santiago* and *Virgen de la Co-pacabana*. La Paz, Bolivia, 2007. Left: maguey, paint, fabric, metal. Right: maguey, paint, cardboard, plastic, fabric, 10" x 7½" (25.4 x 19.1 cm). Museum purchases with funds from Nancy Reynolds and Gloria List, MOIFA.

A few sculpture workshops continue to operate in La Paz today, as seen in these examples. The figure of Santiago is made with similar techniques to those of the early twentieth century, while the clothing of the Virgen de la Copacabana is fashioned from cardboard, plastic, and fabric. This type of image is sold to pilgrims visiting the sanctuary at Lake Titicaca today.[50]

### HUAMANGA REGION, AYACUCHO, PERU

The colonial city of Huamanga (now called Ayacucho) is the capital of the Department of Ayacucho, Peru. When the Spanish settled there in the early sixteenth century, they found the local Andeans carving white stone quarried from a nearby mountain that the Europeans compared to alabaster. Workshops were set up to train the Indian and mestizo carvers to create Christian religious images for upper-class Huamanga society, as well as for export to other areas.[51]

FIG. 2-22 *Virgin of Cocharcas* and *Virgin Mary*. Huamanga, Ayacucho, Peru, late 19th century. Left: stone, paint. Right: stone, 8" x 5¼" (20.3 x 13.3 cm). Private Collection.

As the indigenous population began to adopt aspects of Catholicism into their religious practices in the late seventeenth and eighteenth centuries, mestizo and Indian workshops in the Huamanga region began producing less expensive stone figures of the Virgin Mary and other saints for themselves and other members of the lower class. This continued into the nineteenth century, as seen in these two carvings of the Virgin Mary.

FIG. 2-23 Angelino Alcanta, *San Antonio* and *Virgen de Carmen*, Huamanga, Ayacucho, Peru, ca. 1960. Stone, paint. Largest: 5½" x 1½" (14 x 3.8 cm). Gifts of the Girard Foundation Collection, MOIFA.

A few family workshops in the Huamanga region carried on the stone carving tradition into the twentieth and twenty-first centuries. Due to a decreasing supply of good quality stone and the time-consuming task of carving it, many religious images became smaller in size, as seen in these examples of San Antonio and the Virgen de Carmen produced by Angelino Alcanta in the 1960s.[52]

## HUANCAYO REGION, JUNÍN, PERU

The city of Huancayo, located in the Department of Junín in the central highlands of Peru, gained importance in the late nineteenth century after mining operations began in nearby mountains and newly-laid railroad lines connected it to Lima and other parts of Peru in 1908. As the population grew, it became a market center for the region, and workshops were established to create a variety of products, including small sculptures of Catholic saints and figures from everyday life to place in nativity scenes. As in some workshops in Cuzco, the Huancayo area artists used maguey to sculpt the figures, the tela encolada technique to provide clothing, and gesso or pasta to create additional details. Then the figures were painted in the appropriate colors for the skin, clothing, and other items.[53]

FIG. 2-24 Pedro Abilio Gonzáles Flores. *Santa Rosa de Lima, San Martín de Porras,* and *San Juan Bautista.* Huancayo, Junín, Peru, ca. 1995. Maguey, fabric, gesso, paint. Left: 14 ½" x 4" (36.8 x 10.2 cm). Gift of Sabine Jiménez-Williams, MOIFA. Center: Gift of Martín Jiménez-Williams, MOIFA. Right: International Folk Art Foundation Collection, MOIFA.

One of the local folk artists who became well known for making sculptures in the mid-twentieth century was Pedro Abilio Gonzáles Flores, who learned the craft from his parents and grandparents. He in turn passed his knowledge and skills on to his sons and grandsons.[54] Two of the saints shown here, Santa Rosa and San Martín de Porras, are particularly loved by the Peruvian people as they were both born in Lima in the latter part of the sixteenth century. Santa Rosa came from Spanish parents, and San Martín came from a Spanish military officer and a black Panamanian woman. As part of their good deeds, Santa Rosa and San Martín worked together to help the poor people of Lima.[55]

## MÉRIDA, VENEZUELA

Mérida, founded in 1558, was the colonial center for the northern reach of the Andean mountain range in Venezuela that was under the Viceroyalty of New Granada. Initially, most of the religious artwork used in that region came from the coastal capital city of Caracas, where it was imported from Spain and other Caribbean colonies, or made in local workshops run by Europeans and mestizos. Religious painting and sculpture workshops finally emerged in Mérida and the neighboring state of Trujillo in the mid-eighteenth century. Over the next one hundred and fifty years, folk artists living in towns and villages throughout the region continued to produce religious imagery for local churches and homes.[56]

FIG. 2-25 Left: Patrocino Rangel, *San Ysidro*. La Mucuy Bajo, Mérida, Venezuela, 2004. Wood, paint, leather, 15³/₄" x 21" (40 x 53.4 cm). International Folk Art Foundation Collection, MOIFA. Center and right: Ramon Antonio Moreno, *San Antonio* and *San Benito*. Tabay, Mérida, Venezuela, ca. 1982. Wood, paint. Gifts of Christine and Davis Mather, MOIFA.

The religious folk art tradition is still carried on today, with a younger generation of artists taking over from their parents and grandparents.[57] They produce folk sculptures of well-known saints such as San Ysidro and San Antonio (left and center). One of the most popular saints in Venezuela is San Benito (St. Benedict), a freed African slave who lived in Italy in the sixteenth century (right). As one of the few black Catholic saints, he came to be patron of blacks throughout Latin America, including Afro-Venezuelans. His feast days are celebrated on December 27 and January 6, when thousands of dancers take to the streets playing drums and other musical instruments, as shown in the hands of this figure.[58]

## VENEZUELA AND ECUADOR—IMAGES OF JOSÉ GREGORIO HERNÁNDEZ

José Gregorio Hernández was born in the Andean state of Trujillo, Venezuela, in 1864 and eventually became a physician who dedicated himself to teaching, medicine, and religious practice. He sought priesthood on two occasions but had to withdraw due to his fragile health. Dr. Hernández was known for treating the poor for free and even buying them medicines with his own money. One day, in 1919, while taking medicine to the home of one of his patients in Caracas he was struck by a car and killed. After his death, the legend of Dr. Hernández began to grow in Venezuela and neighboring countries; he became known for performing miracles for those who prayed to him. Since then, he is commonly invoked as "José Gregorio" by both doctors and patients for healing purposes.[59]

FIG. 2-26 *Images of José Gregorio Hernández.* Left: unknown artist, Pujilí region, Cotopaxi, Ecuador, ca. 1990. Plaster, paint. Center left: José Olmos Workshop. Pujilí, Cotopaxi, Ecuador, 1992. Plaster, paint. Center: Miguel Herrera. Azuay, Ecuador, ca. 1990. Wood, paint. Center right: Mariano Rangel. La Mucuy Bajo, Mérida, Venezuela, ca. 2000. Wood, paint, 19½" x 5½" (49.5 x 14 cm). Right: Angel Jesús Rangel. La Mucuy Bajo, Mérida, Venezuela, 2008. Wood, paint. International Folk Art Foundation Collection, MOIFA.

In 1949 Venezuelan Catholic Church officials began the process for the beatification of José Gregorio by the Vatican in Rome. Although they are still waiting, most of his worshippers already consider him a saint. Since the mid-twentieth century, folk artists in Venezuela and Ecuador have created religious images of José Gregorio wearing a black suit and hat that was taken from a photograph of him that appeared in a newspaper in the early twentieth century. However, recently some artists have portrayed him in a white doctor's coat, perhaps to make him look more saintly.

## Portable Altars

The European practice of using small, box-like altars with doors to carry sacred images may have originated with the Greeks and Romans. By the tenth to thirteenth centuries, Christian pilgrims had adopted this type of container to transport small figures of Catholic saints while traveling to important religious sites. In Spain the portable shrines, known as *capillitas de santero*, were used by pilgrims to carry their favorite sculptures of saints on long journeys to religious sites, such as Santiago de Compostela in the northwestern region of Galicia. While at the shrine, they might purchase a small image of St. James (Santiago) in a box-shrine that they could take home. Many churches in Spain also had small images of saints housed in traveling altars that could be carried by devotees during a procession through their town, or by priests transporting the sculptures from one community to another.[60].

This tradition was introduced into the Andes by Spanish priests and European colonists in the sixteenth century. Catholic missionaries utilized the small shrines to facilitate religious teachings in the Indian villages. This practice was recorded in the writing of Hernan González de la Casa, who was assigned to the community of Macha, in the mining region of Potosí, in the 1570s. As part of his work to convert the local Andeans, he brought *imagines de bultos* enclosed in small wooden boxes to carry in religious pilgrimages (*novenas* and *romerías*), between the community church and newly-founded chapels in smaller villages nearby.[61]

Another document, from the 1670s, relates that an indigenous pilgrim visiting the sanctuary of the Virgen de la Copacabana, on the southern shores of Lake Titicaca, purchased a small sculpture of the Virgin contained in a wooden box. He carried the shrine to his home in the Oruro region and began using it to perform religious rituals for local residents.[62] During the eighteenth century, Andean devotion to Catholic images increased. The *caja de imaginero*, or portable shrine, was practical for home use as well as for carrying Christian figures to local churches to receive blessing and to visit the figure of the community's patron saint. It was also a good way for travelers to carry their personal santos, to aid in their work and protect them along the road.[63]

The Republican era of the nineteenth century saw further changes in the lives of the Andean people, who had more freedom to produce the traveling shrines and use them for their own types of Christian practices. These portable altars were put in a special place in the homes of campesinos, where they were worshipped both for protection of the family and for their powerful assistance with the health and reproduction of animals and crops. In many areas of the highlands the people also carried them into the countryside to use in the Fiesta de Herranza, a festival for counting and marking animals owned by the family that took place in March, July, or August depending on the region. This was a time to be with the spirits of the mountains, *wamanis* or apu, who watched over the rituals of counting the animals and putting special identifying bands in their ears. Images of Catholic saints, considered to be patrons of the animals, were brought there to look on and give their blessing.[64]

A small, open-air chapel was constructed out of tree limbs, where the family's portable shrine was placed on a low table. Offerings such as seashells, food, coca leaves, and llama fetuses were brought in a bundle and carefully laid out over a textile on the ground in front of the chapel; a space was designated in front of that for carrying out the rituals. Part of the ceremony included a Catholic mass, along with singing and prayers to the mountain spirits, followed by a celebration with music, food, and drink.[65]

These traditions continued into the twentieth century, and in some areas are still carried on today. The portable altars that have survived from the late nineteenth and twentieth century illustrate a variety of devotional practices, as well as the different styles and materials used in the workshops of the regions where they were produced.

FIG. 2-27 *Portable Altar with Virgen de la Copacabana.* Altiplano region, Peru, or Bolivia, ca. 1675–1700. Maguey, gesso, gold paint, silver. As pictured: 14½" x 15¾" (36 x 40 cm). Collection of the Museo de Arte de Lima.

This seventeenth-century example of a triptych-style caja de imaginero featuring the Virgen de la Copacabana may be more elaborate than the ones purchased by the Indian pilgrims mentioned earlier, but it provides a glimpse of the type of work being made in this region. The image inside the box is a miniature rendition of the altar screen in the Copacabana Sanctuary, with additional figures of saints and archangels applied inside the doors. It was sculpted in maguey with relief detailing done in gesso and then painted in gold leaf. The crown over the altar and the exterior of the box was covered in a thin sheet of silver. It is not known exactly where this portable altar was made, but scholars attribute it to the Altiplano region around southern Lake Titicaca.[68]

### SOUTHERN LAKE TITICACA—PORTABLE ALTARS WITH IMAGES OF THE VIRGEN DE LA COPACABANA

The sanctuary for the miraculous Virgen de la Copacabana, on the southern shores of Lake Titicaca, drew a large number of pilgrims and, as stated earlier, the devotees were able to purchase boxes that contained the Virgin's image to take home with them. Some of these portable altars were probably made in workshops in the Copacabana area. By the nineteenth century, and perhaps earlier, others were produced in the Chucuito region, located to the west of Copacabana along the southern lake Titicaca shoreline.

The Spanish colonial centers for the Chucuito region were Juli and neighboring Pomata, where Dominicans and then Jesuits carried out missionary work among the indigenous communities. The Italian Jesuit-artist Bernardo Bitti was sent from Cuzco to the Chucuito missions in 1576, the year the Jesuits took over from the Dominicans. He made a number of relief sculptures in local churches using maguey and gesso that were painted in gold leaf.[66] It is probable that workshops with mestizo and indigenous artists were established at the time to assist with this work; these workshops may have continued after Bitti left. By the seventeenth century, the Chucuito Jesuits were involved in helping to organize feast day celebrations for the Virgen de la Copacabana, which included bringing a group of musicians from Chucuito to enliven the festivities.[67] The priests may also have been instrumental in having mestizo and Indian artists in the Chucuito region produce portable altars featuring the Virgen de la Copacabana that could be sold at the sanctuary. Extant examples of portable altars made in the Chucuito area in the nineteenth and early twentieth century may be the remnants of a tradition begun by the Jesuits.

FIG. 2-28 *Portable Altar with Virgen de la Copacabana.* Chucuito Province, Puno, Peru, 19th century. Maguey, gesso, wood, gold paint, 18¾" x 27" (47.6 x 68.6 cm). Private Collection.

This nineteenth-century portable altar for the Virgen de la Copacabana was made in the Chucuito Province, Department of Puno, Peru, located to the west of Copacabana along the southern Lake Titicaca shoreline. It was made using the same techniques, features, and layout as the seventeenth-century piece shown above, but there is a reduction in the number of figures portrayed, a simplification in the details, and the absence of silver gilding on the box exterior.

FIG. 2-29 *Portable Altars for Virgen de la Copacabana*. Chucuito Province, Puno, Peru, late 19th century. Maguey, gesso, wood, paint. Left: International Folk Art Foundation Collection, MOIFA. Right: 8½" x 10" (21.6 x 25.4 cm). Gift of Mr. and Mrs. David R. Thornburg, International Folk Art Foundation Collection, MOIFA.

▼ FIG. 2-30 *Portable Altars for Virgen de la Copacabana*. Chucuito Province, Puno, Peru, late 19th–early 20th century. Maguey, gesso, wood, paint. Largest: 16" x 13" (40.6 x 33 cm). Gifts of Connie Thrasher Jaquith, MOIFA.

Over time, there was a shift from the use of gold leaf on the interior of the boxes to a varied palette of brightly-painted details. Chucuito portable shrines dating from the late nineteenth to early twentieth century have been classified into two types.[69] The older, Type A, is a triptych style with molded figures attached to the inside of the doors (figs. 2-28, 2-29). In Type B, these figures have been eliminated and the doors are decorated with brightly-painted floral motifs running vertically from top to bottom (fig. 2-30). By the mid-twentieth century, the southern region of Lake Titicaca fell into economic decline and many residents moved to larger cities to find work. During that time, the Chucuito workshops ceased production.

## DEPARTMENT OF LA PAZ, BOLIVIA

As discussed earlier, sixteenth-century workshops for producing Christian religious sculptures were also established south of Lake Titicaca in the areas around Jesús de Machaca and Tiahuanaco, now part of the Department of La Paz, Bolivia. These were set up by Dominican and Augustinian missionaries, who used indigenous artisans to carve the images in maguey, insert the glass eyes, finish the skin in the encarnación technique, and dress them in rich fabric clothing and silver ornaments. Many of these images were then placed in decorated boxes to make transport easier and to provide shrines for the home altars. These workshops continued to operate throughout the colonial period and into the nineteenth century, when their work became more popular, or folkloric, in style.[70] As in Chucuito, this southern region of Lake Titicaca became economically depressed by the late nineteenth century, and new workshops emerged in the city of La Paz.

FIG. 2-31 *Portable Altar with Virgen de los Remedios.* La Paz, Bolivia, late 19th century. Maguey, gesso, wood, paint, fabric, metal, 17¼" x 15½" (43.8 x 39.4 cm). Gift of Mr. and Mrs. David R. Thornburg, International Folk Art Foundation Collection, MOIFA.

This late nineteenth-century example of a portable altar from La Paz houses an image of the Virgen de los Remedios who had a popular following in the Miraflores district of La Paz.[71] Here, a serrated arch closely frames the figure inside the box and, following the style seen in the seventeenth-century altar (fig. 2-27), the crown over the top of the shrine is cut to match the shape on top of the doors. Also following the earlier model, painted horizontal bands divide the doors into two sections, but here the top is decorated with floral motifs rather than saints.

▲ FIG. 2-32 *Portable Altar with Santiago and Virgin Mary.* La Paz, Bolivia, late 19th early 20th century. Maguey, gesso, wood, paint, fabric, metal, 22" x 25" (55.9 x 63.5 cm). Gift of Connie Thrasher Jaquith, MOIFA.

In the late nineteenth and early twentieth century, portable altars made in La Paz continued to feature sculptures carved in maguey and dressed in elaborate clothing. However, the shape of the boxes changed, becoming squared off rather than having an arch over the top. There is also more space around the figures and the inside walls are covered in printed wallpaper. The shape of the interior archway framing the figures is more ornate and brightly painted with floral motifs. The decoration on the open doors is divided into two sections by horizontal lines.

FIG. 2-33 *Portable Altar with Santiago.* La Paz, Bolivia, early 20th century. Maguey, gesso, wood, paint, fabric, metal, 17½" x 17" (44.5 x 43.2 cm). International Folk Art Foundation Collection, MOIFA.

By the 1930s and into the mid-twentieth century, the decoration on the boxes became more fluid with brightly-painted floral motifs extending in a vertical pattern up and down the doors. This was similar to decorations seen on the Type B portable altars from Chucuito (see fig. 2-30). Small shrines that housed simply-painted, maguey religious figures not dressed in fabric clothing were also made in La Paz during this period.

## DEPARTMENT OF POTOSÍ, BOLIVIA

The other main area for the production of Catholic religious sculpture and portable altars in the southern part of the Viceroyalty of Peru was the wealthy mining region of Potosí, later incorporated into the Department of Potosí, Bolivia. Initially, the workshops there were run by Spaniards who trained mestizo and Indian artists to carve in imported hardwoods and finish the images with sophisticated painting techniques. In the seventeenth century, some of the Andean artisans switched to using maguey. By the following century, indigenous workshops were also producing less expensive sculptures using hand-formed or molded gesso with painted faces, clothing, and other details. Some of the maguey and gesso figures were dressed in the tela encolada technique discussed earlier.[72]

FIG. 2-34 *Portable Altar with Archangel.* Potosí, Bolivia, 18th century. Maguey, gesso, fabric, wood, paint. Collection of the Casa de la Moneda, Potosí, Bolivia. Photograph by Barbara Mauldin.

It is not known what the small portable altars that the priest was using in Indian villages near Potosí in the late sixteenth century looked like, but a larger eighteenth-century example from this region is on display in the Casa de la Moneda museum in Potosí. The figure of an archangel is carved in maguey with the skirt and other details of the clothing created in tela encolada. The arched frame around the figure is decorated with intricate carving and painted gold, as are the interior of the box and the doors.[73]

FIG. 2-35 *Portable Altar with Santiago.* Potosí, Bolivia, ca. 1940. Maguey, gesso, fabric, wood, paint, 10½" x 13½" (26.7 x 34.3 cm). Private Collection.

FIG. 2-36 *Portable Altar with San Antonio and San Juan Bautista.* Potosí, Bolivia, ca. 1940. Maguey, gesso, fabric, wood, paint, metal, plastic, 14½" x 18" (36.8 x 45.7 cm). Private Collection.

FIG. 2-37 *Portable Altar with San Juan Bautista.* Potosí, Bolivia, ca. 1940. Maguey, gesso, fabric, wood, paint, metal, 15" x 16" (38.1 x 40.64 cm). Foundation purchase with funds from Hank Lee and Paul Bonin Rodriguez, International Folk Art Foundation Collection, MOIFA.

By the early to mid-twentieth century, the cajas de imaginero being made in small indigenous workshops in the Potosí region were much more popular in style, similar to what was being produced in La Paz during the same time period (see fig. 2-33). The painted decoration on the doors and the arch framing the central figures featured floral motifs in brilliant colors. The larger santos were carved in maguey and dressed in the tela encolada technique, while smaller religious figures and images of animals were molded or hand-formed in gesso and attached to the back of the box or along the front. The owners placed additional objects in the shrine such as money, notes, paper flowers, and other types of ornaments. The most common saints housed in these portable shrines are Santiago, San Antonio, and San Juan Bautista—patrons of the animals being raised in the rural communities of this region.

## SUCRE AND TARABUCO REGIONS, DEPARTMENT OF CHUQUISACA, BOLIVIA

The Ciudad de la Plata de los Charcas (known today as Sucre) was established in the mid-sixteenth century to oversee the output of the silver mines in Potosí and to have jurisdiction over the southern part of the Viceroyalty of Peru, part of which is now incorporated in the Department of Chuquisaca, Bolivia. Some European artists initially came to this important city to help design and construct buildings, as well as produce religious sculptures. By the seventeenth century, however, most of the religious imagery was being sent from neighboring Potosí. In the following century, there were some local mestizo and Indian craftsmen producing religious sculptures in the pasta and tela encolada techniques[74] and this continued into the nineteenth and twentieth century, when they were freer to create this type of work for the local communities.

FIG. 2-38 *Local couple with portable altars.* Tarabuco, Chuquiscaca, Bolivia, 2006. Photograph by Barbara Mauldin.

One community particularly known for portable altars is Tarabuco, located about 40 miles (65 km) southeast of Sucre. Two small workshops were still operating there in the late twentieth century, one owned by Don Filiberto Mendoza and the other by Don Benigno Sandoval.[75] This photograph shows a Tarabuco couple with portable shrines they had taken to the church to be blessed after Sunday mass.

FIG. 2-39 *Portable Altars with Virgen de Guadalupe.* Tarabuco region, Chuquisaca, Bolivia. Left: ca. 1920. Maguey, gesso, wood, paint, foil, 17" x 12¼" (43.2 x 31.1 cm). Private Collection. Right: ca. 1940. Stone, gesso, wood, paint. Museum purchase with funds from Nancy Reynolds and Gloria List, MOIFA.

A distinguishing feature of the cajas de imaginero from Tarabuco is the painted decoration on the doors with images of local people in their traditional costumes participating in festivals and bullfights. These scenes are sometimes divided by horizontal bands. Images of the miraculous Virgen de Guadalupe, copies of the one housed in the cathedral in Sucre (fig. 2-2), are particularly prominent in the Tarabuco portable altars; the older example shown here, at left, contains a three-quarter relief of her created in maguey and gesso that was carefully painted in gold and other pigments.

In the caja on the right a small image of the Virgen de Guadalupe flanked by Bolivian flags is painted in the center of a large rock that is attached to the back of the box. As discussed earlier, scholars who have studied Christian religious images painted on rocks in Peru and Bolivia have found that the stones themselves are considered to have magical qualities, much like portable huacas. Saints' images painted on the rocks are believed to increase their power.[76] Small pasta figures of sheep and cattle are perched on top of the rock and resting below it. The previous owners of the shrine tied bundles of hair from their own sheep and cattle and placed them behind the rock, along with receipts for the blessings they had paid a priest to give to the altar.

### DEPARTMENT OF COCHABAMBA, BOLIVIA

The Valley of Cochabamba, located in the center of Bolivia, is known for its pleasant climate and large fertile valley that is particularly good for growing corn and wheat. During the height of the silver boom, in the sixteenth to eighteenth centuries, it became the primary food source for miners working in the less hospitable region of Potosí to the south. In exchange, religious artwork for the churches, private homes, and missionary work was brought from workshops in Potosí. Some local production of sculpted and painted religious images also existed in colonial times, and by the nineteenth century there was greater freedom and incentive to create Christian artwork for popular use.[77]

FIG. 2-40 *Portable Altars with Crucifix and Santiago.* Cochabamba, Bolivia, ca. 1940. Stone, gesso, wood, paint. Left: 15¼" x 11" (38.7 x 27.9 cm). Private Collection. Right: International Folk Art Foundation Collection, MOIFA.

These portable shrines produced in the Valley of Cochabamba, in the early twentieth century, have a different style from those seen elsewhere. In both examples the box was designed without doors and the front edge provides a decorative frame painted with repeated floral patterns. The central form is a large stone painted with images of the Crucifix and Santiago, two of the most common Christian images represented on painted rocks.[78] In the one at left a sculpted pasta figure of San Antonio stands behind a row of sheep resting across the front. The caja de imaginero on the right has remnants of flowers that were placed in the shrine, as part of the decoration and offerings to the saints.

## HUAMANGA REGION, DEPARTMENT OF AYACUCHO, PERU

Soon after the Spanish established a colonial settlement in Huamanga, Ayacucho, Peru, in the early sixteenth century, they created workshops to train mestizo and Indian artists to create Christian religious images. During the colonial period, the majority of sculptures were carved in a local stone. By the nineteenth century portable altars were also being made, either entirely in stone or with stone figures placed inside wooden boxes. In the late nineteenth and twentieth century the stone figures were replaced by images made in pasta or gesso.

FIG. 2-41 *Small Portable Altars with Santiago*. Huamanga region, Ayacucho, Peru. Left: late 19th–early 20th century. Stone, paint. Collection of Leslie Goodwin. Right: late 19th century. Stone, paint, 4½" x 3" (11.4 x 7.6 cm). Private Collection.

As seen in the religious sculpture from this region, some of the earliest portable shrines were carved in stone as small plaques that could be easily transported without a box. These shrines were particularly good for travelers on horseback, who wanted to carry with them their patron saint Santiago, who is shown in these two examples.

FIG. 2-42 *Portable Altars with San Antonio*. Huamanga region, Ayacucho, Peru, late 19th–early 20th century. Left: stone, paint. Collection of Leslie Goodwin. Right: stone, paint, wood, 7" x 5¼" (17.8 x 13.3 cm). International Folk Art Foundation Collection, MOIFA.

Other important customers for these portable altars were the arrieros, traveling traders, who transported goods from the Huamanga region, such as tanned leather and quicksilver, to areas west, north, and south as far as Potosí. They wanted to carry a depiction of their patron saint, San Antonio, to protect them from all of the dangers they might encounter during the rugged, year-long trip. These small carvings generally featured an image of San Antonio on the top register, with figures of a cargo-laden mule and the arriero and his dog depicted below. Eventually, these images were carved in three-dimensional forms and placed in small boxes that could function as altars, as seen on the right.

Fig. 2-43 *Portable Altars with Saints and Villagers.* Huamanga region, Ayacucho, Peru. Left: late 19th century. Stone, paint. Right: late 19th–early 20th century. Stone, maguey, paint, 12½" x 15½" (31.8 x 39.4 cm). Private Collection.

As the traveling traders made their way through the circuit of markets in the countryside, they encountered rural communities whose lives depended on raising animals, including llama, alpaca, cattle, and sheep. Through this contact they saw a need to supply the campesinos with portable altars; by the late eighteenth century, mestizo artists in many towns throughout the Huamanga region were producing traveling shrines to serve in the herders' religious practices such as the Fiesta de Herranza discussed above.

This led to the creation of a new type of traveling shrine that came to be known as Sanmarcos, because St. Mark was one of the saints commonly portrayed in them. Similar to the paintings produced by campesinos, in the rural areas around Cuzco (see fig. 2–10),[79] these portable shrines were horizontally divided into two different levels. The top featured the celestial world, with one or more images of the saints who were patrons of animals, while the bottom level portrayed scenes from everyday life.[80] Some of the early Sanmarco shrines were carved entirely in stone as small plaques (left), but later the artists placed the carved-stone figures into boxes divided into two sections (right).[81] In some early examples they were also painting the doors with rural scenes, as seen here.

FIG. 2-44 *Portable Altar with Saints and Villagers.* Huamanga region, Ayacucho, Peru, late 19th century. Stone, maguey, paint, 9¼" x 12" (23.5 x 30.5 cm). Private Collection.

By the late nineteenth and early twentieth century, the scenes in the top and bottom levels were more complex and the boxes became more horizontal in shape. Many of these boxes were made out of maguey and the painted decoration on the doors was divided by horizontal bands.

FIG. 2-45 *Portable Altar with Saints and Villagers.* Huamanga region, Ayacucho, Peru, ca. 1920. Gesso, paint, wood, paper, 11¼" x 18" (28.6 x 45.7 cm). International Folk Art Foundation Collection, MOIFA.

By the early twentieth century, the boxes were constructed in wood rather than maguey and were painted inside and out with simple floral and geometric motifs using bright colors against a white background. The painting on the doors was laid out in a vertical pattern, as seen on early twentieth-century altars from other regions; devotees sometimes added religious prints. The time-consuming job of carving the figures in stone gave way to shaping the images in gesso or pasta and painting them with bright pigments. Some of the older stone figures were used to create ceramic molds that the pasta could be pressed into, making the process go even faster.[82]

As before, the top level generally portrayed the Christian patrons of the types of animals owned by the family that commissioned the shrine. By the twentieth century, a black condor was hung down from the top, symbolizing the presence of wamanis or apu, spirits of the mountain, and in front was a group of domestic and wild animals, along with portrayals of important members of the family or community.

The bottom level evolved into portraying two different types of scenes from the everyday world. One, known as the *pasión,* spoke of the suffering that took place in the lives of the campesinos. It depicts a hacienda owner sitting at a table ordering the punishment of a young man who had stolen some sheep. The thief was tied to a tree with his pants pulled down, and his wife was on her knees nearby, begging for mercy.

The other scene was known as the *reunión,* which showed various people from the village, such as a female cheese-maker with her dog, a man with his bull, men playing different types of musical instruments, a woman spinning yarn, another milking a cow, a traveler with his mule, and a variety of domesticated and wild animals. The artists who created these scenes had some leeway in the images they portrayed and how the figures related to one another.[83]

The Sanmarcos continued to be made into the first half of the twentieth century, but during that time new roads were constructed that created a different type of distribution system for goods made in the Huamanga region. Eventually, the arrieros and their mule trains no longer carried the portable shrines to the rural markets, and the campesinos purchased other types of Catholic images in the larger cities to fulfill their ritual needs. Others joined Evangelistic Christian sects that didn't approve of the "idolatry" of figures that portrayed saints. By the 1940s, many of the shrine makers in Huamanga and the surrounding area converted their art form into something that had a broader commercial market (see figs. 4–168 through 4–175).[84]

## CUZCO REGION, PERU

Throughout the colonial period, Cuzco was a center for producing religious paintings and sculptures to be distributed to other regions of the Viceroyalty of Peru.[85] It seems likely that some of these were housed in small shrines and used by missionaries working in indigenous communities and by individuals and families for their own devotional practices. However, very few examples of portable altars from this region survive today.

FIG. 2-46 *Portable Altar with Virgen de Cocharcas* and *Portable Altar with San Ysidro.* Cuzco region, Peru. Left: mid-20th century. Wood, paint. Right: Julio Mendívil. Cuzco, Peru, 1986. Wood, paint, ribbon, feathers, metal, 15" x 9¼" (38.1 x 23.5 cm). International Folk Art Foundation Collection, MOIFA.

The two Cuzco cajas de imagineria shown here date from the early and late twentieth century, but they may also reflect one of the styles of shrines made in this area in earlier periods. These boxes have no doors, and rather than housing a sculpted figure or painted rock they have a religious image painted on the back wall. Small gesso figures were placed on the floor in front of the painting on the right; the fragile figures that once belonged to the shrine on the left were probably broken and then removed.

The painted image of the Virgen de Cocharcas is flanked by two masked dancers, which is in keeping with the popular religious paintings of the Virgin Mary produced in the Cuzco area in the nineteenth century (see figs. 2-4, 2-5). The more recent altar on the right, with the image of San Ysidro, also has masked dancers painted on each of the side walls.

### CUENCA REGION, AZUAY PROVINCE, ECUADOR

Along with the production of religious sculptures, woodworkers in the Cuenca area of Ecuador also made portable altars for figures. This tradition continued through much of the twentieth century; as a 1989 study indicates, thirty-one *talleres de imagineros* were still operating in the Department of Azuay that year.[86] Craftspeople in the villages of Gualaceo and Sigsig specialized in making *cajónes*, or small, brightly painted wooden boxes, to house the carved saints.

FIG. 2-47 Juan Antonio Supliguichi, *Portable Altars with San Ysidro, Santiago, and San Ramon.* Gualaceo, Azuay, Ecuador, ca. 1980. Wood, gesso, paint. Left: 9½" x 5½" (24.1 x 14 cm). International Folk Art Foundation Collection, MOIFA. Center: Collection of Kisla Jiménez and Jonathan Williams. Right: International Folk Art Foundation Collection, MOIFA. Back: *Portable Shrine without Figure.* Gualaceo, Azuay, Ecuador, ca. 1950. Wood, gesso, paint, 17" x 12" (43.2 x 30.5 cm). Private Collection.

With the absence of closing doors, the façades of the portable altars were decorated to look like the cathedral in Cuenca, complete with pointed steeples and finials. The three smaller examples shown here were made by one of the last santeros working in Gualaceo, Juan Antonio Supliguichi, who carried on the tradition handed down by his father and grandfather,[87] until his death in the late 1990s. The altar in the center features Santiago, the patron saint of Gualaceo.

## Holy Cross and Crucifix

The constellation we call the Southern Cross had been observed and revered in the Andes since early prehispanic times. Priests replicated the figure of the four brightest stars in the constellation in their ritual structures by placing a stone huaca in each of the four cardinal directions. Seeing the similarity of form, Catholic missionaries sought to replace the cult of indigenous veneration with reverence for the Christian cross. They introduced and emphasized the Catholic feast day for the Holy Cross on May 3. A date that falls within the Andean harvest season, this feast day became an important celebration throughout the entire region, and its importance continues today. This devotion is for the Holy Cross itself and not for the Crucifixion that shows Christ's whole body.[88]

**PERU**

FIG. 2-48 *Guardian Holy Cross on the hillside overlooking the town of Huanta, Ayacucho, Peru,* 2008. Photograph by Barbara Mauldin.

FIG. 2-49 *Dressed Holy Cross on the side of the San Francisco Church in Cuzco, Peru,* 2008. Photograph by Barbara Mauldin.

Following traditions established in the colonial era, large crosses are placed on hillsides overlooking towns to serve as guardians for Andean communities, while others are placed outside of churches. These crosses are used in the annual May 3rd celebration, when they are "dressed" and sometimes ornamented with potato plants, cornstalks, and sheaves of wheat to symbolize a bountiful harvest.[89]

FIG. 2-50 Jesús Urbano Rojas, *Holy Cross*. Huamanga, Ayacucho, Peru, ca. 1960. Wood, gesso, paint, glass, fabric, gourd, 16¾" x 9½" (42.5 x 24.1 cm). Gift of the Girard Foundation Collection, MOIFA.

▼ FIG. 2-51 Left: Felipe Gonzáles, *Holy Cross*. Huancayo, Junín, Peru, ca. 1985. Wood, gesso, paint, glass, fabric, 37" x 20" (94 x 50.8 cm). Gift of Diane and Sandy Besser, MOIFA. Right: Joaquin Lopéz Antay, *Holy Cross*. Huamanga, Ayacucho, Peru, ca. 1960. Wood, gesso, glass, paint. International Folk Art Foundation Collection, MOIFA.

In Peru crosses are also placed in private homes and venerated as the "Father of the House." Christ's head is usually shown in the center, with symbols of the instruments of his passion portrayed on the central shaft and across both arms of the cross. Among these are the hammer that drove the nails through his feet and hands and the pliers that pulled them out. The long forms attached diagonally from the arms to the central shaft of the cross represent the holy sponge set on a long reed to offer liquid to Christ while he suffered, the lance used by a Roman soldier to inflict the final wound, and the ladder used to take him down. Other symbols often placed on these crosses are the rooster that crowed after Peter's third denial of Jesus and the dove representing the Holy Spirit.[90]

◀ FIG. 2-52 Jesús Urbano Rojas, *Cross with Sanmarco Scene*. Huamanga, Ayacucho, Peru, ca. 1960. Wood, gesso, paint, 17" x 10½" (43.2 x 26.7 cm). Gift of the Girard Foundation Collection, MOIFA.

Some artists in Huamanga, Ayacucho, Peru, such as Jesús Urbano Rojas, also created crosses for homes that had sculptural scenes at the base. This cross shows St. Mark blessing the animals with an upper-class couple (probably wealthy cattle ranchers) standing on each side.

FIG. 2-54 Nicario Jiménez Quispe, *Cross with Terrorist Scene*. Lima, Peru, ca. 1992. Wood, gesso, paint, 23" x 14" (58.4 x 35.6 cm). International Folk Art Foundation Collection, MOIFA.

In 1980 the Communist Party of Peru began a terrorist movement known as the Shining Path that was centered in Huamanga, Ayacucho. Many families were forced to leave the area and relocate to Lima. Among them was the Jiménez family, who were known for creating portable altars and crosses. Some younger members of the family began making crosses with scenes that would appeal to a growing clientele of tourists and collectors. One example, by Claudio Jiménez, shows the Festival of the Cross with musicians and dancers from Ayacucho. In 1992, after twelve years of bloodshed, his brother Nicario Jiménez created a "bleeding" cross with a terrorist scene and a plea to God to help stop the violence and save his hometown.

FIG. 2-53 Claudio Jiménez Quispe, *Cross with Festival Scene*. Lima, Peru, ca. 1985. Wood, gesso, paint, 23" x 14" (58.4 x 35.6 cm). International Folk Art Foundation Collection, MOIFA.

## BOLIVIA

**FIG. 2-55** *Crucifixes.* La Paz, Bolivia, late 19th–early 20th century. Maguey, wood, gesso, paint, fabric. Largest: 33¾" x 19½" (85.7 x 49.5 cm). Gifts of Tom Wilson, MOIFA.

Sculpture workshops in La Paz produced work for Catholic institutions and mestizo families that wanted more traditional Catholic imagery of Christ on the Cross. The crucifixes were made in the same technique as their other religious figures: using maguey to sculpt the images, the encarnación technique to paint the skin, and rich fabrics to serve as loincloths.

**FIG. 2-56** *Holy Cross* and *Crucifix.* Potosí, Bolivia, early 20th century. Maguey, wood, gesso, paint. Largest: 18½" x 11" (47 x 27.9 cm). Private Collection.

Artists in rural communities in the Department of Potosí, Bolivia, created Holy Crosses for local residents to place in their homes to guard and protect them. Representations of the crucifix are also venerated in this and neighboring regions, as seen here and in the images painted on stones (see fig. 2-40).[91]

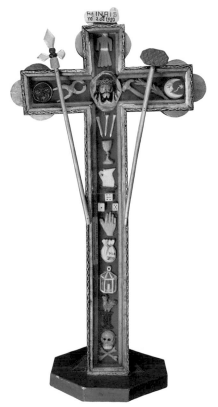

## ECUADOR

FIG. 2-57 *Holy Cross* and *Crucifix*. Cuenca region, Azuay, Ecuador, late 19th–early 20th century. Left: wood, paint, metal, 23½" x 14½" (59.7 x 36.2 cm). Gift of Connie Thrasher Jaquith, MOIFA. Right: wood, paint, cloth, Gift of Peter P. Cecere, MOIFA.

FIG. 2-58 Juan Antonio Supliguichi, *Crucifix*. Gualaceo, Azuay, Ecuador, 1992. Wood, gesso, paint, 29" x 16" (73.7 x 40.6 cm). International Folk Art Foundation Collection, MOIFA.

Artists in Cuenca, Ecuador, have also made Holy Crosses ornamented with symbols of Christ's passion and crucifixes showing him on the cross. Sometimes the crosses include both types of imagery, as seen in figure 2–58. As elsewhere, they are kept on family altars.[92]

◀ FIG. 2-59 Sampedro Workshop, *Processional Cross*. Saquisilí, Cotopaxi, Ecuador, 1980. Wood, gesso, paint, glass, 50" x 25" (127 x 63.5 cm). Gift of Peter P. Cecere, MOIFA.

Large crosses like this one are made in workshops and rented to groups to use during community processions for the May 3rd festival of the Holy Cross.

FIG. 2-60 *Natural Branch Crosses*. Pomasqui, Pichincha, Ecuador, c.1950. Wood, gesso, paint. Left: 31" x 13" (78.7 x 33 cm). Private Collection. Right: Collection of David and Mayi Munsell.

A sanctuary in the town of Pomasqui, north of Quito, houses an image known as El Señor del Arbol, Lord of the Tree. It consists of a sculpted head of Christ placed on top of a large tree trunk with two branches reaching up on both sides. The unusual figure is said to have miraculously appeared there in the early seventeenth century and is credited with performing miracles ever since. Each year,

thousands of pilgrims visit the sanctuary to ask for help, providing a ready market for selling images. By the early twentieth century, local artists were creating crosses in honor of El Señor del Arbol from wood found naturally shaped with a central stalk and two branches. They were usually painted green with floral patterns in red and white and ornamented with carved figures such as the dove of the Holy Spirit, the face of Christ, or angels.[93]

# Reliquaries

Reliquaries are small pendants that traditionally contained relics of saints, such as fragments of bone, fingernails, or teeth. By the sixteenth and seventeenth centuries, the name had become symbolic, and the small silver or gold lockets usually held a miniature painting or sculpture of a saint, rather than any of his or her body parts. This type of devotional jewelry was brought to the Andes by Spanish colonists, who wore them to display their wealth and show their piety and religious sentiments. Silversmiths, painters, and sculptures in the colonial workshops began producing *relicarios* for local clients, including nuns who wore them as badges of their faith and allegiance to their religious order. They were also worn by laypersons, members of Catholic brotherhoods, and soldiers and members of their families, to give protection and inspiration. At times, they were placed around the neck of a favorite saint or hung on a wall as a devotional image.[94]

FIG. 2-61 Left and right: *Reliquaries with Nuestra Señora de la Merced* and *Archangel San Raphael.* Potosi, Bolivia, mid–late 19th century. Oil paint, silver, glass. Largest: 3½" x 2½" (8.9 x 6.4 cm). Top center: *Reliquary with Virgen del Socavón.* Copacabana. La Paz, Bolivia, late 19th century. Mother-of-pearl, paint, silver, glass. Private Collection.

By the nineteenth century, the religious medallions were being worn and used by Indians as part of their devotional practices. During this period, indigenous and mestizo artists in the Potosí region of Bolivia developed miniature painting to an advanced level of popular art. The works are characterized by flattened images filled with intricate, colorful detailing. They were painted on small elliptical plates of silver that were covered in glass and framed in silver, with a ring at the top for suspension from a chain or cord.[95] Often different saints were painted on each side of the plates, so the owner could choose which image to look at on a particular day. Examples are seen here, in the left and right reliquaries, with paintings of Nuestra Señora de la Merced and the Archangel San Raphael. Other examples appear in the earlier discussion on popular religious paintings (see fig. 2-7).

Many devotees acquired relicarios at important pilgrimage sites, such as that of the Virgen de Guadalupe in Sucre and the Virgen de la Copacabana on the shores of Lake Titicaca. By the late nineteenth century, mother-of-pearl (*nacar*) became a favorite surface for painting reliquaries, particularly those acquired at the Copacabana shrine. Some of these miniatures were quite small in size, with exceptionally fine painting said to have been done with a single horsehair.[96] An example is seen here, in the relicario in the top center, which portrays the Virgen del Socavón.

FIG. 2-62 *Reliquaries.* Upper left: *St. Francis.* Huamanga, Ayacucho, Peru, late 19th century. Stone, paint, metal, glass, 2½" x 1½" (6.4 x 3.8 cm). Lower left: *Santiago.* Ayacucho, Peru, late 19th century. Stone, paint, metal, glass. Upper right: *San Jose.* Ecuador, 19th century. Tagua nut(?), paint, metal. Lower right: *Santa Teresa.* Colombia, 19th century. Metal, paint, glass. Private Collection.

Reliquaries were also made and used in other Andean countries in the post-Independence period of the nineteenth century. Artists in Ayacucho, Peru, carved miniature religious images in the local huamanga stone that were covered in glass and encased in silver. The saints were usually portrayed in relief and then either coated with wax or lightly painted to highlight details of their clothing.[97] Some were done in elliptical shapes, as seen in the example of St. Francis (upper left). Others were done in rectangular shapes, such as the Santiago (lower left), and were similar to the small portable altars discussed earlier (see fig. 2-41).

Some artists in Ecuador created relicarios by carving miniature relief images out of a palm nut called tagua. When soft it was easy to carve, and when it hardened it became very durable, somewhat like ivory. The figure of San José in the reliquary from Ecuador (upper right) may have been carved out of tagua. Many beautiful reliquaries were produced in Colombia during the nineteenth century, when painting miniatures became one of the most popular forms of artistic expression. The miniatures featured very delicate images of saints framed in silver lockets that were worn as jewelry,[98] as seen in the medallion with Santa Teresa (lower right).

# Scapulars and Religious Badges

Small cloths embroidered with the Sacred Heart or other Christian images were popular devotional items in the Andes in the late nineteenth and first half of the twentieth century. They were often made by nuns and sold in churches or small shops attached to the convents.

FIG. 2-63 *Scapulars.* Left: *Sacred Heart.* Santa Catalina Convent, Cuzco, Peru, mid-20th century. Fabric, 3" x 2½" (7.6 x 7 cm). Collection of Kisla Jiménez and Jonathan Williams. Right: *Our Lady of Carmen.* Santa Teresa Convent, Potosí, Bolivia, mid-20th century. Paper, fiber. Gift of Carlos Munoz-Flores, MOIFA.

Scapulars are pairs of small rectangular pieces of cloth connected by strings that allow them to hang over a person's neck, with one piece resting on the chest and the other on the back. They are worn by Catholics under their clothes as a testament of their religious devotion.[99] Some are very plain, while others are beautifully embroidered, such as the examples shown here that were made by nuns in convents in Cuzco, Peru, and Potosí, Bolivia.

FIG. 2-64 *Religious Badges.* Left and center left: *Sacred Heart* and *Jesus with Lamb.* Santa Catalina Convent, Cuzco, Peru, mid-20th century. Fabric, metal. Collection of Kisla Jiménez and Jonathan Williams. Center right: *San Martin de Porras.* Lima, Peru, late 20th century. Paper, fabric, thread. Collection of Kisla Jiménez and Jonathan Williams. Right: *Santa Rosa de Lima.* Lima, Peru, ca. 2005. Paper, plastic, metal, 5¾" x 3" (14.6 x 7.6 cm). International Folk Art Foundation Collection, MOIFA.

Other religious badges are known in the Andes as *detentes*, a Spanish word that literally means to stop something bad or evil from hurting the person wearing it. They were made by nuns who carefully embroidered images of the Sacred Heart, Jesus, the Virgin Mary, or saints onto cloth; a small ribbon at the top is used for pinning the badges to the clothing of a devotee. Detentes are worn by groups participating in feast day processions and sold to observers on the sidelines to make money for the event. By the late twentieth century, the quality of these badges had changed and most were made from colored prints of the saints pasted onto cardboard and framed with an embroidered edge. The style of the badges continued to evolve into the early twenty-first century, when plastic gold trim was added to give a more glittery effect.[100]

FIG. 2-65 *Religious Badges.* Left: *Virgen del Socavón.* Oruro, Bolivia, ca. 2000. Paper, plastic, fabric, metal, 4¾" x 3¾" (12.1 x 9.5 cm). Right: *Santiago.* Potosí, Bolivia, ca. 2005. Paper, plastic, metal, fabric. International Folk Art Foundation Collection, MOIFA.

Folk artists in Bolivia have used different materials to create these religious badges. For example, small color prints of the saints were glued to plastic sheets cut to specific shapes, with flat metal images of other religious figures tied to the ribbon on top, allowing them to hang down over the front. Sometimes, additional decoration is created with interwoven string, as seen in the detente of the Virgen del Socavón on the left.

FIG. 2-66 *Religious Badges.* Left: *Virgen de Cisne.* Loja, Ecuador, ca. 2005. Fabric, plastic, 9" x 4½" (22.9 x 11.4 cm). Gift of Nancy Reynolds, MOIFA. Right: *Virgen de Chapi.* Arequipa, Peru, ca. 2005. Fabric, plastic. International Folk Art Foundation Collection, MOIFA.

One of the most recent developments in detentes involves the gluing of colored prints of saints onto fabric that has been stiffened and cut into particular shapes. They are decorated with machine embroidery, including the saints' names and other words of devotion. Some have small, plastic suction cups attached to the ribbon so the badge can be adhered to the inside of a car windshield, as seen in these two examples.

# Milagros

Small metal figures known as *milagros* are used to thank Christian saints for fulfilling requests made by their worshippers in time of need. They fall into a class of devotional objects known as *ex-votos*, which means "by vow" or "according to a promise." They are made in a variety of forms including sacred hearts, human figures, body parts, animals, plants, houses, cars, and other personal items that represent the types of things people ask their saints for help with. Once a prayer is answered, the devotee purchases the appropriate milagro from a vendor of religious items, takes it to the place where an image of the saint resides, and pins it on the figure's robe or something else nearby. This tradition is found throughout Europe and was introduced in the Andes by Spanish colonists.[101]

During the nineteenth century, cottage industries were mass producing metal milagros by casting them in molds or stamping them in sheets. Originally made in silver, milagros were later made from less expensive metals, such as zinc, copper, and nickel that was sometimes coated in silver. The style of the metal figures varied from one region of the Andes to another, and changed over time, as one maker died and others took over the craft.[102]

**PERU**

◀ FIG 2-67 *Milagros*. Lima and northern coastal region, Peru, early 20th century. Silver. Largest: 5¼" x 2¾" (13 x 6.6 cm). Collection of Kisla Jiménez and Jonathan Williams.

FIG. 2-68 *Milagros*. Northern coastal region and Arequipa, Peru, mid- to late-20th century. Mixed metals. Size of group as displayed: 6½" x 7½" (16.5 x 19.1 cm). Collection of Kisla Jiménez and Jonathan Williams.

The milagros in these two groups were made in the *repoussé* technique in which metalsmiths carefully hammered blank sheets of metal into molds to create a relief impression. This method has been used in Lima and other workshops along the northern coast of Peru, as well as in the Andean city of Arequipa. The early twentieth-century pieces in figure 2-67 were made with thin sheets of silver. Those in figure 2-68 were done in a mixture of less expensive metals, which was more common in the mid- to late-twentieth century. Repoussé milagros made in Arequipa are usually square or rectangular in shape and often have a dotted background as seen on some of these pieces.

◀ FIG. 2-69 Maestro Aquino, *Milagros with Photographs*. Piura, Peru, late 20th century. Mixed metals. Largest: 1¾" x 1" (4.4 x 2.4 cm). Collection of Kisla Jiménez and Jonathan Williams.

FIG. 2-70 Maestro Aquino, *Milagros*. Piura, Peru, late 20th century. Mixed metals. Size of group as displayed: 8" x 9" (20.3 x 9 cm). Collection of Kisla Jiménez and Jonathan Williams.

Sometimes devotees attach their photographs to milagros as an additional form of thanks and to make sure the saint knows they have fulfilled their promise. In figure 2-69 we see a photograph of a man pinned to a house milagro and pictures of a young boy and girl that were attached to a milagro depicting lovers. The milagros pictured on the left and above were made by Maestro Aquino—an artisan who cut his images from thin sheets of mixed metals and added simple details with an engraving tool. Aquino grew up in the colonial city of Piura, located in the northwest coastal area of Peru, a region known for its metalwork. He probably learned the craft at a young age and produced thousands of milagros in the "cookie cutter" style, until his death in 2000.

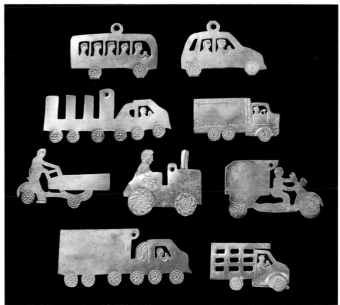

FIG. 2-71 *Milagros*. Northern coastal region, Peru, mid- to late-20th century. Mixed metals. Size of group as displayed: 8½" x 8¾" (21.6 x 22.2 cm). Collection of Kisla Jiménez and Jonathan Williams.

All of these small vehicles were cut out of thin sheets of mixed metals in a similar style as those made by Maestro Aquino. However, the details on the wheels are more intricate than those seen on the vehicles identified as Aquino's. These milagros may be the work of someone who studied under him and developed a slightly different style.

FIG. 2-72 *Milagros.* Otuzco, Peru, mid-20th century. Mixed metals. Size of group as displayed: 8½" x 8" (21.6 x 20.3 cm). Collection of Kisla Jiménez and Jonathan Williams.

Otuzco is located in the Andean foothills east of the northern coastal city of Trujillo, Peru. Artists in this town have produced a distinctive style of milagro made by casting mixed metals and soldering the pieces together. The result is heavy and sometimes layered, as seen in this group. Many of these pieces have small initials engraved in the surface that are probably those of devotees who offered the milagros to their saints. As mentioned earlier, this would assure that their promised gifts were acknowledged.

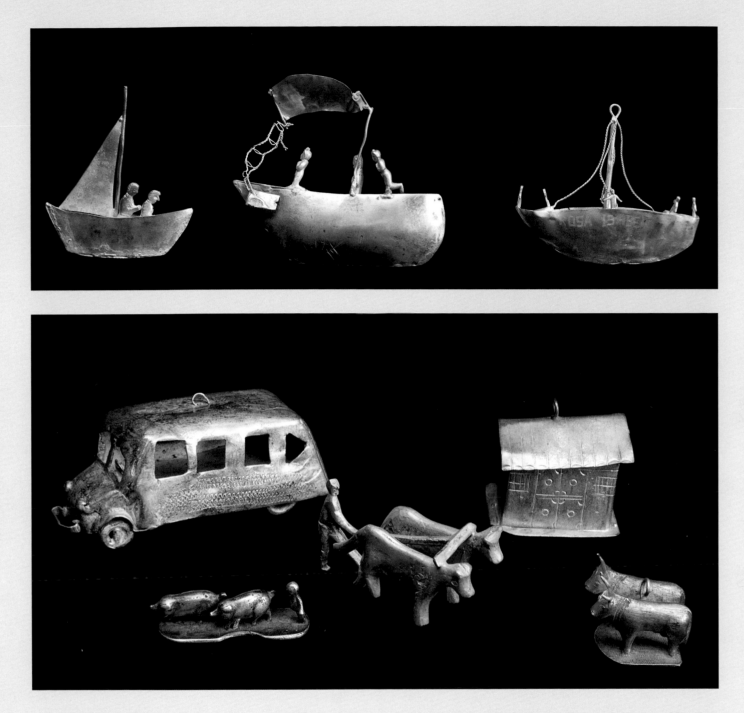

FIG. 2-73 *Milagros*. Motupe, Peru, mid-20th century. Mixed metals. Largest: 5¾" x 5¼" (14.5 x 13.3 cm). Collection of Kisla Jiménez and Jonathan Williams.

FIG. 2-74 *Milagros*. Motupe, Peru, early to mid-20th century. Mixed metals. Largest: 1½" x 3½" (3.5 x 8.5 cm). *Man with Pigs*: Collection of Leslie Goodwin. Others: Collection of Kisla Jiménez and Jonathan Williams.

Motupe is a small village in the northern coastal region of Peru in the Department of Lambayeque. Artists in this town have created a very different style of milagro characterized by three-dimensional forms, some unusually large in size. Most were made by casting, but some have additional details cut from sheets of metal that are soldered onto the other forms. The boats represent a particular concern for the livelihood of fishermen in this village and other towns along the coast.

## BOLIVIA

FIG. 2-75 *Milagros*. Bolivia, early to mid-20th century. Silver. Size of group as displayed: 3½" x 3¾" (8.9 x 9.5 cm). Collection of Kisla Jiménez and Jonathan Williams.

FIG. 2-76 *Milagros*. Bolivia, late 20th century. Silver and mixed metals. Size of group as displayed: 3" x 3¾" (7.6 x 9.5 cm). Collection of Kisla Jiménez and Jonathan Williams.

Not as common in Bolivia as elsewhere, milagros of cast-silver figures were sometimes produced in Bolivian workshops in the early to mid-twentieth century, to serve the needs of devotees. In the late twentieth century, other styles were made available either in the repoussé technique or simply cut out of silver or mixed metals and incised with patterns.

FIG. 2-77 *Milagros.* Cuenca, Ecuador, early to mid-20th century. Silver and mixed metals. Size of group as displayed: 3¼" x 5" (8.3 x 12.7 cm). Collection of Kisla Jiménez and Jonathan Williams.

FIG. 2-78 *Milagros.* Cuenca, Ecuador, early to mid-20th century. Mixed metals. Size of group as displayed: 4" x 8¾" (10.2 x 22.2 cm). Collection of Kisla Jiménez and Jonathan Williams.

The city of Cuenca, Ecuador, is famous for its silversmiths and goldsmiths; some of them have produced milagros cast or cut out of silver and mixed metals.[103] The plant forms are particularly interesting; this type of milagro would be offered to a saint for helping a worshipper with his or her crops.

# Stone Amulets

Andean religious practitioners in the Altiplano region of Peru and Bolivia use stone amulets called illas to perform rituals that seek to ensure well-being and prosperity for indigenous farmers, herdsmen, and their families. Private individuals also keep the amulets in their homes for good luck and to use in their own ceremonies. During colonial times, these objects and rituals were banned by the Catholic Church, forcing their use to be hidden from authorities. The practice reemerged into open view in the post-Independence era of the nineteenth century, when illas once again flourished in the region. The amulets range in shape from flat squares and rectangles to elaborate forms with houses, livestock, and fields. The majority consist of small figures of animals, humans, hands, and other natural forms.

The amulets can be made from any stone, but most are carved from a soft alabaster that ranges in color from white to orange-pink. This material is found in the mountains and the highland lakes area of the Bolivian province of Bautista Saavedra, northeast of Lake Titicaca on the western border with Peru. The alabaster amulets are carved by Qollahuaya (a subgroup of Aymara people) medicine men who live in this region and travel throughout the Central Andes curing people with herbs and performing other types of rituals. The men use the stone amulets in their own ceremonies, as well as selling or trading them to other ritual practitioners and private individuals.

Once acquired, the stone carvings are often coated with llama fat, coca leaves, and blood to make them more powerful. When not being used for ceremonies, the amulets are safely tucked away with the owner's supply of coca leaves, either in a coca bag or cloth. Medicine men keep their amulets carefully folded inside a ritual cloth or bundle, along with llama fat, coca leaves, and other items used in the ceremonies. When the carvings are brought out for certain kinds of rituals, they are placed on a table, or mesa, along with other special offerings for the Andean deities.[104]

## MESAS

FIG. 2-79 *Mesas.* Top left: Tiahuanaco region, Bolivia, 200 BC–AD 1200. Stone, 3½" x 4" (8.9 x 10.2 cm). Collection of David and Mayi Munsell. Bottom center: Bautista Saavedra Province, Bolivia, late 19th–early 20th century. Stone. Right: Bautista Saavedra Province, Bolivia, late 19th century. Stone. Private Collection.

One type of illa commonly used in rituals is a square or rectangular flat stone carved in low relief with geometric lines or patterns. The stones are considered to be "seats" for the supernatural spirits to use when they come to the ritual tables; these stones are also referred to as mesas, or tables.[105] In prehispanic times, the geometric carving was characterized by a series of interlocking rectangles, as shown on the gray stone at left. Some dating from the nineteenth century have bolder geometric shapes; by the late nineteenth and twentieth century, the relief carving became more graphic, with depictions of plants combined with abstract lines, as seen in the mesa in the bottom center.[106]

## HOUSE AMULETS

FIG. 2-80 *House Amulet*. Bautista Saavedra Province, Bolivia, early 20th century. Stone, 1½" x 7" (3.2 x 17.8 cm). Private Collection.

FIG. 2-81 *House Amulets*. Bautista Saavedra Province, Bolivia. Left: early 20th century. Stone. Private Collection. Center: mid-20th century. Stone, pigments, 1¼" x 4" (3.2 x 10.2 cm). Right: early 20th century. Stone. International Folk Art Foundation Collection, MOIFA.

House amulets represent the complete Andean household. They portray the agricultural fields, living structures, and outbuildings flanked on either side by roughly-carved domestic animals (bulls, cattle, rams, sheep, and llamas). In the province of Bautista Saavedra, Bolivia, where the amulets are made, they are given to newlyweds for good fortune in obtaining everything represented. The couple is often shown in a window of the house, or along the side. The husbands and wives who receive these amulets wrap them up with their clothes in the house, so the amulets' magical forces will assist them in all aspects of life.[107] The mid-twentieth-century piece (center, below) has buses in place of animals, reflecting a different type of lifestyle. In some regions of the Altiplano these amulets have come to be known as chacras (fields), and they are used in livestock marking ceremonies to help increase the herds.[108]

## ANIMAL AMULETS

FIG. 2-82 *Animal Amulets*. Altiplano region, Peru or Bolivia, 13th–15th century. Stone. Top and center: International Folk Art Foundation Collection, MOIFA. Bottom: 2½" x 3¾" (6.4 x 9.5 cm). Collection of Leslie Goodwin.

FIG. 2-83 *Animal Amulets*. Bautista Saavedra Province, Bolivia, late 18th–early 19th century. Stone. Back center: 2" x 1¾" (5.1 x 4.5 cm). Collection of David and Mayi Munsell. Others: Gift of Connie Thrasher Jaquith, MOIFA.

Animal amulets—alpacas, llamas, cattle, oxen, horses, and sheep—are primarily used in rituals to help increase the size of herds. Families also have them to help keep their livestock healthy and fertile. In prehispanic times, these amulets were often very flat. By the late eighteenth and early nineteenth century, they had become three-dimensional, but carvers relied on the natural shape of the stone, rather than enhancing the forms. The Andeans could still recognize the species portrayed by a twist of the horns on a ram, or by the elongated shape of a llama's neck.[109]

FIG. 2-84 *Animal Amulets.* Bautista Saavedra Province, Bolivia. Left: early 20th century. Stone. Gift of Connie Thrasher Jaquith, MOIFA. Right: mid-20th century. Stone, 2¾" x 2½" (7 x 9.5 cm). International Folk Art Foundation Collection, MOIFA.

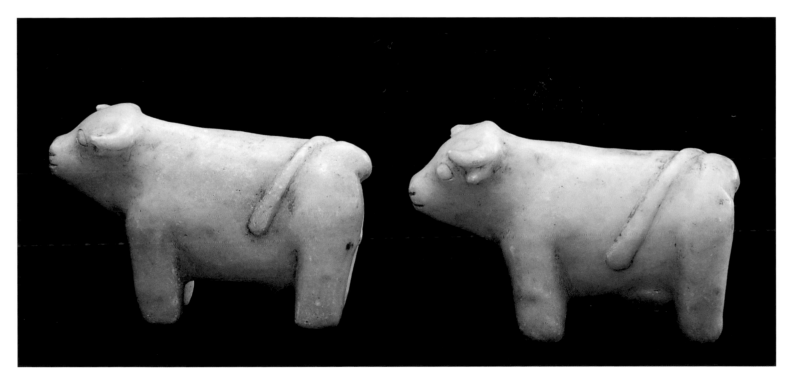

FIG. 2-85 *Bull and Cow Amulets.* Bautista Saavedra Province, Bolivia, or Puno region, Peru, late 20th century. Stone, each 2¼" x 3¼" (5.7 x 8.3 cm). Gift of Kisla Jiménez and Jonathan Williams, MOIFA.

By the twentieth century, more features were depicted in the carvings of animals. The bull and cow portrayed above show carefully finished details, even an anatomically-correct penis cover and udder.

## OTHER TYPES OF AMULETS

FIG. 2-86 *Hand and Corn Amulets.* Bautista Saavedra Province, Bolivia, 19th century. Stone. Top: *Corn.* 1¾" x 3" (4.5 x 7.6 cm). Left: *Hand Holding Weaving Tool.* Right: *Hand Holding Coins.* Private Collection.

Some amulets are kept by individuals to help them with their work. The piece on the left is a hand holding a weaving tool. Women rubbed this amulet on the back of their hands before they started weaving and again when their hands got tired. Other hands held coins, as seen on the right.[110] The corn amulet on the top would help the crops and keep food on the table.

FIG. 2-87 *Amulets with Human Figures.* Bautista Saavedra Province, Bolivia, 20th century. Stone. Left: *Male and Female Couple.* 3¼" x 1½" (8.3 x 3.8 cm). Private Collection. Top center: *Man with Oxen.* International Folk Art Foundation Collection, MOIFA. Right: *Cheese Seller.* Private Collection.

Other stone amulets, made in the twentieth century, portray people from the local environment. Some are used in ceremonies to benefit a person, while others are kept as personal charms. Market vendors carry them to bring good luck with their sales, as seen in the stone carving to the right that portrays a woman selling cheese.[111]

FIG. 2-88 *Amulets. Virgen de Carmen, San Antonio,* and *Santa Inez.* Ayacucho, Peru, mid-20th century. Stone, paint. Largest: 2¼" x 1" (5.7 x 2.5 cm). International Folk Art Foundation Collection, MOIFA.

FIG. 2-89 *Amulet Bottles.* Left: Cuzco, Peru, ca. 1975. Glass, stone, metal, rubber, organic material, liquid. Center left and right: La Paz, Bolivia, 1970. Glass, metal, rubber, fabric, organic material, liquid. Largest: 3½" x 1¾" (8.9 x 4.5 cm). Right: Quito, Ecuador, ca. 1985. Glass, metal, organic material, liquid. International Folk Art Foundation Collection, MOIFA.

By the mid-twentieth century, stone carvers were making miniature figures of Catholic saints that could serve as small amulets.[112] Folk artists in larger cities, such as Cuczo, La Paz, and Quito, began creating another form of amulet using empty injection bottles discarded by local hospitals. The bottles are filled with a variety of materials and liquids said to have magical qualities. Sometimes, miniature stone saints are included, or metal milagros.[113]

## Conopas

Another type of ritual object used by Andeans in the Altiplano region of Peru and Bolivia is generally known as conopa. They are ceramic, stone, wood, or silver sculptures portraying domesticated and other animals important to the everyday life of the people. Examples of the ceramic forms have been found in sites related to the Tiahuanaco culture.[114] Inca carvers also produced beautiful pieces in stone, but these were among the "idols" that Spanish priests sought to destroy. By the late eighteenth and nineteenth centuries, when Andeans were freer to carry out their traditional rituals, conopas were primarily made in clay and the images included llamas, alpacas, cows, bulls, and horses. They are still used today during animal-marking ceremonies to assure protection for the herds and herdsmen, as well as to encourage fertility and increase the number of animals.[115]

Conopas are distinguished by a hole or opening in the back where offerings are placed. Small circular cavities in the Inca stone pieces were filled with a mixture of coca leaves and llama fat. The larger openings in the ceramic forms, known in some regions as *chiwanas*, are filled with a locally made alcoholic drink called *chicha* and coca leaves. These libations are served to the animals, the earth, and the mountains. Sometimes, as part of the ritual, a religious practitioner will carry the vessel to a special place in the mountains where he will bury it for a period of time, inviting the deities to ingest the offering.

FIG. 2-90 *Conopas.* Peru, Inca period, AD 1360–1530. Stone.
Left: *Llama.* Others: *Alpaca.* Largest: 4¾" x 3½" (12.1 x 8.9 cm).
Collection of David and Mayi Munsell.

FIG. 2-91 *Conopas—Llamas.* Cuzco, Peru, 18th–early 19th century. Wood. Left: 4½" x 2½" (11.4 x 6.4 cm). International Folk Art Foundation Collection, MOIFA. Right: Collection of Kisla Jiménez and Jonathan Williams.

Most stone conopas from the Inca period are beautifully carved with details of the animals they portray, such as the bushy hair of an alpaca and long neck of a llama (fig. 2-90). They are generally larger than the pre-Columbian stone animal amulets shown in figure 2-82 but are still small enough to be placed on a ritual table, or mesa, during the ceremonies. A few rare examples of wooden conopas, carved in a similar style, have also survived from colonial times, as seen at left.

FIG. 2-92 *Conopas—Alpaca.* Left: Cuzco region, Peru, 19th century. Ceramic. International Folk Art Foundation Collection, MOIFA. Right: Puno region, Peru, late 18th century. Ceramic, glaze, 7½" x 7" (19.1 x 17.8 cm). Collection of David and Mayi Munsell.

By the late eighteenth and early nineteenth centuries, the use of ceramic conopas became widespread among the rural communities in the southern highlands of Peru and Bolivia. The malleability of the clay allowed potters to decorate them with textured details, such as alpaca hair. There were differences in style from one area to another. For example, conopas from the Puno region were more sculptural in form and coated with a green or yellow glaze made with mineral oxides, as seen in the piece on the right.

FIG. 2-93 *Conopas—Llamas.* Southern highlands, Peru, late 19th century. Ceramic. Left and right: Gift of Connie Thrasher Jaquith, MOIFA. Center back: 8" x 9½" (20.3 x 24.1 cm). Collection of David and Mayi Munsell.

A distinguishing feature of the llama forms, made in the late nineteenth century, continued to be the long neck that was sometimes ornamented with a collar, as seen in the piece on the right. Others had yarn ties added to the ears, as is still done to actual llamas during marking ceremonies. For the most part, the bodies of the ceramic animals were simple bulbous shapes with flat bottoms.

FIG. 2-94 *Conopas*. Cuzco region, Peru, late 19th century. Ceramic, pigment. Left: *Bulls*. Right: *Cow*. 11½" x 6½" (29.2 x 16.5 cm). International Folk Art Foundation Collection, MOIFA.

By the late nineteenth century, many rural people in the southern highlands of Peru had made the transition from tending only alpaca and llama to also herding cattle, sheep, and goats. The bull, seen as a strong and powerful force, became a popular image portrayed in the ceramic conopas, as seen in the two small figures on the left. The bodies of the bulls were sculpted to convey their massive forms and, unlike the earlier pieces portraying llamas and alpacas, they were shown with legs. The two illustrated here were made in workshops in the Cuzco region that specialized in burnishing the clay to create a shiny, copper-colored surface. The larger figure shown at the right represents a cow with spots painted on her hide; although the body is simply shaped, the cow is portrayed with legs.

FIG. 2-95 *Conopas*. Cuzco region, Peru, late 19th–early 20th century. Wood. Left: *Horse*. 5" x 3½" (12.7 x 8.9 cm). International Folk Art Foundation Collection, MOIFA. Center and right: *Bulls*. Collection of Kisla Jiménez and Jonathan Williams.

▼ FIG. 2-96 *Conopas—Bulls*. Bolivia, late 19th–early 20th century. Left pair: mixed metals and wool yarn. Private Collection. Right pair: mixed metals. Each 4" x 3½" (20.3 x 14.3 cm). Gift of Florence Dibell Bartlett, MOIFA.

Some small wooden conopas in the shapes of bulls and horses were produced in the Cuzco area in the late nineteenth and early twentieth century. Small bulls were also made in mixed metals in southern Peru and Bolivia. All of these are similar in form to the small ceramic bulls seen above, with short legs helping to define the animal forms. Their size is similar to the Inca stone conopas (fig. 2-90); they would fit easily on a ritual table along with other ceremonial offerings.

FIG. 2-97 *Conopas—Bulls.* Puno region, Peru, late 19th–early 20th century. Ceramic, glaze. Left: Gift of Kisla Jiménez and Jonathan Williams, MOIFA. Right: 9" x 8" (22.9 x 20.3 cm). Collection of Bob and Gay Sinclair.

Workshops in the Puno region of southern Peru continued to produce ceramic conopas coated in a yellow or green glaze. By the late nineteenth and early twentieth century, they were making bulls in detailed sculptural forms that expressed both the shape and strength of the animals. By the mid-twentieth century, potters in the Pucará area of Puno were particularly well known for creating these figures.

FIG. 2-98 *Conopas—Pumas.* Left: Cuzco region, Peru, late 19th–early 20th centuries. Ceramic, pigment, 11" x 9" (27.9 x 22.9 cm). Collection of Bob and Gay Sinclair. Right: Huayculí, Cochabamba, Bolivia, ca. 1960. Ceramic. International Folk Art Foundation Collection, MOIFA.

Pumas are natural predators in the Altiplano region of the Andes and have been a constant threat to the rural people and their herds. The power and strength of these animals has been admired, much as the bull came to be appreciated in later times. Ceramic conopas portraying pumas were offered to the gods alongside the other animals; this continued into the late nineteenth and twentieth century, as shown in these examples. The figure on the left was made in the Cuzco region, while the animated puma on the right was made in Huayculí, Department of Cochabamba, Bolivia.[116]

## Ritual Offerings

Andeans in the southern highlands of Peru and Bolivia carry out rituals to help bring balance and harmony to their lives and to ensure health, welfare, and productivity for their families, herds, and crops. Most of these ceremonies are performed by a religious practitioner hired by an individual, or family, to help solve a particular problem: provide protection from lightning, bless a new house, prepare a couple for marriage, and a variety of other things. A critical part of the ritual is to put together a special group of items that will be offered to the Andean gods. Traditionally, this consists of things such as flowers, seeds, rice, herbs, cookies, candies, and other foodstuffs, as well as cotton batting, shiny crystals, medals, small Christian crosses, and figures of saints. Llama fetuses and lumps of llama fat are also very important, along with coca leaves and a sprinkling of alcohol.[117]

FIG. 2-99 *Nasario Turpo, a religious practitioner in the Ausangante region of Cuzco, Peru, is preparing a ritual offering*, 2005. Photograph by Andrea Heckman.

These items are generally purchased in *curandero* (healer) shops in large cities and given to a ritual specialist who performs the ceremony. He begins by laying out a poncho or other large cloth and covering that with a smaller ceremonial cloth. Then he will cut paper to a certain size and lay that on top. He selects from the offerings provided by his client and places them on the paper being careful to put them in precise relationships to one another. The fat of the llama is a special delicacy to send to the gods, along with coca leaves that have to be laid down in certain ways. This process can go on for an hour or more, while prayers are said by the religious practitioner. Once he is satisfied with the grouping, he will sprinkle sugar and wine or hard liquor on top of everything. Then the paper is folded into a bundle and tied with a string. At night the bundle will be taken to a special outdoor place, where it will be burned to let the smoke carry the offerings and prayers to the gods. The next morning the ashes may be collected and thrown into a stream or lake.[118]

FIG. 2-100 *Offerings—Tablets with Scenes.* La Paz, Bolivia, 2007. Sugar, wax, paint. Largest: 2¾" x 3" (6.7 x 7.6 cm). International Folk Art Foundation Collection, MOIFA.

FIG. 2-101 *Offerings—Tablets with Scenes.* Oruro, Bolivia, 2000. Clay. Largest: 1½" x 1½" (4 x 4 cm). International Folk Art Foundation Collection, MOIFA.

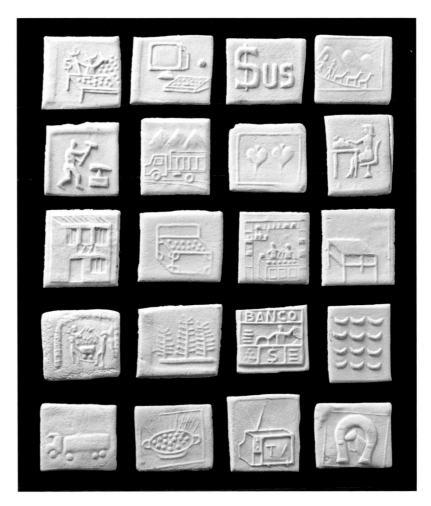

FIG. 2-102 *Offerings—Metal Scenes.* La Paz, Bolivia, 2007. Lead. Largest: 1¾" x 2¼" (4.4 x 5.4 cm). International Folk Art Foundation Collection, MOIFA.

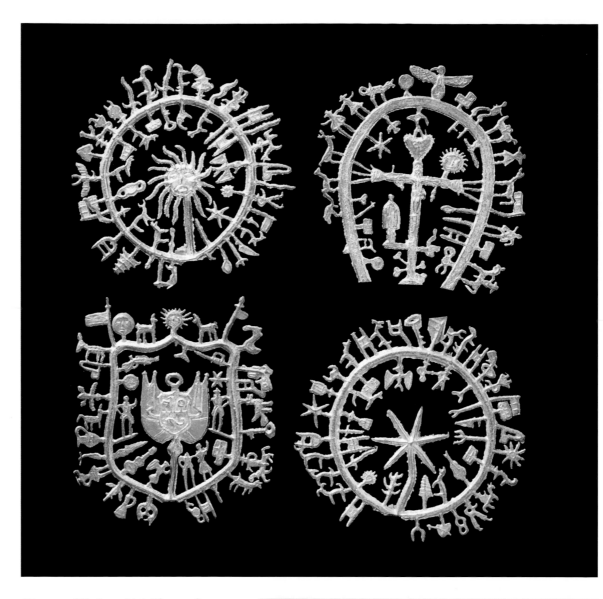

FIG. 2-103 *Offerings—Metal Scenes.* Cuzco, Peru, 1980. Lead. Largest: 3" x 3" (7.6 x 7.6 cm). International Folk Art Foundation Collection, MOIFA.

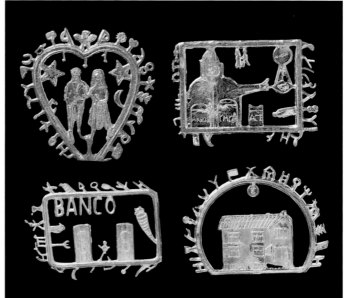

Recently, new types of offerings have become available in the curandero shops. They are scenes portraying the types of things people are asking the gods to help them with. Some of the offerings are painted tablets made from sugar and wax (fig. 2-100), while others consist of small, clay squares stamped with scene (fig. 2-101). Soft lead has also been cast into a variety of pictorial shapes, ranging from animals and crops to houses and lovers. These metal objects and tablets are placed on the ritual paper along with other offerings and later burned.[119]

# Ekeko

Ekeko is considered the Andean god of abundance and prosperity. His origin has been traced to the prehispanic Tiahuanacan culture in the Altiplano region of Bolivia and Peru, where he was represented in small, anthropomorphic figures made in metal, stone, and clay. Archeological evidence shows that the Tiahuanacan people made requests to their deities by offering them miniature representations of what they desired. These practices probably continued to the time of the European conquest, when Spanish priests banned all "idols" and their worship.[120]

FIG. 2-104 *Ekeko Figures.* La Paz, Bolivia, mid-20th century. Plaster, paint, metal, plastic, fabric, foodstuffs. Left: Girard Foundation Collection, MOIFA. Center: 15½" x 12" (39.4 x 30.5 cm). MOIFA. Right: International Folk Art Foundation Collection, MOIFA.

The Ekeko cult resurfaced in La Paz, Bolivia, in 1781, after an indigenous uprising was subdued. The colonial governor, Sebastián Segurola, wanted to make peace with the Andean people and decided to start an annual fair on January 24 to coincide with the feast day of the Virgin of Peace. He was given a figure of Ekeko made by a local artist who revised the traditional characteristics of the deity and made him look like a European man wearing Andean clothing. This became the new image for the god of abundance; as time passed he came to be portrayed loaded down with bags of food, household objects, currency bills, and a variety of other things

that people wanted to make their lives more comfortable. Most families in the Altiplano region have an Ekeko figure in their home and give him offerings of money, food, and other items to keep him happy and ensure their own prosperity.

The annual market to honor Ekeko became known as *alasitas,* taken from an Aymara word that means "purchase me." Today, the fair sprawls along many streets and parks in central La Paz, where miniature versions of money, food, household items, vehicles, and other goods are sold by hundreds of vendors. These toy objects are meant to be given to friends and relatives as gifts. It is believed that recipients of the miniatures will get the represented objects in the course of that year. The popularity of this event has spread to other Bolivian cities and even into southern Peru, where similar markets are scheduled throughout the year.[121]

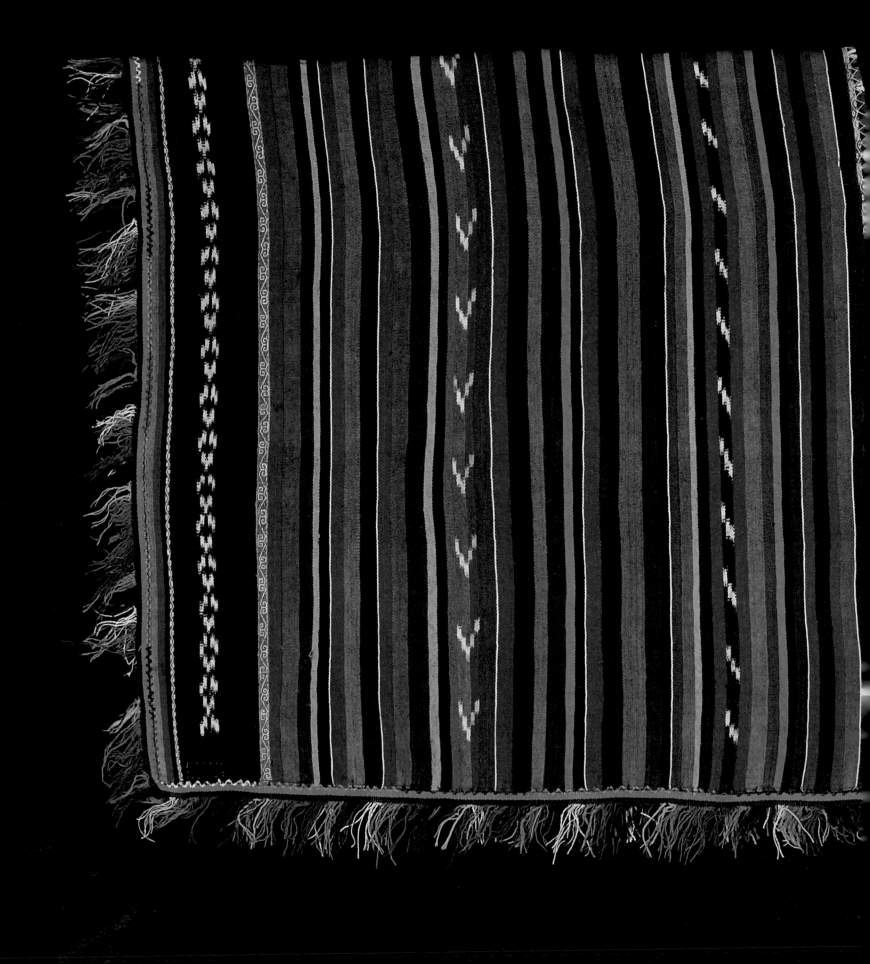

P rehispanic weaving traditions in the Andean highlands evolved after the development of cultivated crops—such as potatoes, corn, and quinoa—that provided the indigenous people of the region with more time to experiment with spinning, dyeing, and weaving techniques. The cold climate made warm clothing essential for survival and animals of the region—llamas, alpacas, vicuñas, and guanacos—offered an abundant source of fiber. Weavers used heddle looms to create different types of garments and accessories; ethnic groups throughout the central Andes developed their own vocabulary of patterns and designs. As weaving evolved, cloth and costumes came to convey such things as gender, age, marital status, social rank, and wealth.[1]

When the Spanish arrived in the early sixteenth century, they were extremely impressed by the richness and beauty of the indigenous weaving and immediately recognized it as a valuable commodity. However, the Europeans brought their own weavers to the Andes and set up workshops, or *obrajes*, where Indians were forced to produce cloth for the overseers. The Spanish introduced foot-treadle looms and new tools to go with them, but indigenous backstrap and horizontal heddle looms were used as well. Flocks of sheep were also brought from Spain and sheep wool, cotton, linen, silk, and metal yarns were all used in the production of various types of cloth.

Andeans were allowed to continue weaving in their own communities, but a series of Spanish laws, enacted from the late sixteenth to the late eighteenth centuries, banned the wearing of traditional garments that were deemed immodest or symbolized indigenous pride among those who fought Spanish rule. Some native men and women of upper ranks were allowed to wear sophisticated Spanish-style clothing, but most Indians were forced to adopt the Spanish-style peasant costume—tailored shirts, pants, skirts, vests, jackets, and hats—often made with fabrics produced in the obrajes. Indians continued to wear some of the old style hand-woven items, such as ponchos, mantles, belts, and bags, along with knitted accessories. They combined the old and new to develop a "traditional" costume they called their own.

The post-Independence era of the nineteenth century allowed for greater freedom among the indigenous people and one aspect of this was a renaissance in weaving. In parts of Bolivia, Peru, and Ecuador a larger number of people were weaving and had access to alpaca fibers, natural dye products, and the technology to produce fine cloth. Most were using the warp-faced technique, and patterns became more and more elaborate. This changed in the latter part of the nineteenth century, when agrarian reforms led to the formation of large agricultural properties leased to foreign companies. Traditional pastoral lands were broken up, causing a decline in breeding and the availability of alpaca fiber. Coarser sheep wool came into widespread use, along with aniline dyes imported from Europe.

Since that time, weavings have been produced and worn in some of the more remote regions of Bolivia, Peru, and Ecuador. The "traditional" costume continues to evolve and incorporate new materials and styles. Even in those areas where people are now wearing European- and American-style manufactured clothing, they continue to create beautiful festival costumes that express their cultural heritage. Today, a few weaving groups have gone back to using alpaca yarns and natural dyes, in order to produce high-quality fabrics for themselves and to sell to an outside market.[2].

## Men's Ponchos

Since early prehispanic times the primary garment for Andean men was a tunic. This was usually made from one piece of cloth folded in half across the warps, with a neck opening created by weaving a discontinuous weft. The sides were sewn up leaving a space for the arms. Tunics continued to be worn through the colonial period and up until the late eighteenth century, serving as an emblem of indigenous identity. In the aftermath of the Indian uprisings, in the 1780s, the Spanish wanted to do away with Indian culture and the tunic became a focus of a new restricted dress code. The Indians were forced to adopt the tailored costume of the eighteenth-century Spanish peasant. In place of the tunic they were told to wear a poncho.

Little is known about the origin of the poncho, but by the seventeenth century it was being worn by Mapuche Indians of south central Chile. This group was notorious for resisting the Spanish; after stealing some of their horses, the Mapuche became adept at breeding them and became equestrians themselves. They may have simply revised the traditional tunic, leaving the sides open, to facilitate use on horseback. The Spanish military quickly recognized the versatility of the poncho for riding and as an all-purpose garment that protected the wearer against cold and rain. By the early eighteenth century, obrajes in Chile were producing thousands of ponchos to export to soldiers and ranchers in other regions of the Spanish colonies. The colonial mestizo also adopted this garment as part of his costume.[3]

The native men were not happy to change their traditional garment; some ponchos woven in the indigenous communities in the late eighteenth and early nineteenth century are small body coverings made from one piece of fabric, similar to tunics. During the wars of independence against Spain, in the early nineteenth century, large ponchos woven with complex striped patterns and embellished with a coat of arms were worn by criollo leaders of the movement, such as General José de San Martín. Indians fighting alongside were impressed by these larger garments; by the mid-nineteenth century, this style had become part of indigenous dress. The larger ponchos were made from two rectangular pieces of cloth sewn together, with a slot left for the neck.[4]

FIG. 3-1 *Ponchito.* Aroma region, La Paz, Bolivia, early to mid-19th century. Alpaca. As pictured: 19¾" x 34¼" (50.2 x 87.6 cm). Gift of Florence Dibell Bartlett, MOIFA.

FIG. 3-2 *Poncho.* Oruro region, Bolivia, mid-19th century. Alpaca. As pictured: 42½" x 64½" (108 x 163.8 cm). Collection of Paul and Elissa Cahn.

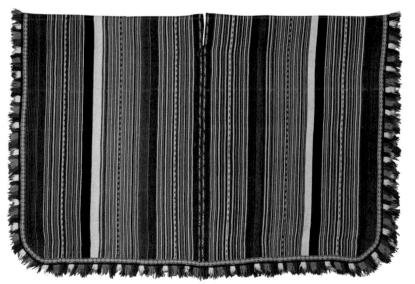

Warp-faced cloth woven by Aymara people in the Altiplano region of southern Peru and Bolivia was traditionally decorated with alternating wide and narrow vertical bands. In colonial pieces monochrome stripes predominated; later, patterned bands became more popular. The ponchos, or *ponchitos*, made in the late eighteenth and early nineteenth centuries, were small squares of cloth with an opening for the head created by weaving a discontinuous weft. One style woven throughout the Aymara region is characterized by a central ground of brown or purple, with wide bands of pink or red near each edge that are broken by three contrasting stripes. Worn for ceremonial occasions, these ponchitos were little more than disguised tunics with open seams. The example above, from the Aroma region in the Department of La Paz, was worn for Sicuri dance ceremonies. Larger ponchos dating from the mid- to late-nineteenth century, were made by sewing two rectangular pieces of woven cloth together, with a slot left for the head. Intricate patterns created with the complementary-warp technique were woven into the bands. However, the weavers continued to use the traditional layout of six bands (three on each side), with solid or bi-colored stripes in between.[5]

FIG. 3-3 *Poncho*. Pisac region, Cuzco, Peru, mid-20th century. Wool. As pictured: 26¾" x 61" (67.9 x 154.9 cm). Collection of Bob and Gay Sinclair.

Quechua weaving traditions in the Cuzco region of Peru are characterized by bands of complex patterns and motifs that often fill the whole cloth. The primary technique used by the weavers is complementary warp that produces a double-faced fabric in which the pattern is the same on both sides, but the colors are opposite. Wide textiles, such as ponchos, often have stripes of varying widths, each combining different motifs. Many of the designs used by the weavers in the Cuzco region today are similar to those found in prehispanic textiles. Other designs have been created in recent decades representing animals, birds, flowers, people, objects, abstract concepts, or an event. The large diamond patterns in this poncho represent multiple lakes of different sizes.[6]

FIG. 3-4 *Poncho*. Potolo region, Chuquisaca, Bolivia, mid-20th century. Wool. As pictured: 21¼" x 47" (54 x 119 cm). Collection of Bob and Gay Sinclair.

Jalq'a weavers in the Potolo region of southern Bolivia also use the complementary-warp technique to create fanciful, two-sided fabrics, but in a different style than found in Cuzco. These fabrics are always woven in red and black and the bands with motifs are usually broken by solid stripes of black or dark brown. The imagery portrays fantastic creatures, such as winged, four-legged figures, headless or multiheaded animals, and even birds wearing human clothing. Many animals have mischievous expressions on their faces. The earliest known examples woven in this style date from the late nineteenth to early twentieth century, when the images were generally more refined and presented in an orderly way. As time progressed, weavers began to experiment with more random patterns, allowing the figures to vary in size and appear upside down or backwards.[7]

### IKAT PONCHOS

*Ikat* patterns are found in ponchos woven in various regions of the Andes. These motifs are created by dyeing the yarn with a design before the weaving begins. Usually, groups of warps are tightly wrapped with another yarn or plant fiber on the sections to be protected from the dye. The Malay-Indonesian word *ikat* is now commonly used in European languages; the technique, however, has a long history in many parts of the world, including in Central Asia and the Middle East.[8] Prehispanic textiles with ikat patterns have been found in sites along the coast of northern Peru and southern Ecuador, but it has been impossible to find a link between those traditions and ikat weavings made in the Andes since the Spanish conquest.[9]

It seems probable that the technique was reintroduced by the Spanish who set up obrajes in many areas of the Andes. At the time of the conquest, the textile industry in Spain was using technology introduced there through seven hundred years of Islamic rule. This had evolved into the Hispano-Moresque and Mudéjar styles of complex, woven fabrics.[10]

Ikat-patterned fabrics came into vogue in Europe in the seventeenth and eighteenth centuries and were produced in workshops there to serve the local clientele.[11] The technique may have been used in some of the eighteenth-century ponchos being woven in the obrajes in Chile and elsewhere. A handful of eighteenth- and early nineteenth-century Bolivian ponchos with ikat patterns have survived. All of them are large and most were woven in cotton, a material used in the Spanish workshops.[12] As with other European art forms, the Indians working in the obrajes would have been able to learn the techniques of ikat dyeing and weaving, passing it on to others who handed it down through the generations. Several Andean communities were making ikat ponchos in the twentieth century and in some regions this tradition is still being carried on today. Most of the ikat patterns are relatively simple, with stepped diamonds and chevrons done in small or very bold motifs.

FIG. 3-5 *Poncho.* Cacha Obraje, Chimborazo, Ecuador, ca. 1965. Cotton. As pictured: 28" x 53½" (71.1 x 135.9 cm). MOIFA.

The ikat technique is used in various parts of Ecuador, but the most elaborate ikat ponchos are made in the town of Cacha Obraje (near Riobamba) in the central highlands. As the name implies, this was once the site of a Spanish-colonial weaving workshop (obraje). Ponchos dating from the first half of the twentieth century were woven in cotton, with indigo-blue dyed yarns providing a striking contrast to the undyed areas of white. In the 1960s thin stripes of red started to appear, as seen in this piece. Later, the weavers began using wool yarn to produce wider bands of red, interspersed with cotton bands of bold blue and white ikat patterns. These ponchos from Cacha Obraje are popular throughout the region, particularly for wearing to fiestas and on other important occasions.[13]

FIG. 3-6 *Poncho.* Ccatca, Cuzco, Peru, mid-20th century. Wool. As pictured: 23½" x 54" (59.7 x 137.2 cm). Collection of Andrea Heckman.

The ikat technique is found in weavings from a number of towns and villages in the Cuzco region of Peru, primarily to the south and east of the capital city. These pieces are made with sheep wool using a warp-faced weave and dyes that are a mixture of natural and aniline pigments. Ponchos from the region of Ccatca are characterized by wide bands of bold, stepped patterns with colorful stripes in between. Fringe is often added as a decorative touch.[14]

FIG. 3-7 *Poncho*. Calcha, Potosí, Bolivia, ca. 1920. Wool. As pictured: 25" x 51" (63.5 x 129.5 cm). MOIFA.

The ikat technique has been used to a limited extent in Bolivia.[15] One of the primary places it continues to be found today is in the town of Calcha, in the southern part of the Department of Potosí. The weavers in this community are known for their ability to spin wool into very fine thread; the cloth they produce is very light. The most elaborate and colorful style of poncho made in Calcha is known as Boliviano. It is woven with many thin stripes of alternating colors, and six of them (three bands on each side of the center seam) are decorated with tiny zigzag and chevron ikat patterns.[16]

FIG. 3-8 *Poncho*. Temuco, Cautín, Chile, late 19th–early 20th century. Wool. As pictured: 26" x 59¾" (66 x 151.8 cm). Gift of Lloyd E. Cotsen and the Neutrogena Corporation, MOIFA.

Mapuche weavers living in various regions of south central Chile had been producing ponchos with finely-spun sheep wool since the late seventeenth and eighteenth centuries. In 1881 this rebellious group was finally subdued by military troops and moved into settlements. The Chilean government instituted a hierarchical system of self government and named *caciques*, or chiefs, to be in charge. These men became very powerful within the Mapuche culture; they began wearing specially-made chief's ponchos as a symbol of their status. Some of the weavers began using the ikat technique to decorate these garments, developing a striking design scheme made up of extremely bold, stepped diamonds and chevrons. The late nineteenth-century examples were usually done in white against dark indigo blue using finely-spun wool. By the twentieth century, the wool fibers became much coarser and other colors, such as aniline red, were sometimes used.[17]

## Women's Mantles

One traditional Andean woman's garment not affected by Spanish-colonial dress codes was the mantle. Composed of two identical pieces of woven fabric sewn together to form a square or rectangular cloth, it is worn across the back and draped over the shoulders. The two edges falling across the chest are held together with a metal pin. The mantle is still used today by women in many regions of the Andean highlands and retains its prehispanic association with the female gender, ethnic identity, and status within local society. These garments are usually ornamented with stripes and bands woven on the loom in a vertical direction. However, when worn the lines are viewed horizontally across the woman's back, a distinction for female garments that can be traced to pre-conquest times.[18] They are generally called *ahuayos* in the Aymara language and *llicllas* in Quechua, but other names are used for mantles worn for special occasions.

FIG. 3-9 *Woman's Mantle*. Aroma region, La Paz, Bolivia, early 19th century. Alpaca, 47" x 41" (119.4 x 104.1 cm). Collection of Paul and Elissa Cahn.

FIG. 3-10 *Woman's Mantle*. Acora region, Puno, Peru, mid-19th century. Alpaca, 42" x 48" (106.7 x 121.9 cm). Gift of William Siegal, MOIFA.

Aymara women in the Altiplano region of southern Peru and Bolivia wore certain types of mantles for religious ceremonies. The one shown opposite, known as *iscayo*, is warp-faced plain weave characterized by a brown or black ground, broken by broad, blue bands. Pink and/or red stripes run across the center of the blue bands and along the edges. The center seam is often elaborately joined. This style was once found in all areas of the Aymara culture but is rarely used today. Another type of warp-faced plain-weave mantle, known as *huallas*, was made in Aymara communities on both sides of Lake Titicaca, where they were worn in marriage ceremonies. In these mantles a plain or mottled ground is broken by groups of narrow stripes (above).[19]

**FIG. 3-11** *Woman's Mantle*. Aroma or Oruro region, Bolivia, second half of the 19th century. Alpaca, 34" x 34" (86.4 x 86.4 cm). Collection of Paul and Elissa Cahn.

The traditional Aymara woman's ahuayo was decorated with a symmetrical arrangement of three groups of complementary-warp patterned bands and color stripes running horizontally across the center and along the edges. Two wide, monochromatic fields in warp-faced plain weave separate the three patterned areas.[20] This fine example is from Aroma or neighboring Oruro and was woven in the second half of the nineteenth century.

**FIG. 3-12** *Woman's Mantle*. Charazani, La Paz, Bolivia, early 20th century. Wool, 32½" x 33½" (82.6 x 85.1 cm). Gift of Laurie Adelson and Bruce Takami, MOIFA.

Weavings from the Charazani region in the Department of La Paz, Bolivia, are often woven in red, pink, or orange yarns with a few darker bands—black, brown, or maroon—added as accents. The patterned areas are usually white and feature zoomorphic and anthropomorphic figures and motifs that represent the environment and lives of the people. Another characteristic of Charazani weavings is the way the terminal areas of the patterned bands are finished off with two- to three-inch sections of no pattern, followed by one or two motifs. As the mantle is composed of two cloths joined together, the terminal areas always appear at opposite ends of the piece.[21]

**FIG. 3-13** *Woman's Mantle*. Bolívar, Cochabamba, Bolivia, mid- to late-19th century. Alpaca and wool, 45" x 48" (114.3 x 121.9 cm). Gift of William Siegal, MOIFA.

During the colonial period, Spanish missionaries imposed the Quechua language and cultural patterns on the Aymara people living in several regions of Bolivia, including Cochabamba. As a result, the decoration on mantles made and worn by women in communities such as Bolívar have wider fields of single, warp-faced colors placed between the three patterned bands of complementary-warp weave. This is similar to the Quechua llicllas from the Cuzco region of Peru (see figs. 3-14, 3-15, 3-16). Women in the Bolívar area handed down weavings such as this one from generation to generation and used them as wedding garments.[22]

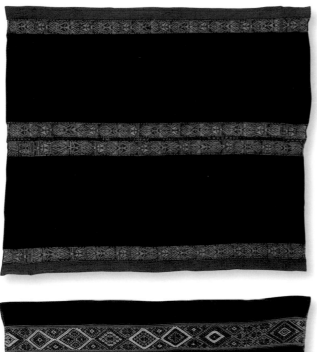

FIG. 3-14 *Woman's Mantle.* Q'ero, Cuzco, Peru, late 19th–early 20th century. Alpaca and wool, 34½" x 38½" (87 x 97.8 cm). Private Collection.

Women's mantles from the Cuzco area typically have outer borders woven in red yarns and two central areas in black. In Q'ero the complementary-warp patterned bands on each side of the black often have different color combinations and sometimes show variations in the design. Motifs used in Q'ero weavings are comparatively few but can be elaborated in a variety of ways; they have also evolved and changed over time.[23]

FIG. 3-15 *Woman's Mantle.* Chahuaytire, Cuzco, Peru, late 19th–early 20th century. Alpaca and wool, 36" x 37" (91.4 x 94 cm). Private Collection.

Weavers in Chahuaytire produce women's mantles with two wide bands of black ground framed by decorated bands of complementary-warp motifs. Some of the primary designs used in their weavings are diamond patterns said to represent flowers and stars. The size and layout of the diamonds can vary from one band to another, creating a lively visual effect when the mantle is worn across a woman's back.[24]

FIG. 3-16 Lidelia Callañaupa Quispe, *Woman's Mantle.* Chinchero, Cuzco, Peru, 2008. Alpaca, wool, 38" x 42" (96.5 x 106.7 cm). International Folk Art Foundation Collection, MOIFA.

In 1996 Nilda Callañaupa Alvarez established the Center for Traditional Textiles of Cuzco, an educational organization for the study and celebration of the weaving traditions of the southern Andes. She learned to weave at a young age in Chinchero, when women still carried on this tradition and wore their traditional dress. However, by the late twentieth century, the art form began to die and younger men and women no longer wore the costume of their villages. Today, Callañaupa Alvarez oversees cooperatives of weavers in nine communities in the Cuzco region, where they are once again using alpaca yarns dyed with natural materials to create extremely fine cloth.[25] This beautiful woman's mantle was woven by Lidelia Callañaupa Quispe, a member of the cooperative in Chinchero. In Lidelia's community, the wide background bands are woven in indigo blue, and identical patterned bands are decorated with tiny motifs.

# Women's Overskirts.

The traditional Andean woman's dress, known as *urku* in Aymara and *aksu* in Quechua, was made from two pieces of woven cloth sewn together to produce a long garment. This was wrapped around the body under the arms, with the top edges pulled over the shoulders and fastened with metal pins. The waist was tied with a wide belt creating a bloused bodice. The long edges of the dress overlapped slightly at the woman's side, but the garment remained open, partially exposing her legs and breasts. The Spanish viewed this as indecent and forced the Andeans to adopt the more modest costume of Spanish peasant women.

In some regions of Bolivia the traditional dress was maintained but slowly modified from a utilitarian garment to a smaller, more decorative piece worn over European-style clothing. In the departments of Cochabamba, Potosí, and Chuquisaca the modified dress was folded lengthwise like an accordion and hung over the belt in the back. The decorative overskirt persisted through much of the twentieth century and in some communities is still worn today. The woven patterns of the two pieces of fabric sewn together are asymmetrical, with one half usually having more design work than the other.[26]

FIG. 3-17 *Woman's Overskirt*. Bolívar, Cochabamba, Bolivia, early 19th century. Alpaca, 56" x 53" (142.2 x 134.6 cm). Collection of Paul and Elissa Cahn.

Overskirts have been worn by women in the Bolívar region of Cochabamba as part of their matrimonial costume. They are considered heirlooms to be handed down from one generation to another. The patterns woven into the two ends are particularly elaborate and colorful.[27]

FIG. 3-18 *Woman's Overskirt.* Potolo, Chuquisaca, Bolivia, early to mid-20th century. Wool, 54½" x 31" (138.4 x 78.7 cm). Collection of Bob and Gay Sinclair.

Jalq'a women in the Potolo region of the Department of Chuquisaca continue to wear the overskirt as part of their outfits today. As in the ponchos, weavers use the complementary-warp technique to create fanciful, red motifs on a black or brown background. The spatial relationship of the images is freeform; by the mid-twentieth century, the figures had become very animated and more randomly arranged, as seen in the top part of this piece.[28]

FIG. 3-19 *Woman's Half Overskirt.* Tarabuco region, Chuquisaca, Bolivia, mid-20th century. Wool and cotton, 30" x 42" (76.2 x 106.7 cm). Collection of Bob and Gay Sinclair.

By the mid-twentieth century, women in the Tarabuco region of the Department of Chuquisaca were wearing half of the aksu for their decorative overskirt, making it less bulky (see fig. 2-38). The patterned area along the bottom was done in the complementary-warp technique, but it is complicated by the use of two different materials for the warp elements. A fine, white, commercial-cotton thread is warped along with coarser, handspun wool. Since the dyed-wool yarns are considerably thicker than the white ones, the color motifs appear in relief. Images of horses and other animals are interspersed with floral and geometric designs.[29]

## Carrying Cloths

A traditional accessory for most Andean women is the carrying cloth, which can be about the same size or larger than a mantle, or as small as a handkerchief. The larger ones are used to carry young children, market items, and even firewood. Medium- and smaller-size cloths hold coca leaves and other foodstuffs. During special ceremonies, they also serve as ground cloths on which to put the ritual table, or mesa, where offerings are laid out for Pachamama and other Andean gods.[30] In the past these cloths were hand woven from alpaca and sheep wool, but today the larger ones are usually commercially made in acrylic yarns woven in colors and patterns that fit the traditional aesthetic.[31]

FIG. 3-20 *Carrying Cloths.* Ocongate region, Cuzco, Peru, mid-20th century. Wool. Largest: 14″ x 14″ (35.6 x 35.6 cm). Collection of Bob and Gay Sinclair.

For the most part, small carrying cloths are still hand woven in one piece of fabric. Some of the finest come from the Ocongate region in the Department of Cuzco, Peru. These cloths, called *unkuñas*, are often used by unmarried women to carry their coca leaves and other personal items for everyday use or for festivals. Special *un-kuñitas*, smaller cloths, are used to store sacred objects that are thought to protect the home.[32] Religious practitioners also use these smaller cloths to hold ritual offerings until they are ceremonially burned.[33] Regardless of the size, the central panel is always ornamented with red and white diamond shapes filled with stylized flower motifs. The edges are decorated with thin vertical lines of alternating colors and the two wider areas between are asymmetrical, woven with bands of neutral tones.

# Woven Bags

The Quechua word for purse or bag is *chuspa*; Andean men and women have used them in different forms for more than 2,000 years. One of their most important functions for men is to carry coca leaves, an essential and sacred plant used in ritual and daily life.[34] Most coca bags are made from a rectangular cloth folded in half across the warps, with the sides sewn up and often covered with a woven border. Small pockets, accessible from the inside, are sometimes woven into the bags using longer warp threads.[35] The pockets can be for carrying lime—used as a catalyst while chewing coca leaves—or for keeping coins; they also add a decorative appearance to the front of the bag.[36] Chuspas woven with elaborate patterns and ornamented with fringe are used for special occasions, or worn as part of dance costumes.[37]

FIG. 3-21 *Coca Bag.* Bolívar region, Cochabamba, Bolivia, late 19th century. Alpaca, wool, 11" x 9¼" (27.9 x 23.5 cm). International Folk Art Foundation Collection, MOIFA.

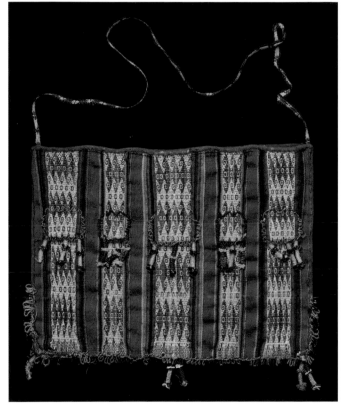

FIG. 3-22 *Coca Bag.* Charazani region, La Paz, Bolivia, late 19th–early 20th century. Alpaca, wool. Without strap: 10½" x 14" (26.7 x 35.6 cm). Collection of Bob and Gay Sinclair.

Coca bags have been made in many different regions of Bolivia, and some of the most elaborate ones come from the southwest area of the Department of Cochabamba around Bolívar and Challa.[38] The example at left is made with a double-cloth weave, known as *corte*. Two small pockets have been woven into the front. The chuspa in figure 3-22 is from the Charazani region of the Department of La Paz. It has been ornamented with small glass beads, similar to the Charazani women's headbands shown in figure 3-29. The intricate scroll pattern in the weave is also similar to that seen in the headbands and represents a land snail that symbolizes fertility for the crops.[39]

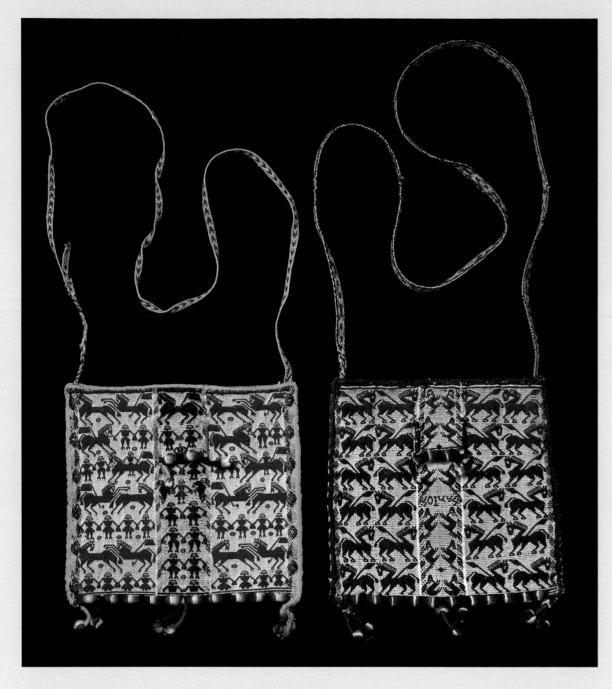

FIG. 3-23 *Coca Bags*. Tarabuco region, Chuquisaca, Bolivia, mid-20th century. Wool and cotton. Left: Gift of Laurie Adelson and Bruce Takami, MOIFA. Right, without strap: 8" x 7½" (20.3 x 19.1 cm). Gift of Cleves Weber, MOIFA.

Coca bags from the Tarabuco region are generally small and flat, ornamented with colorful animals and human figures that stand out against a white-cotton ground. Although maroon, red, and orange on white are the typical colors used in woven clothing from this region, Tarabucans follow the Catholic custom of wearing black during periods of mourning. Everyone has a set of black clothes, called *luto*, which they use on these occasions; included are black-on-white chuspas worn by men, as seen here on the right.[40]

FIG. 3-24 *Coca Bag.* Ingavi Province, La Paz, Bolivia, mid-20th century. Wool, 16" x 18½" (40.6 x 47 cm). Gift of Florence Dibell Bartlett, MOIFA.

Coca bags from the Ingavi region in the Department of La Paz, Bolivia, are characterized by an elongated rectangular shape. They are woven from finely-spun wool yarn dyed with bright aniline colors that are alternated in vertical bands, creating a lively effect. The central band is usually ornamented with pictorial motifs and the two bands on either side are inscribed with words, often the name of the owner.[41]

FIG. 3-25 *Coca Bag.* Taquile Island, Puno, Peru, late 20th century. Commercial wool. Without strap: 7¾" x 8½" (19.7 x 21 cm). MOIFA.

Taquile Island coca bags, dating from the second half of the twentieth century, are generally woven with commercially-spun wool yarn, resulting in a fine, light cloth. Similar to the belt in figure 3-31, this bag was woven with a color scheme of maroon or red warp-faced ground, interspersed with patterned bands of black, white, and sometimes red.

FIG. 3-26 *Coca Bags.* Left: Ollantaytambo region, Cuzco, Peru, ca. 1980. Wool, buttons, beads. Gift of Robert Holzapfel, MOIFA. Right: Pacchanta, Cuzco, Peru, ca. 2000. Wool. Without strap: 13" x 8" (33 x 20.3 cm). Collection of Andrea Heckman.

Coca bags woven in several areas of the Department of Cuzco, Peru, are ornamented with long strands of yarn.[42] Occasionally, chuspas are decorated with plastic buttons and beads, as seen in the example on the left. Two small pockets were woven in the front of this bag and given additional fringe, adding to the festive nature of the piece.

FIG. 3-27 *Money Bags.* Pacchanta, Cuzco, Peru, late 20th century. Wool. Left: Collection of Patricia La Farge. Right, without strap: 15½" x 8" (39.4 x 20.3 cm). Collection of Andrea Heckman.

Another type of bag woven in the Cuzco region was traditionally used by men and women to carry coins. Once the money was put inside it was rolled up, secured with the tie, and tucked away in a pocket or front of a dress. For the most part, their function has been replaced by small, commercially-made coin bags. Today, they are only being woven in the town of Pacchanta in the Quispicanchi Province and are known by the Quechua name *pachaq chaki*, which literally means "one hundred feet," as the bags resemble the shape of a centipede.[43]

FIG. 3-28 Top: *Man's Carrying Bag*. Lampa Province, Puno, Peru, mid-to late 20th century. Llama and sheep wool. Collection of Bob and Gay Sinclair. Left: *Produce Bag*. La Paz, Bolivia, mid-20th century. Llama and sheep wool. Gift of Eloisa Thornburg Jones, MOIFA. Right: *Produce Bag*. Lake Titicaca region, La Paz, Bolivia, late 20th century. Llama and sheep wool, 43" x 25" (109.2 x 63.5 cm). Private Collection.

Another type of bag used daily by men in communities throughout Bolivia and regions of Peru is coarsely woven and features stripes of uniform widths. An example is shown here at the top. The colors are usually that of undyed llama and sheep wool—gray, light and dark brown, and black. Occasionally, one or more stripes will have dyed yarns. Known in Ayamara as *huaycaca* and in Quechua as

*wayaqa*, this type of bag dates to prehispanic times and has remained unchanged in form, aesthetics, and function. It can be used for carrying any item, including coca leaves. Most have no shoulder strap and are carried by tucking into the waistband.[44]

A related bag found throughout the same regions of the Andes is used to transport goods on llama-back, shown here in the bottom (see also fig. 3-35). This larger form also dates to prehispanic times, but since the colonial period they have been referred to as *costales*, the Spanish term for sacks. They are used to carry food, such as potatoes and corn, from the fields to the house and for hauling a variety of produce and other things to and from the markets. The bags are sewn closed with a heavy piece of twine, which is later carefully removed, but not cut, to open the sacks.[45]

## Women's Headbands

Headbands, or *winchas*, were worn by Andean women in prehispanic times, and their use gradually disappeared after the Spanish conquest. The only place they are still found today is in the Charazani region in the Department of La Paz (see fig. 4-1).[46].

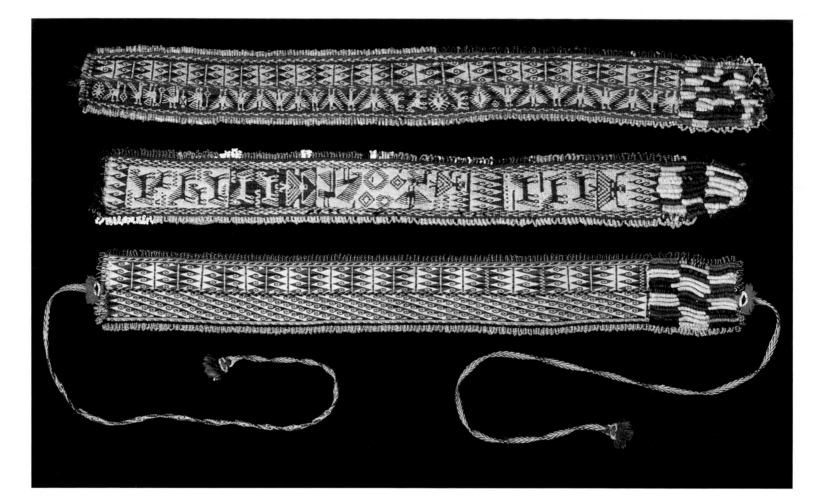

FIG. 3-29 *Women's Headbands*. Charazani, La Paz, Bolivia, late 19th–early 20th century. Wool, glass beads. Top: 21" x 2½" (53.3" x 6.4 cm). International Folk Art Foundation Collection, MOIFA. Center: Gift of Florence Dibell Bartlett, MOIFA. Bottom: International Folk Art Foundation Collection, MOIFA.

Charazani headbands are finely woven with intricate designs and bordered in glass beads. Most of them have been handed down from one generation to another and represent the female lineage.[47] The tiny scroll motif frequently found in Charazani weavings is a stylization of a type of land snail called *churu*. It is regarded as a symbol of agricultural fertility.[48]

# Belts

Belts have been an integral part of Andean costume from very early times. Men originally wore them to cinch the waist of their tunic, and women wrapped them around the waistline of their dress. With the change in clothing styles imposed by the Spanish, men began wearing belts around the waist of their tailored pants, and women wore them with their Spanish-style skirts and dresses.[49] In some regions of Bolivia belts were woven as wide wraps, while in Peru and Ecuador they were generally narrower and longer in length.

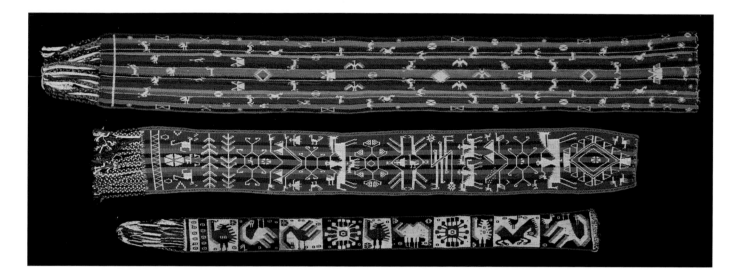

FIG. 3-30 *Belts.* Top: Calamarca, La Paz, Bolivia, early to mid-20th century. Wool, 49" x 5½" (124.5 x 14 cm). Collection of Bob and Gay Sinclair. Center: Pacajes Province, La Paz, Bolivia, early 20th century. Wool. Gift of the Girard Foundation Collection, MOIFA. Bottom: Challa, Cochabamba, Bolivia, mid-20th century. Wool. Gift of Nancy Bloch, MOIFA.

One style of belt that evolved from prehispanic times is known as *huakas.* They are wide bands of cloth created with warp-faced weave and complementary-warp patterning, with braided straps sewn to one end. These belts were still being worn in the twentieth century by Aymara women in certain regions of Bolivia, as part of their ceremonial costume. The top and center belts shown here are good examples of the style found in the Calamarca area and Pacajes Province in the Department of La Paz.[50] The belt on the bottom is from Challa in the Department of Cochabamba, where the belts are not quite as wide and the pictorial motifs are larger in scale, portraying fantastic birds and animals.[51]

▼ FIG. 3-31 *Belt.* Taquile Island, Puno, Peru, late 20th century. Commercial wool, 35" x 6¼" (88.9 x 15.9 cm). Collection of Andrea Heckman.

The wide-belt style is also found in the Department of Puno, Peru.[52] These belts are still being worn by men and women on the Island of Taquile in Lake Titicaca, about 15 miles (24 km) from the Puno Port. Taquile weavers use finely-spun sheep wool to create lightweight fabrics, characterized by broad areas of maroon or red warp-faced weave and narrower bands with complementary-warp pictorial motifs in black and white.[53] One end of the belt has braided straps to help cinch it in place.

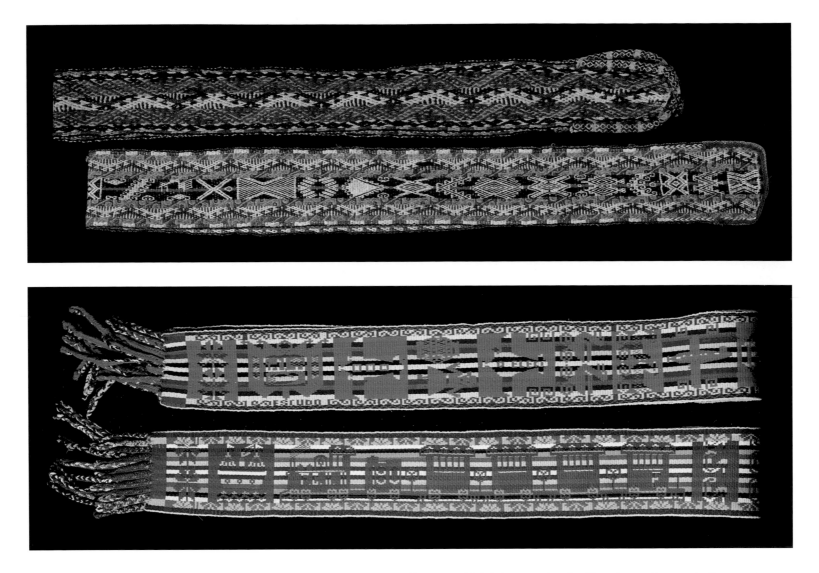

FIG. 3-32 *Belts*. Cotabambas, Apurímac, Peru, mid-20th century. Alpaca and sheep wool. Top: International Folk Art Foundation Collection, MOIFA. Bottom, as pictured folded: 30" x 4" (76.2 x 10.2 cm). Gift of Dr. and Mrs. John Reinhart, MOIFA.

The long narrow belts found in Peru are generally known as *chumpi*, a Quechua word derived from Inca times that refers to finely woven cloth. Although men sometimes wear belts today to cinch up their pants, chumpis are generally used by women to tie the waists of their skirts and to secure babies swaddled in a blanket and carried on the back.[54] In the mid-twentieth century, weavers in the Cotabambas region of the Department of Apurímac specialized in creating belts with complex patterns using alpaca and sheep wool yarns dyed with natural colors.[55]

FIG. 3-33 *Belts*. Viques, Junín, Peru, ca. 1960. Sheep wool and cotton. Longest, as pictured folded: 28" x 3½" (71.1 x 8.9 cm). Girard Foundation Collection, MOIFA.

Weavers in the Viques area of Huancayo in the Department of Junín, Peru, use worsted cotton and sheep wool to create colorful belts worn for festivals and other special events.[56] The yarn is dyed with bright natural and aniline tints and woven in the complementary-warp technique, to create bold, pictorial images of trains and boats, along with fanciful animals and birds. Sometimes, these motifs include the year the weaving was made.

▶ FIG. 3-34 *Belt*. Cañar Province, Ecuador, ca. 1965. Commercial cotton, 96" x 2" (243.8 x 5.1 cm). MOIFA.

Belts are woven in many parts of Ecuador using a variety of techniques. Some of the most elaborate patterns are found on those from the Cañar Province in the central highlands. They are generally long and narrow and are worn by men who tie them around their waist and let the ends hang down to the side. Sometimes, these long belts are used to swaddle babies wrapped in blankets. They are woven by men on small back-strap looms using fine hand-spun wool or commercially-made cotton thread. The bold motifs, created with the complementary-warp technique, feature a wide range of pictorial images—animals, plants, landscapes, humans, religious symbols, and even vehicles. Occasionally, the weaver's name is woven into the design. The traditional colors are wine-red and white, or black and white, or a combination of all three.[57]

## Animal Ornaments

The herding of llamas, alpacas, and other domesticated animals is an important part of rural life in some highland regions of Ecuador, Peru, and Bolivia. As in prehispanic times, these animals are viewed as sacred beings and treated with great reverence.

FIG. 3-35 *A herd of llamas in the Cuzco region of Peru transport goods to market in handwoven sacks called costales. Their ears are adorned with yarn tassels put there during the annual ritual of counting and marking the animals,* 1990. Photograph by A. Tim Wells.

FIG. 3-36 *Animal Ear Ornaments.* Sucre region, Chuquisaca, Bolivia, 2008. Wool. Largest: 5" x 3" (12.7 x 7.6 cm). International Folk Art Foundation Collection, MOIFA.

Families in areas of Bolivia and Peru continue to carry out the annual ritual of counting and marking their llamas and alpacas, along with sheep, cattle, and goats. As part of the ritual, colored-yarn tassels, known as "flowers," are sewn through the animals' ears. In the Oruro region of Bolivia this is referred to as "making the animals bloom."[58]

FIG. 3-37 *Animal Collar.* Ayacucho region, Peru, early 20th century. Wool, 16" x 24" (40.6 x 61 cm). Gift of Florence Dibell Bartlett, MOIFA.

Herd animals, particularly llamas and alpacas, are dressed up to participate in festivals and other special occasions. This embroidered neck collar is from the Ayacucho region of Peru.[59]

FIG. 3-38 *Animal Collar with Bells.* Cuzco region, Peru, mid-20th century. Wool, metal. As pictured: 21" x 15 (53.3 x 38.1 cm). International Folk Art Foundation Collection, MOIFA.

FIG. 3-39 *Animal Collars with Bells.* Highlands Bolivia. Left: early 20th century. Llama and sheep wool, metal. Gift of Laurie Adelson and Bruce Takami, MOIFA. Right: late 20th century. Llama and sheep wool, metal. As pictured: 19" x 18" (48.3 x 45.7 cm). International Folk Art Foundation Collection, MOIFA.

The lead animal in a herd often wears a bell around its neck that makes a tinkling sound as the group moves through the highland pastures. This will let the herder know where to find the animals when it comes time to take them back to the corral. During the marking festival, and other special occasions, the lead animal is adorned with a more elaborate collar. Sometimes a small chuspa (coca bag) will be attached, as seen with the smaller collar pictured upper right.

FIG. 3-40 *Animal Halters.* Cuzco region, Peru, mid-20th century. Left: wool, metal. Right: wool, 11" x 14" (27.9 x 35.6 cm). International Folk Art Foundation Collection, MOIFA.

Sometimes, the animals wear halters; here are two examples from the Cuzco region of Peru. They were probably used when the herd was being led by a man on horseback traveling over a road or trail.

# Women's Adaptation of European-Style Clothing

The prehispanic Andean woman's wraparound dress was left partially open at the side, exposing her legs and breasts. The Spanish viewed this as indecent and forced indigenous women to adopt the more modest costume of Spanish peasant women. In Bolivia and Peru, this process evolved during the sixteenth to eighteenth centuries, but in some parts of Ecuador the traditional dress didn't disappear until the early twentieth century. As women converted to the European-style clothing, they figured out ways to adapt the forms to their own sense of fashion and make a new style of their own. This is still carried on today.

## DRESS, SKIRT, AND BLOUSE

The Spanish-style peasant costume imposed on indigenous women took two forms. One was a long-sleeve dress with a large enough opening at the neck to pull over the head. The other, more common, consisted of a gathered skirt and long-sleeve tailored blouse.

FIG. 3-41 *Woman's Dress.* Calcha, Potosí, Bolivia, ca. 2000. *Dress:* wool, cotton lace, embroidery thread, sequins, 41" x 43" (104.1 x 109.2 cm). *Hat:* felt, cotton lace. Gifts of Nancy Reynolds, MOIFA.

In some communities in the departments of Potosí and Chuquisaca, Bolivian women adopted the European-style, long-sleeved dress called *almilla*, rather than the skirt and blouse. In Calcha they continue to wear these dresses, particularly for festivals and other special events. As shown in this example, the women decorate the neck, wide sleeves, and bottom edge of their festival dresses with lace, embroidery, rickrack, and sequins. They also wear an orange felt hat to set off the outfit.[62]

FIG. 3-42 *Woman's Skirt.* Calamarca, La Paz, Bolivia, early 20th century. Wool, 26 3/8" x 38¼" (67 x 97.2 cm). Gift of Laurie Adelson and Bruce Takami, MOIFA.

When first used, the skirt, or *pollera*, worn by indigenous women in villages throughout the Department of La Paz, Bolivia, were made from traditional cloth. They were woven in exceptionally long pieces and usually ornamented with bold stripes of red, white, and blue on a natural brown or black background. Sometimes, patterned bands were included, as seen in this example from Calamarca. The long pieces of fabric were gathered or pleated to form very full skirts. By the early twentieth century, the handwoven skirts had stopped being produced, but women continued to wear older pieces for ceremonial occasions; the skirts have been handed down through the generations.[60] Today, in many regions of highland Bolivia, women wear gathered skirts made from plain-weave wool, *bayeta,* or other commercial fabrics.[61]

FIG. 3-43 Ciriaco Quispe Auccausi, *Woman's Outfit.* Chinchero, Cuzco, Peru, 2008. Wool, cotton, metal, plastic. International Folk Art Foundation Collection, MOIFA.

Women in many regions of the central and southern highlands of Peru continue to wear gathered skirts made from plain-weave bayeta, or other purchased fabrics. The garments are pleated at the waist and sewn with a band to create a full skirt; several are often worn one on top of another. In the Cuzco region these skirts are usually embellished with woven, multicolored bands sewn around the bottom edge. Skirt lengths vary from reaching the knee to covering the ankle. The tailored, wool shirt worn with the skirts is known in Quechua as *aymilla.* In some towns, such as Chinchero, the wool shirts have been replaced by embroidered cotton blouses, or *camisas.* The women of this village also wear a small matching cotton vest, called a *kurpino.* Short jackets, or *jobonas,* ornamented with rickrack and buttons are often part of the outfit.[63]

FIG. 3-44 *Blouse*. Central Chimborazo Province, Ecuador, ca. 1950. Cotton, embroidery thread, 54" x 31" (137.2 x 78.7 cm). Private Collection.

FIG. 3-45 *Blouse*. Northeastern Pichincha or eastern Imbabura Province, Ecuador, ca. 1980. Cotton, embroidery thread, 45" x 50" (114.3 x 127 cm). Private Collection.

Women in many regions of Ecuador wear gathered skirts and blouses made from wool, cotton, and other fabrics. However, in the provinces of Imbabura, southern Pichincha, and central Chimborazo women continued to wear, into the twentieth century, a version of the prehispanic-style woman's wraparound dress, known in Ecuador as *anaku*. Eventually, a half-length wrapped skirt was adopted and they began wearing long blouses that extended down to the bottom or below the skirt, helping cover the women's legs. The blouses are often beautifully decorated with embroidery on the yoke, sleeves, and sometimes along the bottom edge. The camisa from Chimborazo is an example of the simple patterns and figural motifs being used in that region in the mid-twentieth century. Women in the provinces of northeastern Pichincha and eastern Imbabura developed their own style of embroidered decoration that they applied to the yoke and upper sleeve (also see fig. 4–11). These blouses generally feature intricate floral motifs done in bright, contrasting colors.[64]

### HATS

In prehispanic times, Andean women wore folded cloth to cover their heads, but after adopting the Spanish peasant costume they started wearing European-style hats. Still an important part of the Andean woman's costume today, the hats vary in style from region to region and among different ethnic groups.

FIG. 3-46 *Women's Hats.* Left: Ayaviri, Puno, Peru, early 20th century. Straw, wool, commercial fabrics. Gift of Dr. J. Monroe Thornington, International Folk Art Foundation Collection, MOIFA. Right: Pitumarca region, Cuzco, Peru, early 20th century. Straw, wool, commercial fabrics, 6" x 20" (15.2 x 50.8 cm). Gift of Peter P. Cecere, MOIFA.

Above are two examples of a colonial-style hat still worn in the early twentieth century by women in the Cuzco and Puno regions of Peru. Spanish and criollo women wore this type of broad-brimmed hat in the seventeenth century, to protect their heads and faces from the harsh sun. At first the hats were imported from Europe, but by the eighteenth century they were produced in Jesuit-run workshops. Indigenous women eventually began making similar types of hats themselves.[65] They are constructed from woven straw covered with dark blue or black bayeta (fabric). The top and rim are ornamented with imported brocade fabrics and woven-metallic ribbon. Longer pleated fabrics hang from the sides, offering a decorative effect, as well as more shade for the wearer's head and face.

FIG. 3-47 *Women in Accha Alta, Cuzco, Peru, wear traditional costumes with broad-brimmed hats*, 2008. Photograph by Barbara Mauldin.

FIG. 3-48 *Women's Hats*. Left: Capachica Peninsula, Puno, Peru, ca. 1960. Straw, wool, embroidery thread. 5" x 18" (12.7 x 45.7 cm). Gift of the Girard Foundation Collection, MOIFA. Center: Combapata region, Cuzco, Peru, ca. 1960. Straw, wool, embroidery thread. Gift of Sallie Wagner, International Folk Art Foundation Collection, MOIFA. Right: Raqchi, Cuzco, Peru, 2005. Straw, wool, embroidery thread. International Folk Art Foundation Collection, MOIFA.

This style of broad-brimmed hat is still worn today in many areas of Cuzco and Puno, Peru. It continues to be made from woven straw covered in bayeta. In some communities of the Cuzco region the tops are decorated with applied fabrics, as seen in the photograph of Acha Alta women. In other villages the ornamentation has been simplified to embroidered patterns.[66]

FIG. 3-49 *Women's Hats.* Left: Villa Villa, Chuquisaca, Bolivia, early to mid-20th century. Straw, fabric, thread, sequins, 7" x 16½" (17.8 x 41.9 cm). Gift of Laurie Adelson and Bruce Takami, MOIFA. Right: Tarabuco region, Chuquisaca, Bolivia, ca. 1965. Straw, fabric, thread, sequins. Gift of Eloisa Jones, MOIFA.

Women in the Tarabuco region of the Department of Chuquisaca, Bolivia, wear a slightly different style of hat that derives from Spanish colonial-era fashion. Their hats are also made from straw, but the broad brim flares up on each side rather than laying flat. They are heavily ornamented with embroidery, rickrack, and sequins and are generally worn for festival occasions.[67]

FIG. 3-50 *Women's Hats.* Tarabuco region, Chuquisaca, Bolivia. Left: mid-20th century. Wool, thread, plastic buttons, 14" x 7" (35.6 x 17.8 cm). Gift of Lloyd E. Cotsen and the Neutrogena Corporation, MOIFA. Right: 2007. Wool, beads, sequins. International Folk Art Foundation Collection, MOIFA.

Another type of hat worn by women in the Tarabuco region of Bolivia is a cap that probably evolved from the headwear of Spanish soldiers. The caps are crocheted with a section hanging down the back and are worn as part of a woman's daily costume (see fig. 2-38).[68] The example on the left dates from the mid-twentieth century when the caps had a short brim in front and the space above was ornamented with embroidered floral patterns. By 2007 some caps, such as the one on the right, had broader brims made with wire strung with beads; sequined decoration covered the front and back.

FIG. 3-51 *Women's Hats.* Left: Junín, Peru, 2005. Canvas, paint, ribbon. Center: Cuzco, Peru, 2008. Canvas, paint, satin ribbon. Right: Potosí, Bolivia, late 20th century. Straw, paint, satin ribbon, 8" x 16" (20.32 x 40.6 cm). International Folk Art Foundation Collection, MOIFA.

Woven straw hats were also brought to the Andes by Spanish colonists and were soon being made in local workshops. Eventually, these hats became part of the chola costume and are still worn in many parts of Bolivia, Peru, and Ecuador. Today, this style of hat is also made from stiffened canvas. Those used for festivals and other special occasions are often coated with white paint and decorated with satin or lace ribbons.[69]

FIG. 3-52 *Woman in Puno, Peru, wearing the traditional chola outfit complete with a bowler hat,* 2008. Photograph by Barbara Mauldin.

FIG. 3-53 *Woman's Hat.* La Paz, Bolivia, 2006. Felt, satin ribbon, 7" x 8½" (17.8 x 21.6 cm). International Folk Art Foundation Collection, MOIFA.

The felt bowler hat was first made by London hatmakers in 1849 and quickly became a popular style in both Europe and the Americas. In the 1920s it was introduced into Bolivia and caught the eye of Aymara cholas in La Paz, who adopted it as their own. The fashion quickly spread to cholas living in other cites of Bolivia and in the Puno region of Peru. The wealthiest ladies bought bowlers, or *bombíns,* that were imported from Italy, but lesser quality ones were also made in local hat shops.[70]

FIG. 3-54 *Women's Hats.* Left: Huancayo, Junín, Peru, ca. 2005. Felt, fabric ribbon, 4½" x 15" (11.4 x 38.1 cm). Right: Cuzco, Peru, 2006. Felt, satin ribbon. International Folk Art Foundation Collection, MOIFA.

Many styles of felt hats are worn by chola and indigenous women in Bolivia, Peru, and Ecuador. Most of them are made in local workshops, where customers can go directly to the hatmaker and order the correct size, color, and shape. They are also sold in markets and specialty hat shops. The black hat on the left is a popular style worn by ladies in Huancayo, in the Department of Junín, Peru. The hat on the right is typical of those worn by women in the Cuzco region.[71]

▲ FIG. 3-55 Chalán Guamán family celebrating the grandparents' 50th wedding anniversary. They wear the traditional costumes from Saraguro, Ecuador, including felt hats with black spots under the rim, 2008. Photograph by Luis Gonzalez.

FIG. 3-56 *Women's Hats.* Left: Pomatúg, Tungurahua, Ecuador, 1990. Wool felt, ribbon. Collection of David and Mayi Munsell. Right: Saquisilí, Cotopaxi, Ecuador, ca. 1955. Wool felt, cotton, glass, 3½" x 12" (9.5 x 30.5 cm). Museum purchase with funds from the Folk Art Committee, MNMF, MOIFA.

Felt hats are worn by women throughout highland Ecuador. One of the most distinctive styles is from the town of Saraguro in the southern Province of Loja. The black spots under the broad brims are a result of the felting and ironing process and are considered an integral part of the design. Many hats worn in the central provinces of Chimborazo and Tungurahua have been made in a workshop in Pomatúg, near Pelileo, and sold in the market at Ambato. One of the workshop's popular styles is white with a low crown and narrow brim, shown at left in figure 3–56. When worn for fiestas, these hats are often decorated with a blue ribbon wrapped around the crown and with streamers flowing down to the side.[72] On the right is a woman's wedding hat from Saquisilí made with thick felt. It is decorated with fringe and images of doves, flowers, and the sun made from fabric, beads, and sequins.

## SHAWLS

Many Andean women continue to wear traditional handwoven mantles over the Spanish peasant-style costume adopted during the colonial period. However, other types of shawls are also worn in certain regions of Bolivia, Peru, and Ecuador.

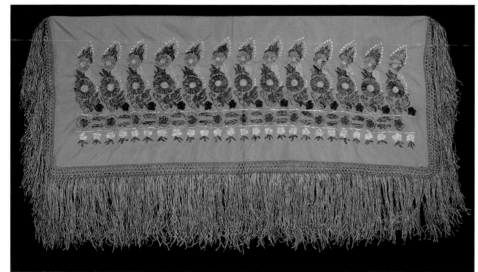

FIG. 3-57 *Woman's Shawl.* La Paz, Bolivia, ca. 1900. Vicuna fiber, 38" x 53" (96.5 x 136.7 cm). Gift of Cleves Weber, MOIFA.

FIG. 3-58 *Woman's Shawl.* La Paz, Bolivia, ca. 1960. Rayon, embroidery thread. As pictured: 32" x 63" (81.3 x 160 cm). Gift of Elizabeth and Duncan Boeckman, MOIFA.

Aymara cholas in Bolivia and Peru were among the first to adopt the dress of lower-class Spanish women. By the eighteenth century, their outfit was distinguished by very full gathered skirts that came down to just above their ankles. They also wore two shawls: a shorter one to cover their shoulders and a long rectangular one that wrapped over this and came down below their waist (see fig. 3-52). The larger shawls are thought to have been inspired by Chinese square-silk shawls that were imported to the Americas from the Far East via the Manila Galleon trade. These shawls, called *mantones de Manila*, were embroidered with floral patterns and had long knotted fringe on all four edges.[73] Some older examples of chola shawls were hand woven in finely-spun yarn from vicuña, a small Andean animal with beautiful brown and white wool. By the mid-twentieth century, most chola shawls were being made with commercial rayon fabrics and embroidered with floral motifs.

FIG. 3-59 *Woman's Shawl*. Calcha, Potosí, Bolivia, ca. 1980. Commercial wool fabric, embroidery thread, sequins, 29" x 33¼" (73.7 x 84.2 cm). Gift of Nancy Reynolds, MOIFA.

Women in the community of Calcha, Department of Potosí, Bolivia, traditionally wear an embroidered aymilla (long-sleeved dress), as well as an aksu (decorative overskirt) and mantle. The latter two garments are hand woven in the beautiful colors and patterns distinctive to their village. They also wear another type of shawl, called a *wayeta*, made from commercially-manufactured wool fabric. It is cut into a long rectangular shape and sewn along one edge to form a square or triangle. Another piece of patterned fabric is sewn to the inside. The outer surface is decorated with sequins and simple embroidered flowers, birds, and other motifs; the two lower edges are ornamented with tassels. The wayeta can be pulled over the head like a hood, or worn around the shoulders like a shawl. They are made in red, green, or purple and add a colorful touch to the rest of the woman's outfit.[74]

FIG. 3-60 Bernabe Garcia Ramos workshop. *Woman's Shawl*. Huancayo, Junín, Peru, ca. 1975. Silk and embroidery thread, 40" x 40" (101.6 x 101.6 cm). International Folk Art Foundation Collection, MOIFA.

Elaborately embroidered silk shawls, known as *paños*, are made in workshops in the Mantaro Valley of Huancayo, Department of Junín, Peru. They are worn as part of the festival costumes for various regional celebrations. The embroidered decoration generally includes an array of colorful flowers, as seen in this example.[75]

FIG. 3-61 *Woman's Shawl.* Gualaceo region, Azuay, Ecuador, ca. 1930. Cotton As pictured: 74" × 30" (119.4 x 76.2 cm). Gift of Nancy Reynolds, MOIFA.

FIG. 3-62 *Woman's Shawl.* Gualaceo region, Azuay, Ecuador, ca. 1930. Cotton. As pictured: 48" × 30½" (122 x 77.5 cm). Gift of Connie Thrasher Jaquith, MOIFA.

Blue and white or blue and blue cotton shawls woven in the ikat technique are found in northern Peru and southern Ecuador. Drawn from European traditions, these paños are rectangular pieces of cloth about 100 inches (273 cm) long and 30 inches (76 cm) wide, finished at both ends with intricate knotted fringe. This type of garment probably dates to the colonial period, when the Spanish obrajes in this region were producing cotton paños; in documents some were described as being blue (from indigo dye).[76] By the mid-nineteenth century, the finest pieces were being made in the town of San Miguel de Pallaques, in the Department of Cajamarca, Peru.[77] They were woven with finely-spun cotton thread that had

been pre-dyed with intricate ikat patterns. The knotted fringe was usually very long and ornamented with birds, floral patterns, inscriptions, and even the national emblem of Peru. Many of them were commissioned by women in the Cajamarca region, while others were marketed in Loja in southern Ecuador during the annual fair held in conjunction with the feast day of the Virgen del Cisne.

In the early twentieth century, weavers in Cuenca and other areas of Ecuador were producing blue and white or blue and blue ikat shawls with much coarser cotton threads. Around 1920, travelers from Cuenca attended the fair in Loja and brought back examples of the beautiful shawls being made in San Miguel. Apparently, this inspired the weavers in Gualaceo and neighboring towns to acquire the finer cotton thread and start producing paños in the Peruvian style. Two examples are shown here.

Production of the shawls continued into the late twentieth century, but the weaving of good quality paños decreased in the 1980s, as clothing styles changed and the price of fine cotton thread and indigo dye rose.

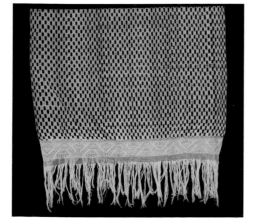

FIG. 3-63 *Woman's Shawl.* Tacabamba, Cajamarca, Peru, ca. 2008. Cotton. As pictured: 40" × 30¼" (101.6 x 76.8 cm). International Folk Art Foundation Collection, MOIFA.

The weaving of ikat shawls in San Miguel de Pallaques had declined by the mid-twentieth century. However, new production started in the neighboring town of Tacabamba. The shawl business is still carried on today, but the cotton thread is not as fine as that used in the earlier pieces from San Miguel, and the knotted fringe is short and simple.

# Knitting

Prehispanic textile artists in the Andes used cross-knit looping and knotting techniques to create objects for ceremonial and everyday use. Although they appear as if they were knitted or crocheted, no needles or hooks were used. True knitting and crocheting tools and techniques were introduced to the region by Spanish colonists and were adopted by the Quechua and Aymara people. Knitting had the advantage of being a mobile craft requiring few supplies; people could knit as they walked, herded animals, or gossiped in the market. Men and women in the highlands of Peru and Bolivia continue to use this technique to produce a variety of items, including caps, bags, arm warmers, and leggings.[78]

### KNITTED CAPS

One of the most common knitted items found in this region is a cap known by the Quechua word *chullu*. Although women and young girls wear these in some regions of Bolivia and Peru, they are primarily worn by men. During the colonial period, chullus replaced other types of woven headgear and became an important item for keeping a man's head warm in the cold climate. Each community developed their own shapes, patterns, and colors, enabling the men to continue the ancient custom of wearing headgear that distinguished one group from another. In the Cuzco area and the Altiplano region of Peru and Bolivia most men knit their own caps, a tradition that may have been introduced by the Spanish, as male knitting guilds were well established in Europe at the time of the conquest. Additionally, chullus communicate identity and pride and many highlanders consider them too personal to be made by anyone else.

Most caps take four to six weeks of intermittent work to complete, and during that process a skillful knitter uses many checks to ensure perfect results. The increases and decreases of stitches must be done carefully to shape a cap correctly and to create even curves and smooth surfaces. Design elements used in chullus are influenced by many factors. Some are drawn from prehispanic woven-textile patterns, such as geometric triangles, stair steps, interlocking waves, stars, and diamonds. Knitters also use stylized images of animals and birds from the local environment, along with motifs of lions and eagles introduced by the Spanish. Sometimes, humans appear in the chullus as static figures standing in rows or riding on horses. The desire to wear a striking and unique cap has inspired young men in some areas to come up with new types of patterns and color schemes. This is particularly true with chullus worn with festival costumes.

FIG. 3-64 *Unmarried men in Cala Cala, Potosí, Bolivia, wear layers of knitted caps draped from the belts of their costumes during Carnival celebrations. Young women in this community decorate their festival costumes with layers of folded mantles draped from belts tied around their chests,* 1996. Photograph by Barbara Mauldin.

FIG. 3-65 *Men's Caps*. Northern region, Potosí, Bolivia, late 20th century. Left: wool, 28" x 10½" (71 x 26.6 cm). International Folk Art Foundation Collection, MOIFA. Center: wool. Gift of Nancy Reynolds, MOIFA. Right: synthetic yarn. Gift of Laurie Adelson and Bruce Takami, MOIFA.

Some of the most complex and colorful knitted patterns are found in caps made by young men in the villages of Llallagua, Cala Cala, and Laymi in the northern part of the Department of Potosí, Bolivia. As the 1996 photograph shows, unmarried men in Cala Cala use their knitted caps, and those of friends and relatives, to decorate their costumes for the annual Carnival celebration. These are traditionally made from handspun sheep wool; in the late twentieth century, men in this region began using extremely fine synthetic yarns dyed in bright colors and very thin needles that allowed them to knit intricate designs and motifs (see the cap at right). Some knitters have experimented with creating bold pictorial images, as seen in the center cap. In recent times, chullus typically featured triangular ear flaps that were knitted separately and sewn on, with pompoms hanging from the ties.

FIG. 3-66 *Woman's and Girl's Caps*. Northern region, Potosí Department, Bolivia, ca. 1980. Wool. Left: 12½" x 13" (31.75 x 33 cm). International Folk Art Foundation Collection, MOIFA. Right: Gift of Nancy Reynolds, MOIFA.

Women in the northern part of Potosí, Bolivia, knit caps for themselves and their young daughters. Their chullus are characterized by a ruffled fringe attached to the bottom, as seen in these two examples.

FIG. 3-67 *Man's Cap.* Taquile Island, Puno, Peru, ca. 1975. Commercial wool yarn, 22" x 11" (55.9 x 27.9 cm). International Folk Art Foundation Collection, MOIFA.

Chullus made in communities on both sides of Lake Titicaca are generally taller than those from other regions of Bolivia and Peru. Men on Taquile Island knit caps for themselves, as well as for their sons and daughters, using finely-spun commercial wool yarn. The color scheme and designs follow that of their woven clothing, such as the belt in figure 3-31. The background color is always carmine or deep wine red, while the patterns are knit in black, white, navy, royal blue, green, and hot pink. The caps usually do not have ear flaps

FIG. 3-68 *Woman's and Girl's Caps.* Left: Ayata region, La Paz, Bolivia, mid-20th century. Wool, 19" x 10" (48.3 x 25.4 cm). Gift of Nancy Reynolds, MOIFA. Right: Llave region, Puno, Peru, ca. 1960. Wool. Gift of the Girard Foundation Collection, MOIFA.

Knitted chullus from the Ayata region in the Department of La Paz, Bolivia, are tall with a deep cuff turned back onto the cap. They are decorated with geometric motifs, along with some pictorial figures of humans, as seen in the example on the left. Women in this area have made and worn these caps as part of their festival costume. In the Department of Puno, on the other side of Lake Titicaca, women knit tall bonnets for their daughters. As shown in the example on the right, they have a wide, white ruffle around the bottom to protect the girl's face from the sun.

FIG. 3-69 *Men's Caps.* Urcos/Ocongate region, Cuzco, Peru, late 20th century. Left: wool, plastic buttons. International Folk Art Foundation, MOIFA. Center, as pictured: wool, glass beads, 34" x 10" (86.4 x 25.4 cm). Gift of Sidney Evans, MOIFA. Right: wool. International Folk Art Foundation, MOIFA.

Men and teenage boys in the Cuzco region of Peru generally knit their own chullus. Caps from the Urcos/Ocongate region are particularly colorful, especially when made for fiesta wear. These caps are ornamented with intricate geometric designs, and in some cases buttons or beads are couched into the pattern outlines. Fancy woven ties or strands of beads are usually attached to the ends of the ear flaps. The cap in the center is an exceptional example of this type of work.

## KNITTED BAGS

In the Andes knitted bags are primarily made and used by women. Different styles appear in various regions of the highlands in Bolivia and Peru.

FIG. 3-70 Left: *Coca Bag*. La Paz region, Bolivia, late 19th–early 20th century. Wool, 12" x 9" (30.5 x 22.9 cm). Gift of Florence Dibell Bartlett, MOIFA. Right: *Coin Bag*. Potosí (?), Bolivia, mid-20th century. Wool, coins, with strap extended: 12" x 6½" (30.5 x 16.5 cm). International Folk Art Foundation Collection, MOIFA.

While men use woven chuspas to carry their coca leaves, many women use knitted bags made specifically for that purpose. An older example, shown at left, was made with natural light and dark sheep wool. The size of the bag and the pictorial imagery suggest it was carried during festival occasions.

Women also use knitted bags to carry their money; most of these bags are produced in the central and southern regions of highland Bolivia. Known as *bollas de moneda*, these money purses range in size from large to very small and are usually worn on the front of a woman's belt. Antique silver coins are often sewn on to the purses as a form of decoration, as seen in the example on the right.

FIG. 3-71 *Coin Bag*. Sucre region, Chuquisaca, Bolivia, mid-20th century. Wool, 13" x 9" (33 x 22.9 cm). Gift of the Girard Foundation Collection, MOIFA.

This style of knitted money bag is used by cholas in the Sucre region of the Department of Chuquisaca. By the mid-twentieth century, the knitters were using coarsely-spun wool yarn dyed with bright aniline tints. The shaped pouches on the front of this bag are similar to those found on some woven chuspas; they are accessible from the inside and used to separate coins from currency.

▲ FIG. 3-72 *Coin Bags*. Left: Ocongate, Cuzco, Peru, late 20th century. Wool. Without tassels: 7½" x 3½" (19 x 8.9 cm). Right: Ccatca, Cuzco, Peru, late 20th century. Wool. Collection of Patricia La Farge.

Small knitted money bags are also used in the Cuzco region of Peru. Both of these examples come from the Quispicanchis Province, the same region where the woven coin bags shown above were made.[79] The purse on the left is ornamented with long yarn fringe, as seen on some of the woven chuspas (fig. 3-26). The bag on the right is knitted with similar colors and designs as seen on the knitted caps from this area (fig. 3-69).

FIG. 3-73 *Pachamama Bags.* Oruro region, Bolivia, early 20th century. Wool, coins. Largest: 12" x 7" (30.5 x 17.8 cm). Museum purchase with funds from the Folk Art Committee, MNMF, MOIFA.

Knitters in the Oruro and Potosí regions of Bolivia make a special type of purse in the form of a woman holding one or more babies. These are known as Pachamama bags, because they often carry amulets and other offerings used in ceremonies to honor the Andean goddess. Sometimes, they are woven in pairs and hung from both sides of a woman's belt. These examples, dating from the 1930s or 1940s, were knitted with finely-plied yarns in natural-gray and dark-brown sheep wool.

FIG. 3-74 *Llama Coin Bag.* Southern La Paz region(?), Bolivia, early 20th century. Wool, coins, 6½" x 7½" (16.5 x 19.1 cm). Gift of Peter P. Cecere, MOIFA.

Some of the most impressive knitted coin bags are those representing three-dimensional people or animals, such as the llama purse seen here. Six pouches knitted into the body of the animal form the head, four legs, and tail.[80]

FIG. 3-75 Left: *Female Coin Bag.* La Paz, Bolivia, ca. 1930. Commercial-wool yarn, coins. Gift of the Girard Foundation Collection, MOIFA. Center: *Pachamama Bag.* La Paz, Bolivia, ca. 1960. Wool. Gift of the Girard Foundation Collection, MOIFA. Right: *Soccer Player Coin Bag.* La Paz, Bolivia, ca. 1975. Commercial-wool yarn, 13" x 6" (33 x 15.2 cm). International Folk Art Foundation Collection, MOIFA.

The small purse on the left in the shape of a chola was made with fine, commercially-spun wool and ornamented with antique coins. A horizontal slit with a drawstring at the back allows other coins to be inserted into the body. The Pachamama bag in the center exhibits the evolution from the early bags shown above. By the mid-twentieth century, aniline dyes had become popular, and the ply of the yarn was generally heavier. In the latter part of the century, knitted bags were being marketed to a broader clientele, and women making them began depicting a more diverse range of subjects, such as the *futbol* (soccer) player seen on the right.

## KNITTED ARM WARMERS AND LEGGINGS

Women in Peru and Bolivia knit other items for men to wear as clothing accessories. Among them are arm warmers and leggings that enrich the men's costumes worn during festivals and other important occasions.

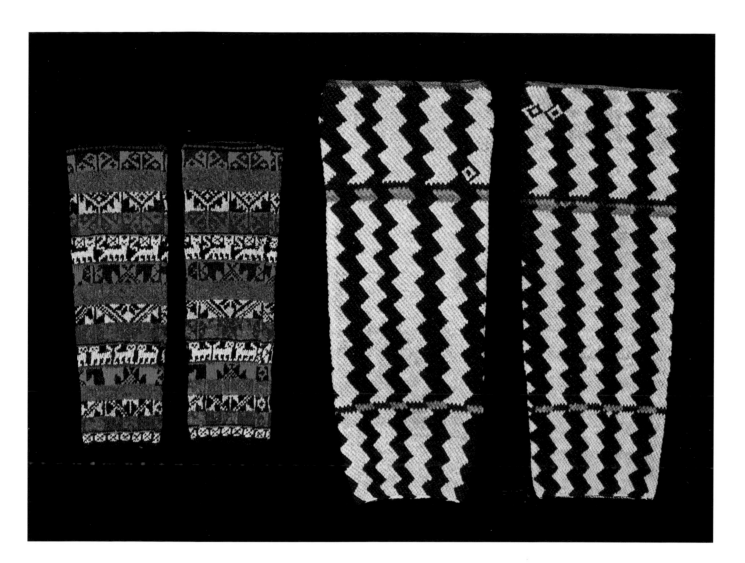

FIG. 3-76 Left: *Arm Warmers.* Huancavelica, Peru, ca. 1960. Wool. Gift of the Girard Foundation Collection, MOIFA. Right: *Leggings.* Pocoata, Potosí, Bolivia, early 20th century. Wool. Each: 22¾" x 9½" (57.9 x 24 cm). Collection of Bob and Gay Sinclair.

Since the mid-twentieth century, women in various regions of the Department of Huancavelica, in the central highlands of Peru, have knitted socks and arm warmers for young men to wear during market days and important regional celebrations. The arm warmers are ornamented with bands of brightly colored geometric motifs, as shown on the left. They create a flamboyant look when pulled over the sleeves of plain colored shirts or jackets. The colors and designs vary from one village to another and help distinguish the men from each community.

Women living in the departments of Potosí and Chuquisaca, Bolivia, knit leggings for men to wear as part of their costumes for certain fiestas. Those made in the Pocoata area of Potosí are longer than leggings made elsewhere and feature a zigzag pattern that was knit with light and dark yarns of natural sheep wool. Some of the finer examples have red and green accents, as seen on the right.

## Looped Fiber Bags

A traditional type of carrying bag used in Ecuador is known as *shigra*; it is made from agave-plant fibers by women who use the prehispanic weaving technique of looping. In agave plants the fibers lie lengthwise in the leaves, and extracting them from the pulp is a tedious process of shredding, soaking, beating, and washing. Sometimes, the leaves are laid out on the road to let cars drive over them to help tenderize the pulp.[81] The finished bags are used for carrying goods to and from the market, to sow seeds in the fields, and to store harvested foods.

FIG. 3-77 *Bag*. Papaurcu, Cotopaxi, Ecuador, late 20th century. Maguey plant fibers, 13½" x 14¼" (34.3 x 36.2 cm). Collection of Patricia La Farge.

FIG. 3-78 *Bags*. Cotopaxi region, Ecuador, late 20th century. Maguey plant fibers. Left: Gift of Nancy Reynolds, MOIFA. Right: 12" x 12" (30.5 x 30.5 cm). Collection of Patricia La Farge.

Shigras, found in many regions of highland Ecuador, are made from the native Andean agave plant (*Furcraea andina*) that grows wild in a variety of terrains. The leaves are stiff and narrow and the fibers taken from them are coarse. As a result, the bags are somewhat rough and stiff. At some point, women in the Cotopaxi Province began processing leaves from another type of agave plant that was originally brought to Ecuador from Mexico, in the late colonial period. This species, generally known as *Agave americana*, has fleshy bluish-green leaves that are wider and more curved than the native variety. The fibers are also more supple and easier to use in the looping process; the bags made in this area of Ecuador are generally finer, as shown in these examples. The shigra on the left is from Papaurcu, where women traditionally ornament them with three or more bands of geometric designs in red, pink, brown, and black against the undyed fiber. In the late twentieth century, women in the Cotopaxi region began creating bolder geometric and pictorial motifs to sell to an outside tourist market, as seen above.

## Double Bags

A type of double bag, the *alforja*, was introduced by Spaniards in the early colonial period; production began in different regions of the Andes with a variety of weaving techniques. The name derives from the Arabic *al-khurj*, suggesting that the form was originally brought to Spain by Islamic people, who controlled that region of Europe for seven hundred years. It is characterized by two large pouches connected by one wide band of cloth. In some regions of the Andes it has been used across the backs of pack animals, but in many areas the alforja is used as a shoulder bag by people.

FIG. 3-79 *Double Bags*. Left: Chota, Cajamarca, Peru, ca. 1960. Cotton, wool. Gift of the Girard Foundation Collection, MOIFA. Center: Highland region, Cajamara, Peru, ca. 1890–1910. Wool, cotton, silk, metallic thread. As pictured: 26" x 19½" (66 x 49.5 cm). Gift of the Girard Foundation Collection, MOIFA. Right: Monsefú, Lambayeque, Peru, mid-20th century. Cotton. Collection of Bob and Gay Sinclair.

Some of the finest alforjas come from the departments of Lambeyeque and Cajamarca in northern Peru. They are woven by specialists who produce one long rectangular cloth, fold the ends toward the center, and finally sew the sides closed. This creates deep pockets at either end that are decorated with the same designs in opposing directions. Alforjas are worn over one shoulder of the men and women who use them to carry a variety of items.

Plainer bags are used at home and in the agricultural fields, while those with ornate decorations are taken to markets and fairs. Some are decorated specifically for women. The bag in the center, for instance, is an ornate example of a female alforja made in the late nineteenth or early twentieth century. The designs on double bags from the coastal town of Monsefú in Lambayeque (see the bag at right) often portray the coat of arms of Peru and have inscriptions across the top bands. Those made in Chota in Cajamarca (see the bag at left) are usually ornamented with blue or red on a white background. The decoration on the pockets is divided into three horizontal sections filled with pictorial and floral motifs. Among the most popular images used on the Chota bags is the peacock.[82]

# Embroidered Costumes

The techniques and tools used to ornament cloth with embroidery were introduced in the colonial period; by the nineteenth and twentieth century, embroidery had become an important part of costume decoration. Originally, this was done by hand, but today sewing machines are often used to create elaborate patterns and motifs.

FIG. 3-80 *Girls from the Pisac region in the Department of Cuzco, Peru, wearing their embroidered festival costumes*, 2008. Photograph by Barbara Mauldin.

FIG. 3-81 *Hat and Vest.* Colca Canyon, Arequipa, Peru, late 20th century. Wool felt, cotton fabric, thread. *Vest*: 17" x 18⅞" (43.2 x 47.9 cm). International Folk Art Foundation Collection, MOIFA.

Women in villages along the Colca River Valley in the Department of Arequipa, Peru, adopted Spanish peasant-style clothing in the eighteenth century; this is the costume still being worn there today. It consists of a long gathered skirt, blouse, short vest, jacket, and hat. By the twentieth century, the garments were richly ornamented with embroidery done by men on treadle sewing machines. The embroidery typically features geometric and pictorial motifs done in bright, contrasting colors. These striking outfits are worn every day as well as for festival occasions.[83]

FIG. 3-82 *Girl's Festival Outfit*. Cuenca, Azuay, Ecuador, 1992. Wool, rayon, embroidery thread, sequins, straw. *Skirt*: 15" x 28" (38.1 x 71.1 cm). International Folk Art Foundation Collection, MOIFA.

Indigenous women in Azuay Province, in the southern highlands of Ecuador, wear gathered skirts (polleras), tailored blouses, and a rectangular shoulder-wrap (*lliglla*). Today, the outfits are made in clothing workshops in Cuenca and sold in shops around the Diez de Agosto and San Francisco markets.[84] Everyday garments have some decoration done with machine embroidery, but those worn for festivals are more heavily ornamented with embroidery and sequins. Miniature versions of the costumes are made for young girls, who wear them in the annual Pase del Niño parade that takes place during the Christmas season.

FIG. 3-83 *Sleevelets*. Huancayo, Junín, Peru, ca. 1960. Wool, cotton, embroidery thread. Each: 12½" x 6" (31.8 x 15.2 cm). Gift of the Girard Foundation Collection, MOIFA.

Hand embroidery is used by women in the Huancayo region of the Department of Junín, Peru, to decorate sleevelets (*manguitos*) worn as part of a festival outfit. They utilize a variety of stitches to create colorful floral patterns interspersed with tiny human figures and animals.[85]

FIG. 3-84 *Dance Capes.* Huayucachi, Junín, Peru, ca. 1960. Cotton, silk and cotton embroidery thread, sequins. Each: 30" x 18" (76.2 x 45.7 cm). Gifts of Lloyd E. Cotsen and the Neutrogena Corporation, MOIFA.

Another type of embroidery from the Huancayo region is found on capes worn by male dancers in the annual fiesta for the Virgen de Cocharcas in Sapallanga. These costumes are made by men and their families as a cottage industry and rented to dancers who participate in the Sapallanga festival from different villages in the Huancayo area. The embroidery technique, known as stump work, involves wrapping the thread around wooden forms or other stuffed shapes to create a three-dimensional surface texture. The subject matter portrayed in the embroidery has evolved since the nineteenth century; many express themes related to South American military history. For example, the panel on the left portrays General José de San Martín, who helped Peru win its independence from Spain. The piece on the right probably shows a ship captain who fought Chile in the War of the Pacific (1879–1884). There is also a fascination in portraying modern technology, as shown with the airplanes flying overhead in both scenes.[86]

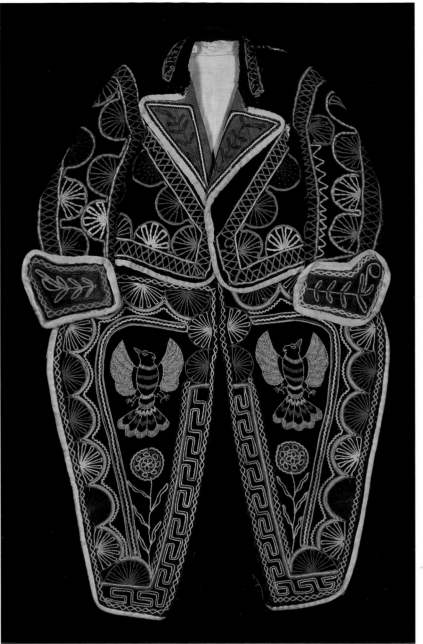

FIG. 3-85 *Man's Festival Costume.* La Paz, Bolivia, ca. 1950. Wool, cotton, embroidery thread, 47" x 31" (119.4 x 78.7 cm). Gift of the Girard Foundation Collection, MOIFA.

*Ch'uta* is a popular festival masquerade worn by men in the capital and other communities of the Department of La Paz. The Ch'uta character represents an Indian man born and raised in La Paz during the colonial period, so the masqueraders wear short jackets and pants in imitation of the styles worn during that time. These outfits are made in workshops in La Paz and rented to the dancers. They are always heavily ornamented with embroidery, as seen in this lively example from the mid-twentieth century.[87]

# Featherwork

The art of mosaic featherwork can be traced to the prehispanic Tiahuancan culture that developed in the southern region of Lake Titicaca and spread north into Peru. Examples dating from AD 600 display a rich array of abstracted figural images, such as monkeys, pumas, and other symbolic animals. In the early twentieth century, a handful of Aymara artists living on the east side of Lake Titicaca in Bolivia were still carrying on this tradition.

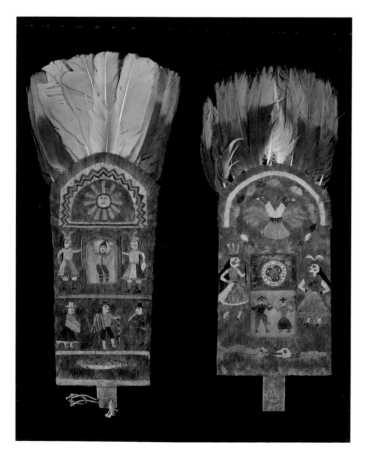

FIG. 3-86 *Dance Costume Shoulder Bands.* Lake Titicaca region, La Paz, Bolivia, early 20th century. Wood slats, tropical-bird feathers, fiber, natural glue. Largest: 36" x 12" (91.4 x 30.5 cm). Gifts of Lloyd E. Cotsen and the Neutrogena Corporation, MOIFA.

FIG. 3-87 *Dance Costume Headpieces.* Lake Titicaca region, La Paz, Bolivia, early 20th century. Wood, tropical-bird feathers, natural glue. Largest: 15½" x 5½" (39.4 x 14 cm). Gifts of Lloyd E. Cotsen and the Neutrogena Corporation, MOIFA.

The primary focus for featherwork in recent times has been the ornamentation of costume pieces worn in ceremonial dances for the Quena-Quena, in which dancers represent mythological warrior-musicians who wear breastplates made of jaguar skin and play out aggressive acts of war. In some Bolivian villages around Lake Titicaca their costumes include colorful headpieces, pectorals, and shoulder bands decorated with mosaic featherwork. Feathers from parrots, macaws, and hummingbirds have been carefully pasted to wood, creating pictorial images. Some of these portray prehispanic symbols such as the Andean sun god and butterflies, lizards, insects, fish, and snakes. Other images on these pieces depict the Hapsburg double eagle and rampant lions found on many of the Spanish coats of arms. Aspects of contemporary festival activities are also shown. For example, a man on horseback wears a feathered headdress, and dancing men and women wear fiesta costumes and masquerades.[88]

A Diversity of Folk Art

# Jewelry

Women throughout the Andes adorn themselves with distinctive jewelry, primarily fashioned from silver. However, gold, brass, coral, glass beads, and cut pieces of colored glass have also been used. The forms and styles of jewelry vary from one geographic and cultural region to another, reflecting prehispanic traditions, as well as the technology, materials, and styles of ornamentation introduced by the Spanish.

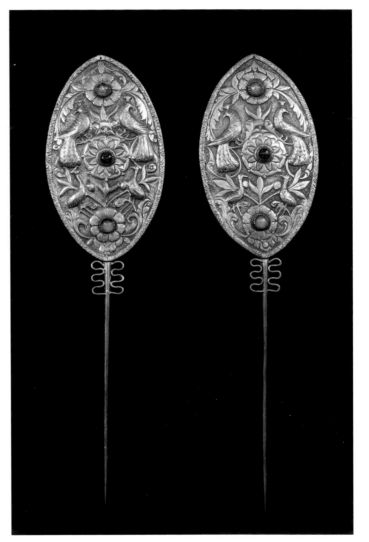

### PERU AND BOLIVIA

FIG. 4-1 *A woman from the village of Charazani, in the Department of La Paz, Bolivia, is wearing a ceremonial costume with two large vertical pins (tupus) attached to the shoulders of her dress and another horizontal pin (ttipqui) secures the mantle across her chest*, 1975. Photograph by Bruce Takami.

Archeological excavations and historic documents from various regions of highland Peru and Bolivia show that garment pins have a long history, dating back almost 2,500 years. They have always been used to secure the women's traditional wrapped dress and mantle. In prehispanic times, most pins had a flat circular or crescent-shaped head attached to a thin pointed shaft. Under Spanish influence, the shape of the head underwent changes and gradually became more ornate. This evolution continued into the post-Independence period of the nineteenth century, when indigenous women could once again take pride in wearing their "traditional" costume.[1] Most of the nineteenth-century garment pins were made in the Cuzco and Puno regions of southern Peru and in the Lake Titicaca area of the Department of La Paz, Bolivia.

As we can see in this photograph, two large pins are used to attach the fabric of the wrapped dress over the woman's shoulders. These pins, called *tupus*, were always made in pairs and worn with the large heads facing downwards. The single pin, or *ttipqui*, that secures the mantle across the woman's chest is worn in a horizontal position.[2]

FIG. 4-2 *Pair of Dress Pins*. Altiplano region of Peru and Bolivia, late 18th–early 19th century. Silver, glass, each: 17" x 4½" (43.2 x 11.4 cm). Gift of Florence Dibell Bartlett, MOIFA.

Although the traditional woman's wrapped dress was viewed as indecent and banned by the Spanish, women in some regions of Bolivia continued to wear it over other garments. Elaborate matching tupus were used for ceremonial occasions to pin the top of the dress over a woman's shoulders, with the two large heads facing downwards. This pair dates from the late eighteenth or early nineteenth century, when silversmiths were using the repoussé technique to cover the entire surface of the head with ornate motifs, such as the birds and flowers seen here.[3]

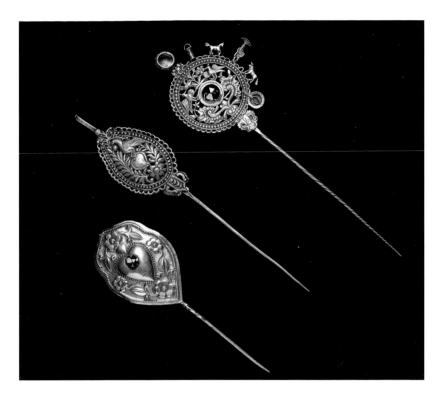

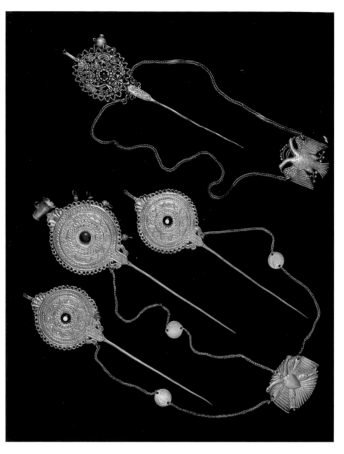

FIG. 4-3 *Mantle Pins*. Cuzco region, Peru, 19th century. Left: silver, glass. Museum purchase with funds from Connie Thrasher Jaquith, MOIFA. Center: silver. Private Collection. Right: silver, glass, 12" x 4 ⅛" (30.5 x 10.5 cm). Museum purchase with funds from Connie Thrasher Jaquith, MOIFA.

All of these are single pins, ttipquis, used to fasten a woman's mantle across her chest. Using repoussé and casting techniques, nineteenth-century silversmiths in the Cuzco region decorated the heads of pins with elegant birds and floral motifs. Sometimes, they attached miniature figures (top pin), such as festival dancers, horses, bulls, and household objects across the curved edge that would be on top when worn horizontally.

FIG. 4-4 *Wedding Pins*. Top: Cuzco region, Peru, 19th century. Silver, glass. Private Collection. Bottom: Late Titicaca region, Bolivia, late 19th century. Silver/metal alloy, glass beads, glass. 12¾" x 4" (32.3 x 10.1 cm). Gift of Florence Dibell Bartlett, MOIFA.

Pins with long chains attached are worn for weddings and other special ceremonial occasions.[4] The group on the bottom has two tupus to fasten the shoulders of a woman's wraparound dress and a single ttipqui (center) to secure the mantle.

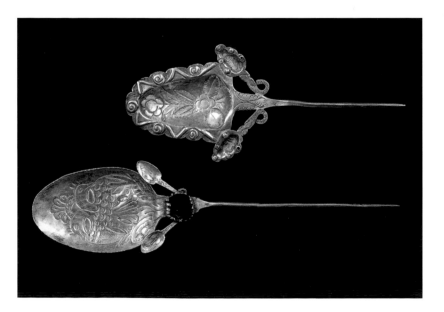

FIG. 4-5 *Mantle Pins*. Cuzco region, Peru, 19th century. Top: silver. International Folk Art Foundation Collection, MOIFA. Bottom: silver, glass, 9¼" x 2¾" (23.5 x 7 cm). Gift of Florence Dibell Bartlett, MOIFA.

After the indigenous uprisings of the early 1780s, the Spanish prohibited Indians from wearing clothing that identified them with their Inca past. The simpler mantle pins worn for everyday use became a focus of this prohibition. To disguise their continued use, silversmiths in the Cuzco region began making pins in the shape of *cucharas* (spoons); this style remained popular into the nineteenth century.[5]

FIG. 4-6 *Mantle Pins.* Top left: Cuzco region, Peru, 19th century. Silver, glass beads, glass, 9¾" x 10¼" (24.8 x 26 cm). Gift of Florence Dibell Bartlett, MOIFA. Top right: Cuzco region, Peru, 19th century. Silver, glass beads. Private Collection. Bottom: Department of La Paz, Bolivia, late 19th–early 20th century. Silver, glass. Gift of Florence Dibell Bartlett, MOIFA.

By the mid-nineteenth century, chola and rural indigenous women were freer to express their aesthetic preferences. Some of the horizontal mantle pins in the Cuzco region were made without the circular head and the top of the shaft was ornamented with miniature scenes (see top left and right). Among the images portrayed were animals, birds, and singing mermaids. Small charms were attached to the ends of thin chains that hung from the bottom of the shaft. The charms portrayed miniature objects from the house and kitchen, which led them to become known as ttipquis *comida* (food).[6] Silversmiths in the Department of La Paz, Bolivia, copied this style of pin, using larger figures on the top of the shaft with coins instead of charms hanging from the chains (see bottom).

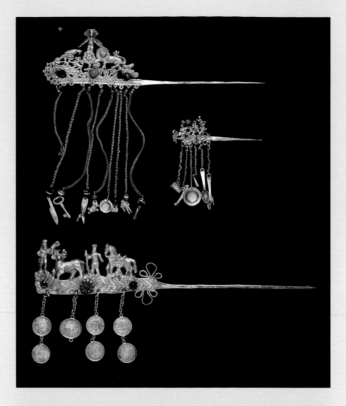

FIG. 4-7 *Mantle Pins.* Left: Paucartambo, Cuzco, Peru, late 19th–early 20th century. Silver, glass. Right: Lake Titicaca region, Peru, or Bolivia, late 19th–early 20th century. Silver, glass, 8¾" x 2¾" (22 x 7 cm). Gifts of Florence Dibell Bartlett, MOIFA.

Some late nineteenth- and early twentieth-century mantle pins, worn by Aymara cholas in the Lake Titcaca region of Peru and Bolivia, didn't have a shaft at all. They were made in a European style with a large, central figure group framed by other patterns and motifs. Silversmiths in Paucartambo, in the Department of Cuzco, altered the conventional-style pin by adding thin chains to the bottom with figures of fish from Lake Titicaca (left). Similar pins made in workshops of the Lake Titicaca region of Peru and Bolivia used smaller peacocks or other forms on the top and large fish with joined bodies hanging below (right).[7]

FIG. 4-8 *Earrings.* Department of La Paz, Bolivia, early 20th century. Silver. Left: 6" x 2½" (15.2 x 6.4 cm). Museum purchase with funds from Connie Thrasher Jaquith, MOIFA. Right: Gift of Florence Dibell Bartlett, MOIFA.

Earrings were not a traditional form of jewelry for prehispanic women in Peru and Bolivia; in most regions they are still not worn today. However, they were adopted by the Aymara cholas, who copied the earrings used by the Spanish. Large, dangling earrings are worn with the chola festival costumes.

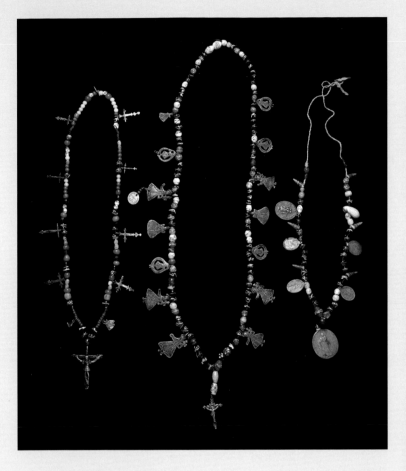

FIG. 4-9 *Rosario Necklaces*. Cuzco area or Lake Titicaca regions, Peru or Bolivia, late 19th century. Glass beads, silver, metal, shells, cord. Left: Private Collection. Center: 21½" x 3½" (54.6 x 8.9 cm). Gift of Connie Thrasher Jaquith, MOIFA. Right: Private Collection.

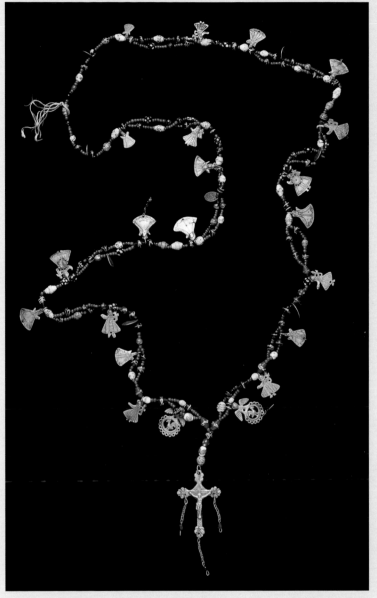

FIG. 4-10 *Rosario Necklace*. Lake Titicaca region, Bolivia, late 19th century. Glass, silver, cord, 42¾" x 3¾" (108.6 x 9.5 cm). Private Collection.

Traditionally, necklaces are not used as part of a woman's costume in highland Peru and Bolivia. However, families in some communities in the Cuzco region and around Lake Titicaca do own necklaces, known as *rosarios*, to keep in their homes, put on images of saints, and wear for special occasions. They are usually strung with glass beads, silver crucifixes, and religious medals (4-9, left and right). Some of the rosarios are also ornamented with small silver figures of the Virgin of Copacabana, whose shrine is at the southern end of the lake (center). Larger and more elaborate rosarios with figures of the Virgin of Copacabana are worn for special ceremonial events (above).[8]

ECUADOR

**FIG. 4-11** Rosaelena de la Torre and her daughters wear traditional clothing and jewelry. Ilumán, Imbabura, Ecuador, 1984. Photograph by Shari Kessler.

Unlike in Peru and Bolivia, women in many parts of highland Ecuador wear necklaces as part of their everyday costume. This photograph shows Rosaelena de la Torre and her daughters, from the Otavalo region, in the northern Imbabura Province, wearing necklaces made from gilded-glass beads manufactured in Czechoslovakia as Christmas ornaments. A woman may wear as many as four necklaces, each with ten to fifteen strands of beads strung at slightly varying heights, so they hang from below her chin to the middle of her chest. Rosaelena is also wearing traditional arm wraps made from long strands of the same type of beads.[9]

FIG. 4-12 *Necklace.* Salasaca, Tungurahua, Ecuador, early 20th century. Coral and glass beads, string, 9" x 9" (22.9 x 22.9 cm). Private Collection.

FIG. 4-13 *Necklace.* Central Cañar Province, Ecuador, early 20th century. Glass beads, metal coins, string, 9" x 5½" (22.9 x 14 cm). Private Collection.

Women in communities of the central and southern regions of highland Ecuador also wear elaborate necklaces. Those worn in Salasaca, Tungurahua Province, are particularly spectacular. They are made from red coral and Venetian-glass beads with strands strung at varying lengths, so the necklace covers all of the woman's neck. Having become very scarce, the antique beads are handed down from generation to generation and kept in the family.

Chokers worn by women in the central part of the Cañar Province are made with two or more strands of different types of beads, ranging from antique European-glass trade pieces to more modern glass and plastic ones. Sometimes, antique coins are interspersed. No single color or type predominates; usually there are several colors combined in a strand. Women in Saraguro, in the southern province of Loja, make a different style of necklace from tiny, glass, seed beads imported from Europe and the United States. These are sewn together with a netting technique that creates zigzag rows of different colored patterns. It is worn like a collar over the top of a woman's blouse (see fig. 3-55).[10]

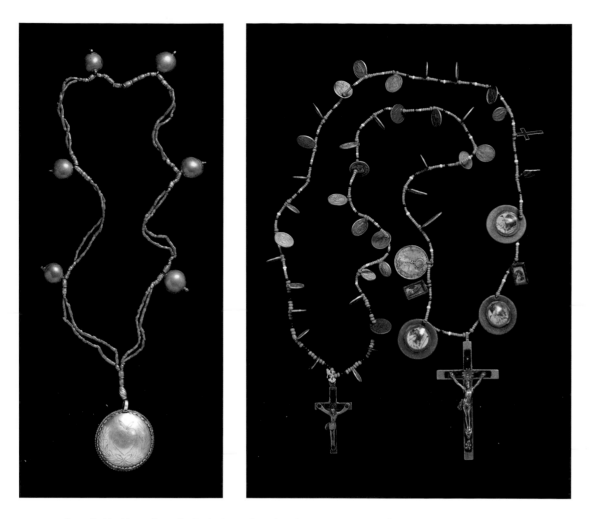

▲ FIG. 4-14 *Rosario Necklace.* Otavalo, Imbabura, Ecuador, late 19th century. Coral, brass, silver, string, as pictured: 19" x 3¾" (48.3 x 9.5 cm). Private Collection.

Rosario necklaces from the Otavalo region of northern Ecuador consist of a long strand of red-glass, coral, and brass beads. They are often ornamented with silver and brass charms, coins, crosses, and occasionally a reliquary. Although they were once more frequently worn, today their use is generally restricted to weddings and festivals when male sponsors wear them as part of their official outfit.[11]

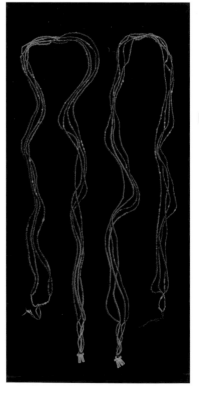

▶ FIG. 4-15 *Wedding Necklace.* Riobamba region, Chimborazo, Ecuador, mid-20th century. Glass beads, metal coins, plastic, string, as pictured: 36¾" x 3" (93.3 x 7.6 cm). Gift of Connie Thrasher Jaquith, MOIFA.

Another type of rosario necklace comes from the Riobamba region, in the Chimborazo Province of central Ecuador, and is worn by a bride and groom during their wedding ceremony, with each end of the necklace draped over their heads. The long strand consists of small, blue and green seed beads interspersed with old coins. Brass or silver crucifixes on each end are meant to rest on the chests of the wedding couple. Other charms may be added for good luck, such as blue and green plastic poker chips that have small religious prints glued to their centers.[12]

FIG. 4-16 *Earrings.* Otavalo, Imbabura, Ecuador, late 19th century. Coral and glass beads, brass, string, as pictured: 24" x 7" (61 x 17.8 cm). Private Collection.

In the 1940s it was popular in Otavalo and other towns to wear long strands of beaded earrings that hung below a woman's waist, while today they are generally worn shorter. They are made from coral and glass beads with loops of string that pass through holes in a woman's ears.[13]

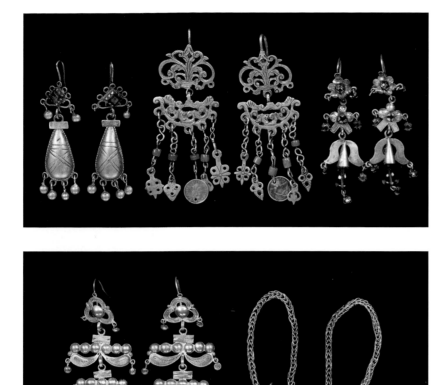

FIG. 4-17 *Earrings*. Southern Highlands, Ecuador, early 20th century. Left: silver, glass. Center: silver, coral, 4½" x 1¾" (11.4 x 4.4 cm). Right: silver, glass. Museum purchases with funds from Connie Thrasher Jaquith, MOIFA.

European-style metal earrings ornamented with coral beads and cut glass were worn by Spanish and criollo ladies during the colonial period. By the nineteenth century, this type of jewelry had been adopted by mestiza and chola women in the Cuenca area as part of their costume. In the mid-twentieth century, these earrings also became popular with indigenous women in southern Chimborazo, Cañar, and Azuay provinces.[14]

FIG. 4-18 *Earrings*. Saraguro, Loja, Ecuador, late 19th–early 20th century. Silver. Left: 6½" x 1¾" (16.5 x 4.4 cm). Museum purchases with funds from Connie Thrasher Jaquith, MOIFA.

Unlike other indigenous groups in southern Ecuador, women in Saraguro only wear two specific types of silver earrings. One, called *kurimolde*, often has graduating tiers of horizontal, beaded bars with filigree wings. Those with three or more tiers are worn for festivals and other special occasions (left). The other style is called *media luna* (half moon), because the center part of the earring is ornamented with a crescent shape (right). Both styles often have a silver chain attached to the top near the hook, which is worn around a woman's neck to keep the earrings from getting lost if they slip out.[15]

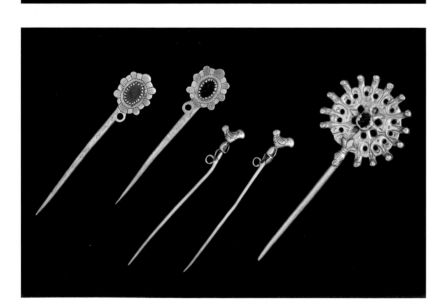

FIG. 4-19 *Dress and Shawl Pins*. Left: Tungurahua Province, Ecuador, early 20th century. Silver, glass. Center: Highlands, Ecuador, early 20th century. Silver. Right: Saraguro, Loja, Ecuador, 2008. Silver, glass, 7½" x 3¼" (19.1 x 8.3). Private Collection.

Women in some regions of Ecuador continued to wear their traditional-style wraparound dress into the twentieth century. As part of this costume, they used paired metal pins (known in Ecuador as *tupos*) to fasten the cloth over their shoulders. A single pin (also called tupo) was used to hold their shawls across their chests. Some women still wear the wraparound dress and use the traditional tupos, or substitute modern safety pins. Others have changed their costume and wear a blouse and wraparound skirt. As the paired tupos were no longer needed for the dress, they began wearing the matching pins on their shawls. The pairs shown here (left and center) have small holes where strings were attached; the strings draped around the back of the woman's neck, so she wouldn't lose the pins if they fell out. The heavier tupo (at right) is typical of those worn in Saraguro (see figure 3-55), where they are made from nickel coated in silver, and usually have a piece of colored glass inserted in the center. They also often have a chain attached to one side that is worn around the neck to prevent loss.[16]

CHILE

The Mapuche Indian nation was never conquered by the Spanish, and it was only in the late nineteenth century that they were finally subdued by the Chilean army. The various bands were rounded up and placed in settlements in a region known as La Frontera in the southern Andes of central Chile. Although they were not controlled by the Spanish, the Mapuche adopted the art of silverwork from the Europeans during the colonial period. They melted coins and other silver objects obtained from the Spanish and began making various forms of silverwork using the sandcasting technique. Mostly, they created horseback-riding equipment and jewelry for the women. In the early twentieth century, the women's clothing began to change, and the jewelry once worn for everyday use was only brought out for special occasions. Heirloom pieces, handed down from mother to daughter, are proudly worn as a symbol of Mapuche culture.[17]

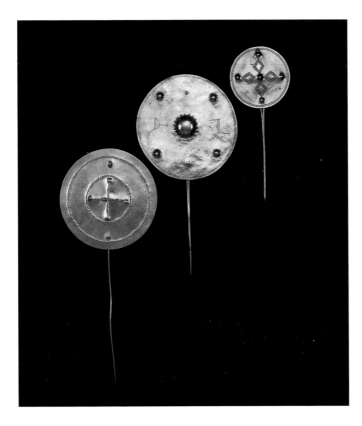

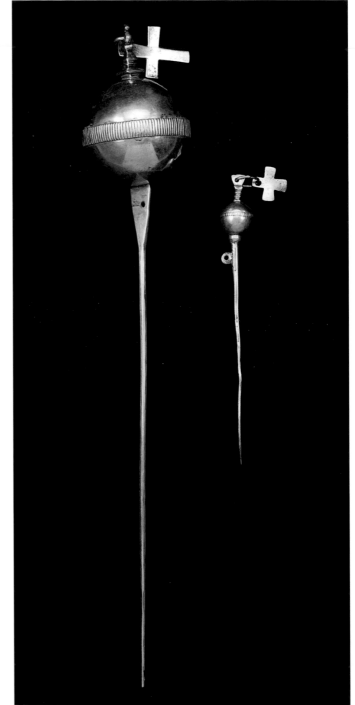

FIG. 4–20 *Garment Pins*. La Frontera region, Chile, late 19th century. Silver. Largest: 10" x 4½" (25.4 x 11.4 cm). Gifts of Edith Page Skewes-Cox, MOIFA.

FIG. 4–21 *Garment Pins*. La Frontera region, Chile, late 19th century. Silver. Largest: 14" x 2¼" (35.6 x 5.7 cm). Gifts of Edith Page Skewes-Cox, MOIFA.

Mapuche women have worn two types of garment pins. One style has a flat disk attached to a pointed shaft. Known by the Quechua term tupu, they were used to fasten a woman's dress over one shoulder and attach other jewelry to the front of the garment. The discs, which are ornamented in relief with simple patterns, vary in size and can be as large as 4 inches (10 cm) in diameter. The other type of pin, known as *punshon*, evolved in the late nineteenth century. It has a round ball on the end of the shaft made from two half spheres soldered together. Usually, it has a small Greek cross attached to a projection above the ball.

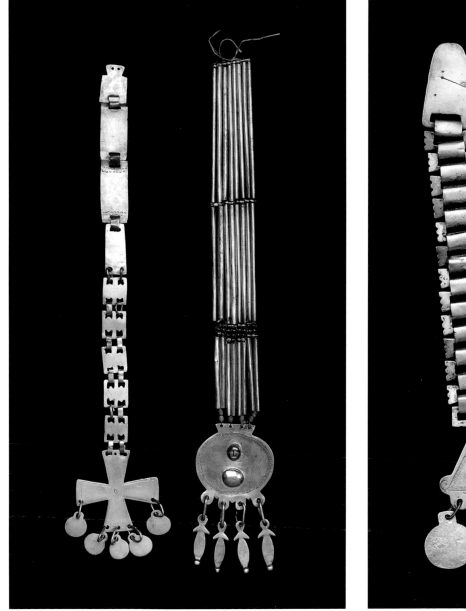

FIG. 4-22 *Pectorals.* La Frontera region, Chile, late 19th century. Left: silver. Right: silver, glass beads, 16" x 2¾" (40.6 x 7 cm). Gifts of General and Mrs. Barksdale Hamlett, MOIFA.

FIG. 4-23 *Brooch.* La Frontera region, Chile, early 20th century. Silver, 10" x 4½" (25.4 x 11.4 cm). Gift of Mr. and Mrs. Thomas Pearce, MOIFA.

By the late nineteenth century, Mapuche women were wearing long pectorals on the front of their costume. Made in different styles, the long form was usually wider at the bottom with small pendants dangling underneath. The pectorals were attached to a neckband or collar made of leather decorated with tiny beads of silver. The silver brooch was a later form of chest ornament that evolved from the thin pectoral. These pins became a prominent form of jewelry for Mapuche women in the twentieth century.

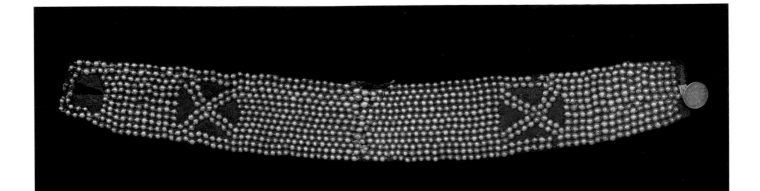

FIG. 4-24 *Collar/Headband.* La Frontera region, Chile, mid-19th century. Leather, silver, 2¼" x 17" (5.7 x 43.2 cm). Gift of General and Mrs. Barksdale Hamlett, MOIFA.

Strips of leather ornamented with tiny silver beads were worn as collars around women's necks. A similar piece was sometimes worn across women's foreheads to frame their face between the two bands.

FIG. 4-25 *Headbands/Necklaces.* La Frontera region, Chile, early 20th century. Silver. Top: Gift of General and Mrs. Barksdale Hamlett, MOIFA. Bottom: 2½" x 23¼" (6.4 x 59.1 cm). Gift of Sallie Wagner, International Folk Art Foundation Collection, MOIFA.

Linked silver bands with numerous pendants hanging from the bottom are another traditional style of headband. In the twentieth century, some Mapuche women started attaching the two ends of the headband to their dress or shirt just below the top of their shoulders, so they hung over their chest like a necklace.

FIG. 4-26 *Earrings.* La Frontera region, Chile, late 19th–early 20th century. Silver. Top left: 4¼" x 3¾" (10.8 x 9.5 cm). Gift of Skip Holbrook, MOIFA. Top right and bottom left: International Folk Art Foundation Collection, MOIFA. Bottom right: Gift of Edith Page Skewes-Cox, MOIFA.

The oldest style of earrings worn by Mapuche women were large rectangular plates with special attachments to prevent their ear lobes from tearing. Later, trapezoid-shaped earrings came into fashion (top left). In the late nineteenth and early twentieth century, they adopted the European-style crescent-shaped earrings that often had small pendants dangling from the bottom (see bottom left and right). Mapuche silversmiths continued to experiment with other styles of earrings and eventually developed the elongated rectangular form with cutout geometric patterns (see top right).

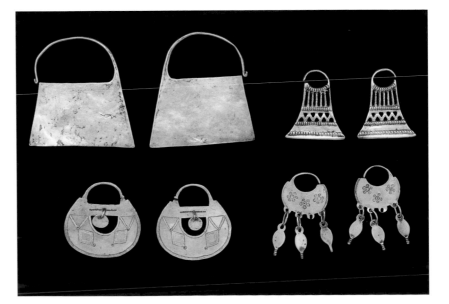

## Staffs

Silver and mixed metals have also been used to create or decorate staffs.  These are carried by men to symbolize the important role they play within the community political system or as sponsors for local festivals.  Some staffs are ornamented with similar items found in women's jewelry such as old coins, cut glass, and articulated fish.

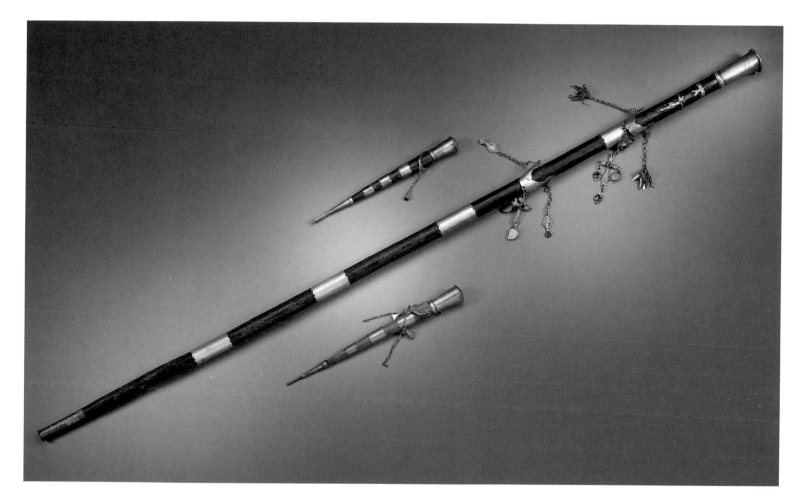

FIG. 4-27 *Authority Staffs.* Top: Peru, early 20th century. Wood, silver. MOIFA. Center: Cotopaxi, Ecuador, mid-20th century. Wood, silver, 44" x 1½" (111.8 x 3.8 cm). Gift of Tom Wilson, MOIFA. Bottom: Peru, early 20th century. Wood, silver. Gift of David R. Thornburg, MOIFA.

One type of staff found in central Ecuador, southern Peru, and the Department of La Paz, Bolivia, is known as *bastón de mando* (cane of authority). They were copied from staffs used by Spanish officials during the colonial period. By the nineteenth century, indigenous mayors, *alcaldes*, and council members throughout these regions were carrying bastónes de mando to symbolize their power within

their communities. Most are made from wood that is extremely hard and dark in color, taken from a certain species of palm (*astrocaryum chanto*) found in the Amazon rainforest and considered sacred. Silver sheeting is used to cover the handle and tip of the staff and evenly spaced bands decorate the shaft. Most have thin chains hanging from one or more of the bands, with small crosses and ornaments attached.[18] Today, staffs are also used as symbols of sacred power during ceremonial rituals (see fig. 2-1).

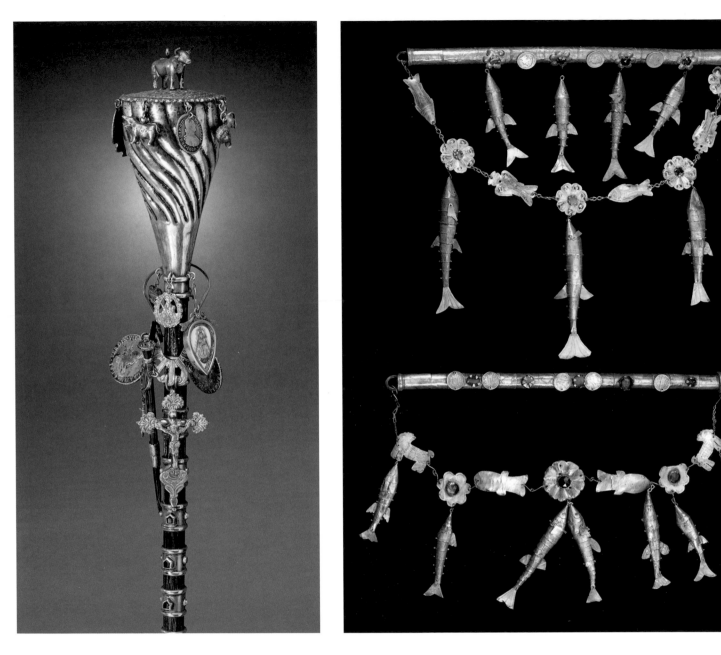

FIG. 4-28 *Dance Staff* (detail). Department of La Paz, Bolivia, late 19th century. Wood, metal, glass. Fullsize: 40" x 3½" (101.6 x 8.9 cm). Private Collection.

Elaborate staffs are carried by *priostes* during important festivals. A complex social structure, known as the festival-cargo system, was established in colonial times to organize large public celebrations that marked religious feast days and civic events. The system is still in use today and new priostes are elected each year to sponsor a particular fiesta. The tradition includes collecting money from various groups in the community and assuring that the processions, dance groups, bands, bullfights, food, and drink are all organized and presented in a lavish manner. Priostes usually head the procession carrying ornate dance staffs as symbols of their authority. Often made by special silversmiths, these staffs are owned by wealthy families who rent them out for use in the festivals.[19] The shaft is carved from the same palm wood as the authority staffs; the silverwork and ornamentation are much more intricate.

FIG. 4-29 *Dance Staffs.* Department of La Paz, Bolivia, mid-20th century. Silver, glass. Top, as pictured: 16½" x 18" (42 x 45.7 cm). Gift of the Girard Foundation Collection, MOIFA. Bottom: Gift of David R. Thornburg, MOIFA.

Dance staffs carried by festival sponsors in some communities around Lake Titicaca are made in a different style. The ornamented silver shaft is carried in a horizontal position, with several long articulated fish hanging below, symbolizing the fish from Lake Titicaca, an important aspect of the culture in this region.[20]

# Woodwork

Many high-altitude regions of the Andes have stark landscapes with no forests or groves of trees. In these areas wood is a valued commodity brought from forests in the foothills along the western coast, or tropical jungles to the east. Woodworking was an important craft in prehistoric times, but artists used basic implements that limited both form and ornamentation. The Spanish introduced more sophisticated tools and techniques in the sixteenth century, setting up woodshops to produce furniture and utilitarian items for churches, convents, private homes, and other secular settings. Following the style of European woodwork, the objects were often decorated with carved, incised, inlaid, or painted patterns and motifs. Production in large and small woodshops continued into the nineteenth and twentieth century.

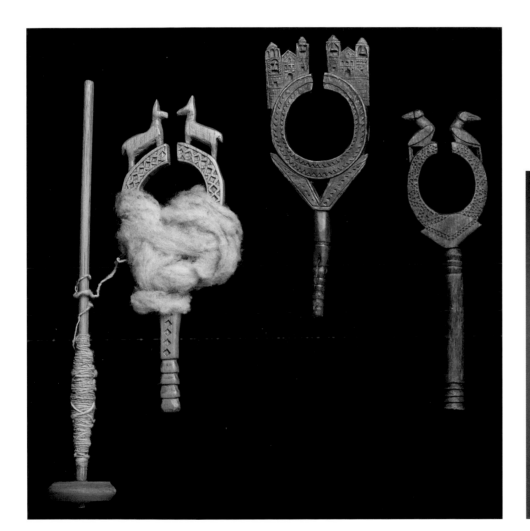

FIG. 4-30 *Distaffs*. Sarhua, Ayacucho, Peru. Left: *With Drop Spindle*, 2007. Wood, wool. International Folk Art Foundation Collection, MOIFA. Center: mid-20th century. Wood, 10½" x 4" (26.7 x 10.1 cm). Collection of Kisla Jiménez and Jonathan Williams. Right: mid-20th century. Wood. Collection of David and Mayi Munsell.

FIG. 4-31 *Canes* (detail), Sarhua, Ayacucho, Peru, mid-20th century. Wood. Largest, full size: 31" x 3¼" (78.7 x 8.3 cm). International Folk Art Foundation Collection, MOIFA.

Sarhua is a small rural village in the western part of the Department of Ayacucho, Peru. Artists in this community make a variety of utilitarian items out of wood decorated with sculptural forms and minutely carved geometric patterns. The examples shown at left are distaffs used to hold raw wool as it is wound onto a drop spindle. The Sarhua woodworkers also make canes with artfully carved handles portraying humans, animals, birds, and fish. The shafts are incised with images of the canes' owners and their families, engaged in different activities (right). Similar imagery is found on Sarhua house beams painted with narrative scenes portraying family members at home and work (see fig. 4-119).[21]

FIG. 4-32 *Stirrups.* Left: Chile, late 19th century. Wood, metal. Right: Bolivia, late 19th century. Wood, metal, 8" x 8" (20.3 x 20.3 cm). Gifts of David R. Thornburg, MOIFA.

▼ FIG. 4-33 *Stirrups.* Left: Ecuador, late 19th century. Wood, 8" x 7½" (20.3 x 19.1 cm). Private Collection. Right: Bolivia, late 19th century. Wood, metal. Gift of David R. Thornburg, MOIFA.

In the late nineteenth and early twentieth century, woodworkers in some parts of the Andes were producing elaborate stirrups ornamented with intricately carved patterns and motifs. One popular image carved on them was a dog's face, probably originating in the colonial period. Unfortunately, the Spanish colonizers brought fierce mastiffs to the Andes in the sixteenth century, to aid in the conquest of
indigenous people. They may have worn stirrups shaped like the head of a mastiff to remind the Indians of this threat.[22]

FIG. 4-34 *Tray and Small Chest.* San Juan de Pasto, Nariño, Colombia, late 19th century. Wood, pasto varnish. Largest: 4½" x 16" (11.4 x 40.6 cm). Gifts of Peter P. Cecere, MOIFA.

San Juan de Pasto is the capital of the Department of Nariño in southwestern Colombia. When the Spanish arrived in this region in the early sixteenth century, they were impressed by a varnishing technique used by the local Indians to decorate gourds. The method was adopted by Spanish artists to decorate wooden objects for the colonists; the technique is still being used today. It is practiced with a type of rubber extracted from a local tree known as *mopa-mopa.* The rubber is processed and colored with vegetal dyes and precious metals. It is then stretched out into sheets, and artists use special knives to cut out patterns and designs that are applied to wood surfaces. The rubber sticks and then hardens, providing a durable and protective coating.[23]

FIG. 4-35 *Small Chest.* Peru, 19th century. Wood, metal, 12¼" x 17¼" (31.1 x 43.8 cm). Private Collection.

FIG. 4-36 *Small Chest.* Ecuador, 19th century. Wood, metal, 12½" x 20" (31.8 x 50.8 cm). Private Collection.

FIG. 4-37 *Small Chest.* Quito, Ecuador, 19th century. Wood, metal, 10" x 17" (25.4 x 43.2 cm). Collection of Earl and Shari Kessler.

Wooden chests were probably the earliest and most widespread form of furniture in the Andean colonies and, in certain places, they continued to be made and used into the twentieth century. They served the dual function of transporting and then storing one's possessions. The dome-topped piece from Peru was made using a recessed carving technique and is ornamented with animals, birds, and floral motifs. The woodworkers of Ecuador often used the chip-carving method to decorate the sides of chests with geometric patterns. Wood inlay was also used in some regions of the Andes to decorate chests and boxes. A few nineteenth-century workshops in Quito specialized in this technique, utilizing different colored woods to create floral patterns and pictorial scenes.

## Leather and Hide Trunks

Ornate leatherwork, produced in Spain since the time of Islamic occupation, persisted into the sixteenth century, when it was used to cover furniture and chests. The technique involves moistening sheets of leather and then applying heated metal plates that have been embossed with elaborate designs. An alternative method involves pressing the leather between two molds. The decorated leather would then be sewn and tacked onto the frame of a simple wooden chest and the surfaces might be further embellished with hand-tooled details that were painted and varnished.[24]

FIG. 4-38 *Trunk*. Huamanga, Ayacucho, Peru, 18th century. Wood, leather, metal, paint, 7½" x 17" (19.1 x 43.2 cm). Private Collection.

▶ FIG. 4-39 *Trunk*. Huamanga, Ayacucho, Peru, 18th century. Wood, leather, metal, paint, 8½" x 21" (21.6 x 53.3 cm). Private Collection.

FIG. 4-40 *Document Box*. Huamanga, Ayacucho, Peru, 18th–19th century. Wood, leather, metal, 5" x 15½" (12.7 x 39.4 cm). Private Collection.

Skilled craftsmen traveling to South America in the eighteenth century brought the leatherwork technique with them and opened up workshops in places such as the Ayacucho region of Peru, where there were abundant supplies of cowhide. All of the pieces shown here were made in the style of traveling trunks, or cases, with flat tops and overhanging flaps. In figures 4-38 and 4-39 the embossed leather is covered with ornate scrolls and floral patterns. The top of each has a double-eagle motif—a symbol of the Hapsburg royal family that controlled Spain during the sixteenth and seventeenth centuries. The double eagle became a popular motif used in Spanish coats of arms and decorative arts. The trunk in figure 4-39 has the same image repeated on the front, flanked by two fantastic animals. The shapes and sizes of the iron locks complement the decoration; they were obviously viewed as an integral part of the overall design. The large trunks were painted with bright contrasting colors, while the smaller document box was left a solid brown.

FIG. 4-41 *Trunk.* Huamanga, Ayacucho, Peru, 19th century. Wood, leather, 12½" x 21½" (31.8 x 54.6 cm). Private Collection.

This larger traveling trunk, known as a *petaca*, was used for transporting goods. It is made from two layers of raw, untanned cowhides, each a full quarter of an inch thick. Hides were soaked in water and then stretched and lashed over frames in the shape of a box and lid. Once dry, the rawhide was very strong and had the permanent shape of a trunk and lid. Finally, the outside layers were decorated with patterns and designs cut into the hide. The Hapsburg double-headed eagle appears twice on the front of this petaca.

▲ FIG. 4-45 *Plates.* Top row: Cuzco, Peru, early 20th century. Ceramic, pigments, glaze. Largest: 2¾" x 9¼" (7 x 23.5 cm). Bottom row: probably Pucará region, Puno, Peru, early 20th century. Ceramic, pigments. Largest: 2½" x 9½" (6.4 x 24 cm). International Folk Art Foundation Collection, MOIFA.

Majolica *platos* (plates) in the shape of shallow bowls were one of the most common items made in Cuzco and Pucará. The centers were painted with a variety of images including bulls wearing banners and other festive decoration, as seen in these five pieces. A comparison of the painting styles and color of the opaque background of the two plates in the bottom row suggests that they were made in Pucará.

FIG. 4-46 *Plates.* Cuzco, Peru, early 20th century. Ceramic, pigments, glaze. Largest: 2¾" x 10" (7 x 25.4 cm). International Folk Art Foundation Collection, MOIFA.

This group shows some of the images typically used to decorate majolica plates. The one at top left is decorated with *suche*, a type of fish found in Lake Titicaca. The pattern on the plate at lower left looks like a ladder, or stylized floral motif, but residents of Cuzco say that it represents a llama.

FIG. 4-47 *Plates.* Pucará region, Puno, Peru, ca. 2000. Ceramic, pigments, glaze. Largest: 3" x 10" (7.6 x 25.4 cm). International Folk Art Foundation Collection, MOIFA.

Some ceramic workshops in the Pucará region are still making the traditional plates, but they no longer use the tin glaze that creates the opaque white background when fired. Instead, they coat the interior of the plates with a thin veneer of white clay and then paint over that, a technique known as *engobe*. The decorated area is then coated with a lead glaze and fired. The painted surface of the finished pieces does not have the same quality and durability as majolica; today, the plates are used as a colorful substitute on festival occasions.

FIG. 4-48 *Majolica Cooking Pots*. Chordeleg, Azuay, Ecuador, early 20th century. Ceramic, pigments, glaze. Largest: 11" x 13" (27.9 x 33 cm). Collection of Bob and Gay Sinclair.

These three ollas exemplify one type of vessel made in the majolica workshops in Chordeleg, Ecuador. Each has a line of three ceramic loops coming down from two sides of the rim onto the shoulders. These loops are decorative but also can be used to fasten a leather strap that serves as a handle (see center). The opaque white background has a yellow tinge, and the painted decoration usually covers half the body, or sometimes comes all the way down to the base (see right).

◀ FIG. 4-49 *Majolica Jars*. Chordeleg, Azuay, Ecuador, early 20th century. Ceramic, pigments, glaze. Largest: 13¼" x 12½" (33.7 x 31.8 cm). International Folk Art Foundation Collection, MOIFA.

Long-necked majolica jars were also made in Chordeleg, but the body on these vessels is fatter than those on the jars from southern Peru. The opaque background on these two examples is much whiter than on the ollas in figure 4-48.

FIG. 4-50 *Majolica Bowl and Pot*. Chordeleg, Azuay, Ecuador, early 20th century. Ceramic, pigments, glaze. Left: Private Collection. Right: 10" x 16" (25.4 x 40.6 cm). International Folk Art Foundation Collection, MOIFA.

The majolica workshops in Chordeleg made different types of vessels that were decorated on the inside rather than the exterior. Some were bowls, as seen here on the left. The large olla on the right was used for serving chicha—an alcoholic beverage of fermented corn—during fiestas and other special events.

## Carved Gourds

Andeans have been making containers from dried *calabaza* fruit since early prehispanic times. Many of them were small cups known in the Quechua language as *mati* or *mate*. By the time the Spanish arrived, in the early sixteenth century, this term was also being used to refer to the gourd material itself. Calabaza is grown in hot dry climates, and different species produce a variety of shapes and sizes. The technique of preparing and decorating the gourds has not changed much since early times, with the exception of using more sophisticated tools. Once the fruit is thoroughly dried, the exterior surface is cleaned and smoothed with sand and water, or sandpaper. Then the design is carved into the skin with a sharp pointed tool, such as a burin or graver. Traditionally, the carved surface of the gourd was then coated with a black stain, made from a mixture of charcoal and grease, rubbed into the incised areas and absorbed. After this mixture was cleaned off the smooth, golden-colored skin, the recessed lines stood out in dark contrast.[26]

### YERBA MATE

A popular drink in the southern regions of South America is *yerba mate*, made with hot water and leaves from a species of holly (*Ilex paraguariensis*) native to subtropical climates. As mentioned, the word *mate* derives from the Quechua word for cup and in particular refers to the small cups made from dried calabaza that indigenous peoples of the region found to be the perfect vessel for their cherished drink.[27]

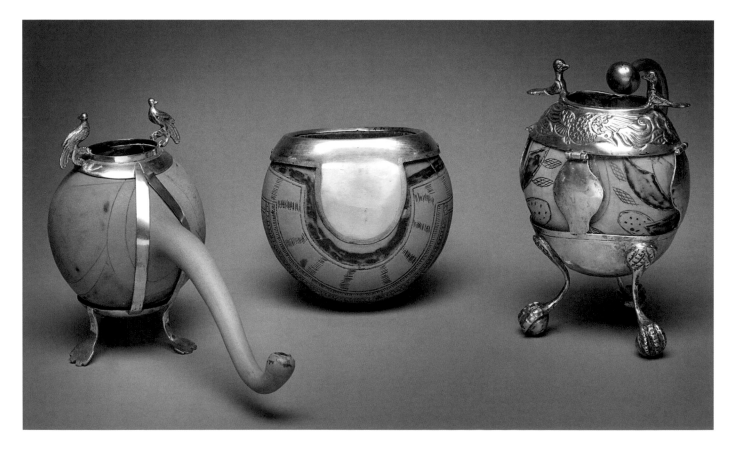

FIG. 4-51 *Cups.* Left and center: Bolivia, 19th century. Calabaza and silver. Largest: 4¾" x 6¾" (12.1 x 17.1 cm). Gifts of Edith Page Skewes-Cox, MOIFA. Right: Peru, 19th century. Calabaza and silver. Gift of the IBM Corporation, MOIFA.

These different-shaped gourd cups used for drinking yerba mate were decorated with simple carved designs using the techniques described above. Once the Spanish discovered the pleasure of yerba mate, they began decorating the gourd cups with silver, as seen in these nineteenth-century examples from Bolivia and Peru.

## GOURD CARVING IN THE LOWER MANTARO RIVER VALLEY, PERU

Calabaza grows naturally in the temperate climate of the Lower Mantaro River Valley that runs through the departments of Huancavelica and Ayacucho, Peru. After the Spanish discovered the ideal climate and resources of this region, in the early sixteenth century, they established a colony here with the capital city of Huamanga. As the population grew, Spanish and criollo families moved into the Lower Mantaro River Valley, where they planted sugar cane and raised cattle. During the Republican period, in the mid-nineteenth century, some artists in the towns of Huanta and May-occ started using the dried calabaza, or mate gourds, to make household items such as *azucareros* (lidded sugar containers) and *platos* (curved plates). This production continued into the early twentieth century.[28]

FIG. 4-52 *Plates.* Lower Mantaro River Valley, Ayacucho or Huancavelica, Peru, 1920s. Calabaza. Largest: 2¾"x 7½" (7 x 19.1 cm). Gifts of the Girard Foundation Collection, MOIFA.

Inspired by the popularity of nineteenth-century costumbrismo paintings and prints that portrayed everyday life, the gourd artisans developed their skills to decorate the curved shapes with intricate designs and scenes of the countryside. Elegant arabesques and geometric curves ornamented the center of the plates, while broad bands around the sides were filled with scenes of people tending their cattle and participating in weddings and other festivals. Some of the clothing and other details were enhanced with red pigment applied with a brush.[29]

FIG. 4-53 *Sugar Container.* Lower Mantaro River Valley, Ayacucho or Huancavelica, Peru, late 19th century. Calabaza, 6"x 8" (15.2 x 20.3 cm). Gift of Mr. and Mrs. Guy Edwards, MOIFA.

Gourd artisans also showed an interest in Peruvian history, particularly battle scenes, as shown in the decoration on this late-nineteenth-century azucarero that portrays the 1879 Guerra del Pacifico when Peru lost its southern region to Chile. As seen here,

the circular tops and bottoms of sugar containers were delineated and ornamented with arabesques and curves, while the crowded-pictorial scenes were confined to broad bands around the sides. Many of the decorated gourds also had narrow bands with inscriptions, including phrases from poetry, titles relating to the scenes portrayed, and dedications to the people who received the gourds as gifts.[30]

## GOURD CARVING IN THE UPPER MANTARO RIVER VALLEY, PERU

The upper part of the Mantaro River Valley, in the Department of Junín, has a rugged terrain with higher elevation and colder climate; the people living there remained somewhat isolated until 1908, when a new railroad line connected the region to the rest of Peru. Shortly thereafter, a highway was constructed through the mountainous area that brought modern forms of transportation, as well as interested visitors. The Sunday trade fair in the capital city of Huancayo had always been important to the region, but its importance increased as new goods were brought in by outsiders and neighbors came to acquire things to take home to other areas. Among those coming to take advantage of this lucrative market were the *materos,* gourd carvers, from Huanta and Mayocc in the Lower Mantaro River Valley. They inspired artists living near Huancayo, particularly in the villages of Cochas Grande and Cochas Chico, to learn the techniques of gourd carving and to produce items such as azucareros and platos for themselves. Since calabaza did not grow in this colder climate, different varieties of the fruit were acquired from the coastal region of northern Peru.[31]

FIG. 4-54 Catalina Sanabria, *Sugar Container.* Cochas Chico, Junín, Peru, 1921. Calabaza, 5"x 10" (12.7 x 25.4 cm). Gift of Mr. and Mrs. Guy Edwards, MOIFA.

FIG. 4-55 Sixto Sequil, *Plate.* Cochas Chico, Junín, Peru, 1958. Calabaza, 3³/₈"x 15" (8.6 x 38.1 cm). Gift of the Girard Foundation Collection, MOIFA.

Women were among the early gourd carvers in the Huancayo region. Initially, they copied the style of ornamentation seen on the pieces from Huanta and Mayocc. This azucarero, made by Catalina Sanabria in 1921, has decoration on the circular top and bottom consisting of fluid curves and geometric motifs. The central band around the side of the gourd was filled with intricate floral motifs, as well as figures of upper-class men dressed in suits from that time period. To distinguish her work from that of the Lower Mantaro River Valley, Catalina left the incised areas white rather than darkening them with the charcoal and grease mixture. Also, rather than painting details on the images, she used a smoldering branch of the *quinwal,* or eucalyptus tree, to burn brown and black colors into the golden hue of the gourd's skin.[32]

Gradually, the artists in the Upper Mantaro River Valley developed their own style of ornamentation, as seen on the bottom of this plate made by Sixto Sequil in 1958. In this work, the scene runs horizontally across the circular gourd rather than around the rim. Also, the images are bolder and less crowded. Sequil has portrayed the mountainous region with the new forms of transportation—railroad, highway with buses, trucks, and cars, and an airplane in the sky—and has pushed the traditional arrieros, traveling traders with their llamas, down to the bottom of the scene. The sacred Andean condor looks down from above. Large areas have been cut away from the gourd's surface to expose the white background, and details were added in a variety of burned colors using the smoldering-branch technique.

FIG. 4-56 *Sugar Containers.* Cochas Chico, Junín, Peru. Left: Bertha Aquino, ca. 1960. Calabaza. Right: Evaristo Medina, 1968. Calabaza, 5½" x 7½" (14 x 19.1 cm). Gifts of the Girard Foundation Collection, MOIFA.

Gourd carvers in the Upper Mantaro River Valley continued to experiment with different styles of decoration. The azucarero on the left, made by Bertha Aquino, shows a local funeral scene with bold images laid out in a wide horizontal band around the body of the gourd. Large areas of the background were carved out of the surface. These areas and the more detailed incisions were darkened using the traditional charcoal and grease mixture.

Bertha married another gourd carver, Evaristo Medina, who was the son of Catalina Sanabria. In the late 1960s Evaristo was dyeing the surface of gourds with aniline colors, such as red, and leaving the incised areas white to create a lively contrast. Some of the details were painted pink, yellow, and blue. In the azucarero on the right he portrayed local men wearing striped ponchos with a group of llama below.[33]

FIG. 4-57 Francisca Medina de Flores Vilcacoto, *Plate.* Cochas Chico, Junín, Peru, 1972. Calabaza, 4"x 14" (10.2 x 35.6 cm). Gift of H. M. Monroe Thorington, International Folk Art Foundation Collection, MOIFA.

By the 1970s, many of the carvers had started creating more complex scenes, as shown here on a plate by Evaristo Medina's cousin, Francisca. Following the earlier Upper Mantaro River Valley style, the image is laid out horizontally across the wide gourd with mountains along the top and houses and fields below. In the foreground Francisca portrayed a local festival scene with musicians, dancers, and a bullfight. The color details were done with the burning technique.

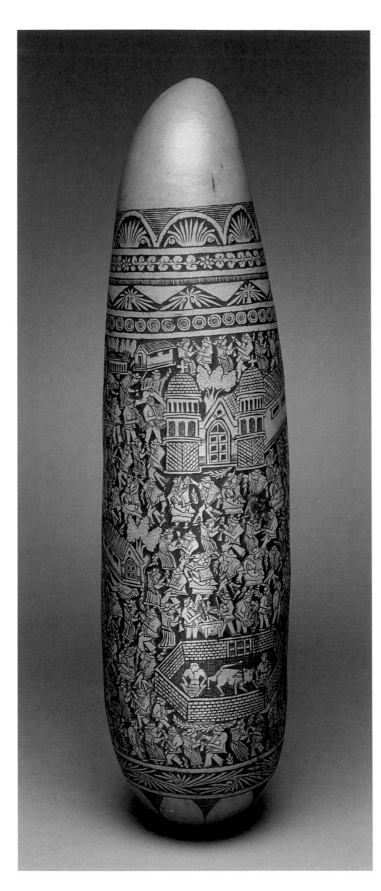

FIG. 4-58 *Decorative Gourd.* Cochas Chico, Junín, Peru, 1973. Calabaza, 15½" x 3¾" (39.4 x 9.5 cm). International Folk Art Foundation Collection, MOIFA.

▶ FIG. 4-59 Bertha Medina, *Decorative Gourd.* Cochas Chico, Junín, Peru, 2009. Calabaza, 12" x 10" (30.5 x 25.4 cm). International Folk Art Foundation Collection, MOIFA.

As time went on, artists in the Upper Mantaro River Valley began decorating gourds with no functional purpose; the elongated and globular shapes seen here became popular for that type of work. Beginning in the 1970s, another trend began that returned to the more detailed style of decoration seen in the Lower Mantaro River Valley work, including the use of black carbon and grease coloring to bring out the contrasts. In these gourds most or all of the surface was covered with miniature scenes of Peruvian life, pushing the art of carved mate to new limits and requiring patience and skills beyond what had come before. The piece in figure 4-59 was made by Bertha Medina, daughter of Bertha Aquino and Evaristo Medina.[34]

## Flasks and Drinking Cups

During the nineteenth century, travelers on horseback often carried horn flasks filled with water to quench their thirst along the road. They also carried non-breakable drinking cups made from cow horn or coconut shell that made it easy to drink water from a flask.

FIG. 4-60 *Flasks.* Bolivia, 19th century. Left: cow horn, silver. Gift of Florence Dibell Bartlett, MOIFA. Right: silver. Without chain: 13" x 4⅞" (33 x 12.4 cm). Private Collection.

These *chifles* (flasks) were usually made from cow horns that were hollowed out and fitted with a metal covering on the large end and a silver cap on the opposite end. Metal chains attached to the sides were used to fasten the chifles to saddles. The fancier flasks were ornamented with bands of decorated silver; in some cases, the entire piece was made of silver shaped like a cow horn, as seen here on the right.[35]

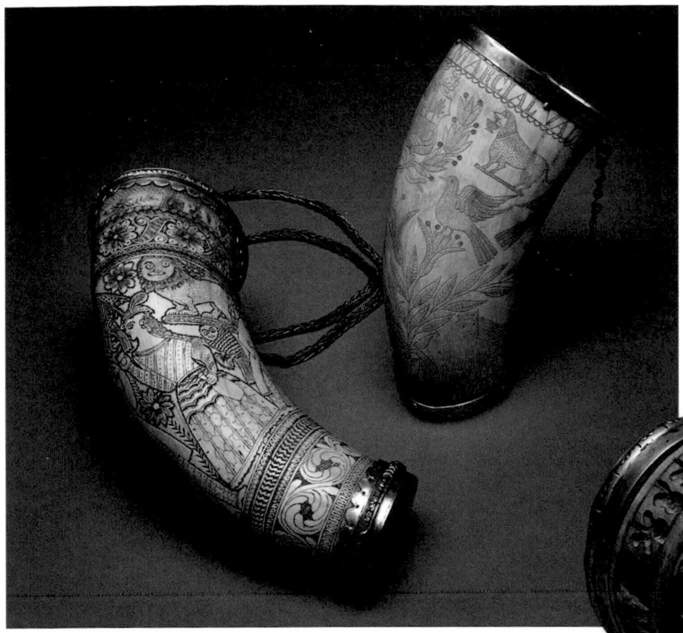

FIG. 4-61 *Drinking Cups.* Lower Mantaro River Valley, Ayacucho, Peru, late 19th century. Horn, metal. Left: 3½" x 8½" (8.9 x 21.6 cm). Gift of John Lunsford in Honor of Elizabeth Boeckman, MOIFA. Right: private Collection.

▶ FIG. 4-62 *Drinking Cups.* Argentina. Left: 19th century. Horn, metal, 9" x 2¾" (22.9 x 7 cm). MOIFA. Right: ca. 1910. Horn. International Folk Art Foundation Collection, MOIFA.

Drinking cups made from cow horn, *chambaos*, were the complement to the chifles. The two examples in figure 4-61 were made in the Lower Mantaro River Valley, in the Department of Ayacucho, the same area where the carved gourds were made (see figs.4-52, 4-53). The horn cups are ornamented with relief carving in a similar style to the gourds; also like the gourds, the cups portray scenes of daily life, along with decorative motifs and inscriptions. The two cups in figure 4-62 are from Argentina, where artists decorated the chambaos with a deeper relief carving. The late-nineteenth-century cup on the left was made in a similar fashion as those from Peru, with silver bands on both ends. The carved image depicts a mounted soldier and the inscription around the top has a line from the Argentine national anthem: "Los Laureles Sean Eternos" (May the Laurels Be Eternal). The cup on the right was probably made in the early twentieth century, when the style for the horn cups had become smaller and lacked the silver ornaments. The relief carving on this cup depicts a couple embroiled in a terrible fight, with a humorous inscription below: "Excenas de la Vida Conyugal" (Scenes from the Life of a Married Couple).

FIG. 4-63 *Drinking Cups.* Left: Ecuador, 19th century. Coconut shell, metal, 5½" x 5" (14 x 12.7 cm). Private Collection. Right: Colombia, 1872. Coconut shell, metal. Gift of Elizabeth Wallace, MOIFA.

Drinking cups used by travelers in Ecuador and Colombia were made from coconut shells that were typically decorated with detailed relief carving. A hook and chain were attached to one end so the cups could be hung from a saddle or belt.

FIG. 4-68 *Candleholders*. Bolivia, 19th century. Silver. Largest: 7" x 4¾" (17.8 x 12.1 cm). Collection of Judy Espinar and Nancy McCabe.

FIG. 4-69 *Candleholders*. Bolivia, late 19th century. Mixed metals, wood. Largest: 10¼" x 5½" (26 x 14 cm). Private Collection.

Silver candleholders were popular decorative items in homes, as well as serving the function of holding candles to illuminate rooms at night. The pair in top photo was made in the same caliber of workshop that produced the cups and goblets shown on the previous page. The examples in figure 4-69 were done in a more primitive style, probably by indigenous silversmiths working in their own villages. The bodies of the pieces are made from a sheet of mixed metals that was cut and attached to shaped-wooden forms. The metal was ornamented with bold patterns and motifs using the repoussé technique. Cylindrical candleholders were attached to the top and the wooden bases were painted.

FIG. 4-70 *Incense Burners.* Left: Chile, mid-19th century. Silver. Gift of the IBM Corporation, MOIFA. Right: Peru, mid-19th century. Silver, 8" x 5³/₈" (20.3 x 14.3 cm). International Folk Art Foundation Collection, MOIFA.

FIG. 4-71 *Incense Burners.* Peru or Bolivia, mid-19th century. Silver. Largest: 5³/₈" x 8¹/₂" (13.7 x 21.6 cm). International Folk Art Foundation Collection, MOIFA.

Domestic incense burners, known as *sahumadores*, were used to burn aromatic and purifying substances that perfumed the air of the home. They also served as decoration; silversmiths made them in a variety of imaginative forms ornamented with intricate detailing. The burners were usually attached to a small tray, or *salver*, that protected the surfaces on which the burners were placed by catching ash from spent coals. The roosters below do not have the attached trays, so they were probably placed on one large tray or plate when used.

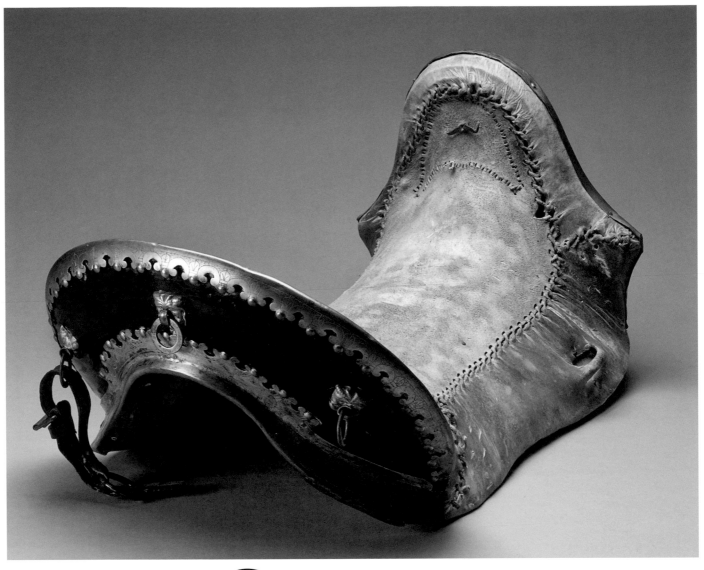

FIG. 4-72 *Saddle Tree*. Bolivia, 19th century. Wood, rawhide, silver, fabric, metal, leather, 10¼" x 18" (26 x 45.7 cm). Gift of Eloisa Brown Jones, MOIFA.

FIG. 4-73 *Quirt*. Argentina, 19th century. Silver, metal, leather. Handle: 17¼" x 1¼" (44 x 3 cm). International Folk Art Foundation Collection, MOIFA.

Silversmiths working in the nineteenth century produced many pieces used in horseback riding, a popular sport with both men and women. Quirts (*rebenques*) were made in a variety of styles. This example is typical of those carried by gauchos in Argentina.

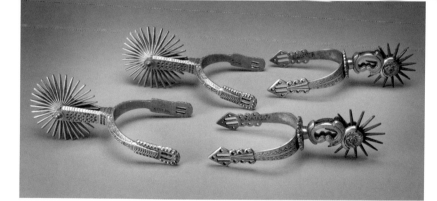

**FIG. 4-74** *Stirrups.* Argentina, mid- to late-19th century. Left: silver, leather, gold. Gift of David R. Thornburg, MOIFA. Right: silver, leather, 26" x 4¼" (66 x 10.8 cm). International Folk Art Foundation Collection, MOIFA.

▼ **FIG. 4-75** *Woman's Sidesaddle Stirrups.* Left: Argentina, early 19th century. Silver. International Folk Art Foundation Collection, MOIFA. Right: Bolivia, early 19th century. Silver, 5" x 8¾" (12.7 x 22.2 cm). Gift of Lucia Fox Edwards, MOIFA.

Stirrups, *estribos*, were (and continue to be) an important part of horse-riding gear; many were made in ornamented silver. Often, the leather straps that attached them to the saddle were also decorated with sections of silver, as seen at left. Most women rode sidesaddle and only used one stirrup for the foot on the outside leg. Usually, they were designed like a slipper and came to be known as *estribos sandalias* (below).

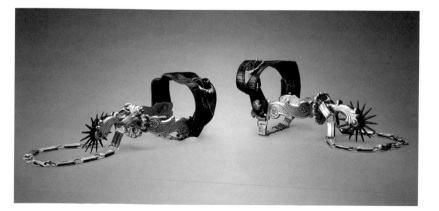

**FIG. 4-76** *Spurs.* Left: Argentina, late 19th century. Silver, 3³/₈" x 8" (8.6 x 20.3 cm). Right: Chile, mid-19th century. Silver, steel. Gifts of David R. Thornburg, MOIFA.

**FIG. 4-77** *Dance Spurs.* Argentina, mid-19th century. Silver, leather, 2¼" x 9½" (5.7 x 24.1 cm). International Folk Art Foundation Collection, MOIFA.

Spurs, *espuelas*, are worn on the heel of the riding boot and used to urge the horse along. The form and ornamentation of silver spurs dating to the nineteenth century vary from region to region. The pair of espuelas in figure 4-77 was worn for dancing. Leather straps went over the front of the boot and chains attached to the back were looped around the ankle to help hold the spurs in place.

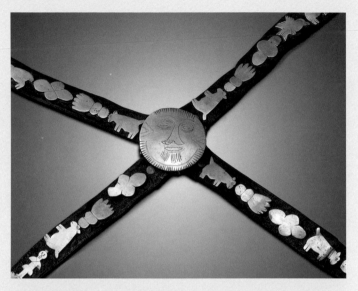

▲ FIG. 4-78 *Horse Headstall*. Central highlands, Ecuador, late 19th–early 20th century. Leather, silver, 20½" x 8" (52.1 x 20.3 cm). Collection of Leslie Goodwin.

FIG. 4-79 *Horse Breast Collar*. Central highlands, Ecuador, late 19th–early 20th century. Leather, silver, 67" x 47" (170.2 x 119.4 cm). Collection of Leslie Goodwin.

FIG. 4-80 *Horse Blinders*. Ayacucho, Peru, early to mid-20th century. Leather, silver. Largest, without straps: 3¾" x 17" (9.2 x 43.2 cm). Top: MOIFA. Center and bottom: International Folk Art Foundation Collection, MOIFA.

Silverwork has been used to ornament leather horse trappings. Some of the more elaborate examples are worn by horses for special riding competitions and festival parades.[40] The headstall and breast collar in figures 4-78 and 4-79 were acquired in the Riobamba region of Chimborazo Province, located in the central highlands of Ecuador. They are ornamented with silver figures of humans, animals, and birds created in a wonderful folk style. The blinders, *anteojeras*, in figure 4-80 were attached to a bridle and hung down on each side of the horses' eyes. The intention is to restrict the animals' vision to the rear and sides and keep them focused towards the front. They were often used on horses that were pulling carriages or wagons, to keep them from being distracted or spooked. All three of these blinders are from the Ayacucho region of Peru.[41]

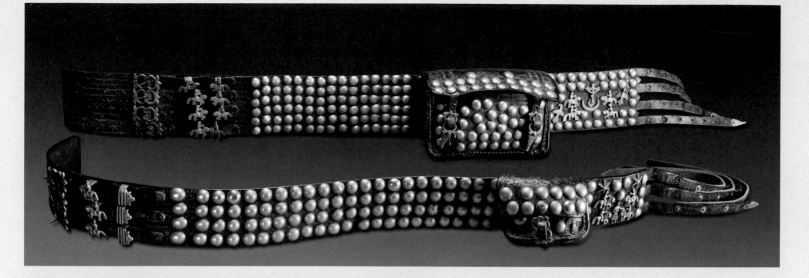

FIG. 4-81 *Belts*. Saraguro, Loja, Ecuador. Top: Early to mid-20th century. Leather, brass. Gift of Lloyd E. Cotsen and the Neutrogena Corporation, MOIFA. Bottom: Late 19th–early 20th century. Leather, silver, 3" x 51" (7.6 x 129.5 cm). Collection of Bob and Gay Sinclair.

In a few regions of the Andes, metalworkers have ornamented leather items worn by men. Here are two examples of men's leather belts from Saraguro, in the southern Province of Loja, Ecuador. They are made in different widths with three to six buckles and small pouches sewn to one side. Rows of circular studs, made from old silver or brass coins that have been hammered into the desired form, are used to decorate the belts. Small, silver figurines ornament both ends.[42]

FIG. 4-82 *Bags*. Cuzco, Peru, late 19th–early 20th century. Leather, silver. Left: 32" x 7" (81.3 x 17.8 cm). Collection of Bob and Gay Sinclair. Right: Private Collection.

During the post-Independence era of the nineteenth century, wealthy Indian men in the Cuzco region started carrying leather bags ornamented with silver figurines, rosettes, stars, and coins. A miniature silver version of the Peruvian national coat of arms was usually featured in the center. These bags, known as *chuspa de coquera,* replaced the handwoven wool bags for carrying coca leaves.[43]

## Miner's Lamps

In the deep recesses of silver mines, where there was no natural daylight, miners needed a form of artificial light to work. In prehispanic times, the workers carried torches made from cloth. When the Spanish began exploring the mines, they used candles, but they were not reliable and kept blowing out. Finally, by the late sixteenth century, they devised a miner's lamp adapted from oil lamps used in churches and homes.

FIG. 4-83 *Miner's Lamps.* Bolivia, early 20th century. Iron. Largest: 25" x 5" (63.5 x 12.7 cm). International Folk Art Foundation Collection, MOIFA.

The portable lamp has a hook at the top for attaching to the workers' clothing or belts, allowing the miner to keep his hands free to chip the rock or carry buckets full of ore. The lamps usually had a central shaft with a cup at the bottom that held oil or other combustible liquid. A flame was lit at the end of a length of wool or cotton string that wicked the oil up from the bottom of the cup. The shafts of the lamps were ornamented with Christian and Andean religious images, to protect the miners from dangers encountered in the underground work. The lamps used by the Spaniards in the colonial period were often elaborate and made of silver. However, most of the lamps used by the miners throughout the colonial period, and into the early twentieth century, were made of iron, as seen in these examples.[44]

# Tinwork

Metalworkers in the Andes made utilitarian items from silver and other metals throughout the colonial period; however, in the late eighteenth century, some began using tinplate, or *hojalata*. In English these objects are generally referred to as tinwork, but they are actually made from sheets of steel or aluminum coated with tin. Originally, the pieces were left unpainted so they would have a shiny look similar to silver; by the early twentieth century, some folk artists were painting the tinwork to create a different look. Two cities particularly known for their *hojalatería* are Cuenca, in the southern province of Azuay, Ecuador, and Huamanga, in the Department of Ayacucho, Peru.

FIG. 4-84 *Picture Frames*. Cuenca, Azuay, Ecuador, early 20th century. Tinplate, paint. Largest: 25" x 15" (63.5 x 38.1 cm). International Folk Art Foundation Collection, MOIFA.

FIG. 4-85 *Staff Finials*. Cuenca, Azuay, Ecuador, early 20th century. Tinplate, paint. Largest: 16" x 9" (40.6 x 22.9 cm). International Folk Art Foundation Collection, MOIFA.

By the early twentieth century, there were many workshops in Cuenca, Ecuador, creating objects from tinplate. Most of them produced unpainted utilitarian ware, such as lanterns, candleholders, braziers, buckets, scoops, and other simple tools. However, some craftsmen made more elaborate items, including portable shrines for religious sculptures and frames to hold religious prints. This tinwork was often painted in contrasting colors to complement the sacred image. The wide pedestal bases were filled with small pebbles or sand to keep the structures from tipping over.

Another item made with painted tinplate was a finial for the tops of staffs carried by Catholic priests or members of religious brotherhoods. The finials were often cut in the form of a cross and the Sacred Heart or initials of Jesus were painted in the center.

FIG. 4-86 *Candleholder*. Cuenca, Azuay, Ecuador, mid-20th century. Metal, paint, 21½" x 21" (54.6 x 53.3 cm). International Folk Art Foundation Collection, MOIFA.

Painted tinwork continues to be made in Cuenca, with some artists specializing in creating ornate candleholders. Typically, they are adorned with flowers and birds and painted in lively colors. The wide base is filled with sand, or other heavy materials, to keep the candleholders stable.[45]

FIG. 4-87 *Candleholders*. Huamanga, Ayacucho, Peru, ca. 1965. Metal, paint, 19" x 17" (48.3 x 43.2 cm). Gift of the Girard Foundation Collection, MOIFA.

FIG. 4-88 Desiderio Loayza, *Holy Cross*. Huamanga, Ayacucho, Peru, ca. 1980. Metal, paint, 27½" x 15½" (69.9 x 39.4 cm). International Folk Art Foundation Collection, MOIFA.

Workshops in Huamanga, Ayacucho, Peru, started working with tinplate in the late eighteenth century and created inexpensive candleholders and other things that imitated silverwork. These items continued to be made through the nineteenth and into the twentieth century. In 1950 collectors from Lima began asking the artists to paint the tinwork and make it look more decorative, thus starting a new trend that continues today. The artisans primarily make candleholders and crosses; as in Cuenca, the bases are weighted so they won't tip over. Some of the Ayacucho tinworkers, such as Desiderio Loayza, moved to Lima to be closer to the commercial market. Others, such as Teófilo Araujo, remained working in Huamanga.[46]

## Ceremonial Drinking Vessels

Since prehispanic times, indigenous people living in the Andean highlands of Bolivia, Peru, and Ecuador have made special vessels to use for drinking alcohol during ceremonial events. The most common form of drink is chicha, made from fermented corn, but grain alcohol also started to be produced after the Europeans introduced wheat as an agricultural crop. The vessels are meant to be filled with an alcoholic beverage and shared with one person, or passed around to community members participating in a celebration. Religious practitioners also use some of these vessels in their rituals for the Andean gods, which involves the offering and consumption of alcohol. Drinking vessels from different regions have been made in a variety of shapes and materials, including painted-wood cups, unpainted carved-wood bowls, delicately crafted silver bowls and cups, as well as ceramic bowls, pitchers, and bottles.

FIG. 4-89 *Carved Queros.* Cuzco region, Peru, early 16th century. Wood, each: 4½" x 3¼" (11.4 x 8.3 cm). Private Collection.

Wooden cups known as *queros* are shaped liked European beakers, but they were widely used in the Andes prior to the Spanish conquest. Under the Inca, they were usually made in pairs for a toast between two people. By using matched vessels, there was parity in the amount drunk, and it symbolized an amicable and reciprocal relationship. At the time of the conquest, these wooden cups were usually decorated with geometric motifs.[47]

**FIG. 4-95** *Wooden Cocha.* Bolivia, 19th century. Wood, 4" x 9½" (10.2 x 24.1 cm). Collection of David and Mayi Munsell.

Another type of ceremonial drinking vessel is known as a *cocha*, taken from the Quechua word *qucha* that means pond or lake. The bowls have small figures of cattle or oxen, and sometimes humans, attached in the center. When filled with chicha the bowl becomes a symbolic pond with the figures immersed in the liquid. In some areas of southern Peru and Bolivia it is believed that domesticated animals originated in miniature form out of highland springs; as the alcohol is drunk from the bowl, the figures appear to be emerging from such a spring or pond.[48] In this cocha an Andean man is playing a flute behind five cattle, two of which are shown copulating, representing the wish for fertility among the animals. This bowl still has the residue of chicha from many years of use.

**FIG. 4-96** *Wooden Cocha.* Bolivia, early–mid-20th century. Wood, 4¾" x 16¼" (12.1 x 41.3 cm). Private Collection.

Wooden cochas are generally found in Bolivia, where they are used in festivals and ceremonies to serve alcohol to the whole community. Women who help put on these events carry jugs of chicha in one hand and the bowls in another and go from person to person offering a drink to each of them. Before taking a sip, everyone offers a libation to Pachamama by pouring some of the chicha on the ground. This is a particularly large example of a cocha, featuring two pairs of yoked oxen facing in opposite directions.

FIG. 4-97 *Wooden Cochas*. Bolivia, early–mid-20th century. Wood. Back: 8½" x 10" (21.6 x 25.4 cm). Girard Foundation Collection, MOIFA. Far left, left center, right center: Gifts of Peter P. Cecere, MOIFA. Far right: Gift of David R. Thornburg, MOIFA.

As this group illustrates, cochas are made in a range of sizes with different styles of carving and ornamentation. Yoked oxen are the most common figures depicted in the center; in smaller bowls, a bull or cow is represented by itself. Occasionally, the oxen or cattle are shown copulating, or a young calf is portrayed with its mother.

FIG. 4-98 *Ceramic Cochas*. Southern Peru, late 19th–early 20th century. Ceramic. Largest: 4" x 9" (10.2 x 22.9 cm). International Folk Art Foundation Collection, MOIFA.

Cochas are used in communities in southern Peru, where they are ceramic rather than wood. The figures portrayed in the center are primarily cattle that are often shown copulating. In others, mothers are shown with their calves. And in some, people are portrayed carrying out rituals with their cattle, as seen here (center). All three types of scenes are petitions for fertility among the animals.[49]

FIG. 4-99 *Silver Cochas*. Bolivia. Left: mid-20th century. Silver. Gift of Connie Thrasher Jaquith, MOIFA. Center: late 19th–early 20th century. Silver, 1½" x 4" (3.8 x 10.2 cm). Private Collection. Pair on right: 19th century. Silver. Gift of Connie Thrasher Jaquith, MOIFA.

Silver has been used in Bolivia to make ceremonial drinking vessels; they are very small and used for drinking grain alcohol, rather than chicha. These cochas are often used by religious practitioners as part of the mesa, or ceremonial table, where ritual offerings for the Andean deities are placed.

FIG. 4-100 *Silver Cups*. Bolivia, 19th century. Silver. Left: International Folk Art Foundation Collection, MOIFA. Center: 3¾" x 2½" (9.5 x 6.4 cm). Gift of Connie Thrasher Jaquith, MOIFA. Pair on right: Private Collection.

All of the drinking vessels in this group are miniature versions of silver cups used by the Spanish in the colonial era. The one in the center was copied from chalices used to offer wine during mass. By the nineteenth century, these small chalice-like cups were known as *copas challadoras*, because they were used by the indigenous people in *ch'allas*, or special drinking rituals, to ask for fertility, good health, and prosperity from the Andean gods. The pair of cups at right is typical of those used on ceremonial tables.[50]

FIG. 4-101 *Multi-Chamber Wood Vessels.* Bolivia, late 19th–early 20th century. Wood. Left: Collection of David and Mayi Munsell. Right: 3" x 10½" (7.6 x 26.7 cm). Private Collection.

Multi-chamber ceremonial drinking vessels gained popularity in the nineteenth century. Alcohol was poured into a bowl with connecting tubes that allowed the liquid to run into four or more chambers around the edge. These vessels were passed around during a community festival, or ceremony, and individuals drank out of the different chambers. In Bolivia they were made in various sizes and were often carved in wood, as seen here.

FIG. 4-102 *Multi-Chamber Ceramic Vessels.* Left: Yura, Potosí, Bolivia, late 19th–early 20th century. Ceramic, glaze. Gift of Kisla Jiménez and Jonathan Williams, MOIFA. Center: Cuzco region, Peru, late 19th–early 20th century. Ceramic, glaze, 4" x 10½" (10.2 x 26.7 cm). International Folk Art Foundation Collection, MOIFA. Right: Cuzco region, Peru, ca. 1960. Ceramic. Gift of Kisla Jiménez and Jonathan Williams, MOIFA.

Ceramic multi-chambered vessels were used for community drinking rituals. The one on the left, from the northern region of the Department of Potosí, Bolivia, has a small bowl in the center with tunnels underneath that allow the liquid to run to four spouts around the edge. The other two are from the Cuzco region of Peru, where the multi-chambered vessels are known by the Quechua word *paccha* (the earth).[51] These are made with two smaller bowls placed inside the larger one, and each has a tunnel that connects to three spouts on one side of the rim. Many of them were made with the majolica tin-glaze technique, as seen in the center piece. The unglazed paccha on the right has a small bull in the center bowl, similar to the cochas shown earlier (see figs. 4-95 through 4-99).

FIG. 4-103 *Ceramic Pitchers.* Checca Pupuja, Puno, Peru, early 20th century. Ceramic, pigment, glaze. Largest: 14" x 7" (35.6 x 17.8 cm). International Folk Art Foundation Collection, MOIFA.

In the eighteenth century, a large number of Spanish colonists settled in the Puno region of southern Peru. Because they needed plates and other vessels for their homes, they began commissioning glazed ceramics from pottery workshops in Santiago de Pupuja and Checca Pupuja, villages already making conopas, as discussed earlier (see figs. 2-92, 2-97). After Peru gained independence from Spain, in the early nineteenth century, the potters continued to produce glazed ceramics for mestizos living in Puno, as well as for Indians in rural villages. By the early twentieth century, the green-glazed pottery had become quite ornate, particularly those vessels used during fiestas and ceremonial occasions. Among the most popular forms were pitchers used to serve chicha and other types of alcohol. They often depicted men on the top—drinking while seated or riding a horse—as seen in these two examples.[52]

FIG. 4-104 *Ceramic Cups.* Cuzco region, Peru, late 19th–early 20th century. Ceramic, pigment. Each: 3½" x 3" (8.9 x 7.6 cm). Gift of Kisla Jiménez, MOIFA.

This pair of ceramic drinking vessels was made in the shape of small shoes to be used by a bride and groom to toast each other during their wedding ceremony. They were made in the same type of pottery workshop in the Cuzco region that produced the small, burnished bull conopas shown earlier (see fig. 2-94).

FIG. 4-105 Mamerto Sánchez, *Ceramic Bottles.* Quinua, Ayacucho, Peru, ca. 1960. Largest: 14" x 3½" (35.6 x 9 cm). Gifts of the Girard Foundation Collection, MOIFA.

One of the most important potters in Quinua, in the Department of Ayacucho, Peru, is Mamerto Sánchez. Since the mid-twentieth century, he has made a variety of figural pieces to use as drinking vessels and as roof ornaments (see figs. 4-114 through 4-117).

Among the first group are narrow-shape human forms used as bottles for drinking chicha and other alcoholic beverages. These often portray band members who play for a community ceremony during the annual cleaning of irrigation ditches in late August or early September.[53] During the event, each musician is presented with a bottle; a figure in uniform playing the musician's particular instrument, such as a rasp, drum, or horn (left). Sometimes, the women who serve chicha are given drinking bottles portraying themselves in the act of serving (right).

# House Blessing Ornaments

The use of house blessing ornaments is a tradition found in several communities in Ecuador and Peru, and to a lesser extent in Bolivia. Placed on the roof, these ornaments take on a variety of forms ranging from painted and unpainted metal crosses to ceramic animals, humans, and churches. In one Peruvian community the center roof beam inside a home is painted with religious and secular scenes. For devout Catholics, roof crosses are a symbol of their faith and a blessing of their home. For many Andeans, however, the crosses and other forms of ornamentation serve as petitions to the gods for fertility and prosperity of the family, as well as for protection from severe storms and other calamities.[54]

Scholars have not identified a European source for the Latin American practice of putting crosses on the roofs of private homes.[55] The tradition may have been influenced by the use of crosses on the tops of small private chapels attached to houses on the properties of large haciendas. Once the strict rules of the Catholic Church subsided in the nineteenth century, the local people began putting the crosses on their own structures to add a decorative feature to their architecture and bring good luck to their homes.

**ECUADOR—ROOF ORNAMENTS**

FIG. 4-106 *Roof Crosses.* Cuenca, Azuay, Ecuador, 1992 and 1993. Wrought iron, paint. Left: International Folk Art Foundation Collection, MOIFA. Right: 35" x 14" (88.9 x 35.6 cm). Collection of David and Mayi Munsell.

Cuenca, capital of the southern highland province of Azuay, Ecuador, was known for its ironwork in the colonial period; the craft continues to be practiced today in an old part of town on Calle de las Her-

rerías, or Street of the Blacksmiths. These artisans specialize in making iron crosses that are painted black. They are placed on the roof of a new home on the day the owner has his friends over to attend a housewarming.[56] Some of the crosses are ornamented with the symbols of the Instruments of the Passion of Christ (see figs. 2-50, 2-51), while others are decorated with birds and floral motifs.

FIG. 4-107 *Roof Crosses.* Latacunga, Cotopaxi, Ecuador, early 20th century. Wrought iron, paint. Largest: 31¼" x 10¼" (79.4 x 26 cm). Gifts of Connie Thrasher Jaquith, MOIFA.

Latacunga is the capital of the Cotopaxi Province in the central highlands of Ecuador. Mestizo families in this town may have adopted the roof-cross tradition from Cuenca; by the late nineteenth and early twentieth century, they were commissioning iron crosses from local workshops. One example shown here, dated 1921, served a dual purpose as a cross and weather vane. Another family had a rooster placed on the top of their cross framed by the initials "MR."

FIG. 4-108 *Plastic baby doll roof ornament on house in the mountains above Latacunga, Cotopaxi, Ecuador,* 1993. Photograph by Barbara Mauldin.

Indigenous families living in smaller towns outside of Latacunga adopted the tradition of decorating their roofs, but instead of metal crosses they used ceramic figures of animals to bless their homes. One family living high up in the mountains above the valley even felt inspired to place a plastic baby doll on their roof, perhaps in hopes of bringing more children into their lives.

## PERU—METAL ROOF CROSSES

FIG. 4-109 *Roof Cross.* Cuzco or Junín, Peru, late 20th century. Sheet metal, paint, 23½" x 16¼" (59.7 x 41.3 cm). Collection of Kisla Jiménez and Jonathan Williams.

FIG. 4-110 *Roof Crosses.* Left: Llave, Puno, Peru, ca. 1980. Metal, paint. International Folk Art Foundation Collection, MOIFA. Center: Pampachiri, Apurimac, Peru, 2000. Metal, paint, 31" x 14½" (78.74 x 36.8 cm). International Folk Art Foundation Collection, MOIFA. Right: Antonio Prado. Huamanga, Ayacucho, Peru, 1958. Metal. Gift of the Girard Foundation Collection, MOIFA.

FIG. 4-111 *Roof Crosses.* Left: Ayacucho, Peru, 2000. Metal, paint, 48½" x 24" (123.2 x 61 cm). Center: Apurimac, Peru, 1996. Metal, paint. Right: San Jeronimo de Tunan, Junín, Peru, 1979. Metal, wood, paint. International Folk Art Foundation Collection, MOIFA.

The tradition of putting crosses on the rooftops of homes is carried on today in many regions of Peru. They are usually made from iron, rebar, and tinplate in local metalshops. Some are decorated with the Instruments of the Passion of Christ, while others are ornamented with birds, bulls, floral motifs, and the Peruvian flag. An inscription of the year is also a popular feature. Once the various pieces are soldered together, the crosses are usually painted in bright colors.[57]

After several years of exposure to the rain and bright sunshine, the paint on the roof crosses disappears, and the sheet metal rusts; at this point the owner of the home often decides to get a new one. Sometimes they are purchased and carried in a procession for the May 3rd celebration of the Feast of the Cross and afterwards they are placed on the roof as a renewed blessing.[58]

## PERU—CERAMIC ROOF ORNAMENTS

FIG. 4-112 *Roof ornamented with metal cross flanked by two ceramic bulls, Cuzco, Peru*, 2006. Photograph by Barbara Mauldin.

FIG. 4-113 *Bull Figures.* Checca Pupuja, Puno, Peru, ca. 1960. Ceramic, pigments. Largest: 13" x 16" (33 x 40.6 cm). Gifts of the Girard Foundation Collection, MOIFA.

An interesting tradition that developed in the Cuzco region is the placement of two ceramic bulls on each side of the roof cross. These ceramic figures are made in Checca Pupuja near Pucará, in the Department of Puno, in southern Peru. The bulls were originally made to be used as ceremonial vessels, or conopas, as shown earlier in figure 2-97. However, tourists passing through Pucará on the railroad from Cuzco to Puno, in the early to mid-twentieth century, became enchanted with the sculptural forms and wanted to take the bulls home as souvenirs; to meet this demand artisans began producing larger decorative figures for that purpose.[59] Eventually, these figures made their way into the markets of Cuzco, where local residents placed them on their roofs, adding to the architectural ornamentation and bringing increased blessings to their homes. Wheat and cornstalks are placed in the opening on the bulls' backs or between the figures, as offerings to the gods in hopes of abundant food on the family's table.

FIG. 4-114 *Roof ornamented with ceramic church flanked by two ceramic musicians, Quinua, Ayacucho, Peru,* 2008. Photograph by Barbara Mauldin.

FIG. 4-115 Mamerto Sánchez, *Church Figures*. Quinua, Ayacucho, Peru, ca. 1960. Ceramic, pigments. Largest: 24" x 14" (61 x 35.6 cm). Gifts of the Girard Foundation Collection, MOIFA.

FIG. 4-116 *Male Musician Figure*. Quinua, Ayacucho, Peru, last quarter 20th century. Ceramic, pigments, 18½" x 9" (47 x 22.8 cm). Gift of Lloyd E. Cotsen and the Neutrogena Corporation, MOIFA.

A ceramic form commonly seen on the rooftops of homes in Quinua, Ayacucho, Peru, is a church with two bell towers and clocks on the sides. Large churches, or cathedrals, such as this are not found in Quinua, or in the neighboring city of Huamanga; they are created from the artists' memory of churches they have seen in cities such as Cuzco and Lima. They intentionally fashion the towers to rise out of a narrower base to accentuate the perspective of height. The church is usually embedded in plaster on top of the roof gable, with other ceramic figures, like musicians, on each side.[60]

# Figures from Everyday Life

During the colonial period, sculpture workshops throughout the Andes produced religious art-work for churches and convents, as well as private homes. Some of the images they created were used in nativity scenes set up for Christmas. In the sixteenth and seventeenth centuries, the crèche figures usually included Mary, Joseph, the infant Jesus, and the three kings. Following trends in Italy and Spain, the nativity scenes started to get larger in the eighteenth century. They began to include other figures, many taken from everyday life,[63] ranging from upper-class citizens to lower-class market vendors to a great variety of animals. During this time, nuns in convents of some cities assembled very large nativities for public viewing during the entire Christmas season. Both the nuns and private citizens wanted to show a diverse and interesting mix of characters in their Christmas displays.[64]

The interest in using a range of figures in crèches led to a new form of sculpture that portrayed an engaging spectrum of people and animals as seen on the city streets and in the rural countryside. By the late eighteenth century, many mestizo and indigenous sculpture workshops were creating this type of work. Production continued into the nineteenth and twentieth century, when the sculpted figures from everyday life began to be recognized as folk art. A new clientele developed and began to purchase the images for use as decorative objects or toys.

**PERU**

FIG. 4-120 *Animal Figures*. Huamanga, Ayacucho, Peru, late 19th century. Stone, paint. Largest: 3" x 2½" (7.6 x 6.4 cm). Gifts of Florence Dibell Bartlett, MOIFA.

FIG. 4-121 Elias Curi, *Male Figures*. Huamanga, Ayacucho, Peru, ca. 1960. Stone, paint. Largest: 6½" x 2¾" (16.5 x 7 cm). Gifts of the Girard Foundation Collection, MOIFA.

Stone carvers in Huamanga, Ayacucho, Peru, were among the first to make small secular images that portrayed people and a variety of animals. The figures were skillfully carved in the local white stone and painted with details.[65] This tradition was carried on into the twentieth century by artists such as Elias Curi, who created small figures portraying people from Ayacucho wearing traditional clothing.

FIG. 4-122 Leocino Tineo Ochoa, *Group of Men.* Huamanga, Ayacucho, Peru, ca. 1960. Ceramic, paint. Largest figure: 6½" x 3⅛" (16.5 x 7.9 cm). Gift of the Girard Foundation Collection, MOIFA.

FIG. 4-123 Mamerto Sánchez, *Human and Animal Figures.* Quinua, Ayacucho, Peru, ca. 1960. Ceramic, paint. Largest: 7" x 5½" (17.7 x 14 cm). Gifts of the Girard Foundation Collection, MOIFA.

Sculptors working in ceramic, in Huamanga and the neighboring town of Quinua, also made figures of people and animals from the local environment. Often the sculptors portrayed humorous subject matter, such as a couple in bed being visited by a tortoise (lower left).

FIG. 4-124 Julio Villalobos, *Group of Musicians*. Cuzco, Peru, ca. 1960. Pasta, paint, 5¼" x 9" (13.3 x 22.9 cm). Gift of the Girard Foundation Collection, MOIFA.

FIG. 4-125 Hilario Mendívil Workshop, *Boxers and Market Women*. Cuzco, Peru, ca. 1960. Pasta, wire, paint. Largest: 6½" x 2½" (16.5 x 6.4 cm). Gifts of the Girard Foundation Collection, MOIFA.

By the late eighteenth century, some mestizo and indigenous workshops in Cuzco were producing small, secular figures to place in nativity scenes. They were made of maguey and dressed in fabric coated in gesso, with additional detailing done in pasta—a malleable material made of dried potato or wheat, gesso, and various forms of liquid. This figural tradition was carried on into the twentieth century by families such as the Villalobos and Mendívils whose work is seen here. Another well-known folk artist who created genre figures in Cuzco during this period was Santiago Rojas (see figs. 5-11, 5-12). By the twentieth century, many of the small secular figures were sculpted entirely in pasta, with the details, such as clothing and other items, painted onto the surface.[66]

FIG. 4-126 Pedro Abilio Gonzáles Flores and Felipe Gonzáles, *Male and Female Figures*. Huancayo, Junín, Peru, ca. 1960. Maguey, gesso, fabric, paint. Largest: 5½" x 6¾" (14 x 17.1 cm). Gifts of the Girard Foundation Collection, MOIFA.

FIG. 4-127 Pedro Abilio Gonzáles Flores and Felipe Gonzáles, *Musicians and Female Figure*. Huancayo, Junín, Peru, ca. 1960. Maguey, gesso, fabric, paint. Largest: 6" x 3" (15.2 x 7.6 cm). Gifts of the Girard Foundation Collection, MOIFA.

In the early twentieth century, small workshops in the Huancayo region of the Department of Junín, Peru, began making secular figures for nativity scenes. They used maguey to sculpt the images, the tela encolada technique (gessoed fabric) to provide clothing, and gesso or pasta to create additional details. Then the figures were painted with appropriate colors for the skin, clothing, and associated items. One of the local folk artists who became well known for this work was Pedro Abilio Gonzáles Flores. He learned the craft from his parents and grandparents and passed his knowledge and skills on to his sons and grandsons. Their figures portray people from the local environment who wear traditional clothing and perform everyday activities as seen in the streets and markets.[67]

## BOLIVIA

FIG. 4-128 *Market Vendors*. La Paz, Bolivia, ca. 1960. Maguey, gesso, fabric, pasta, paint. Largest: 2¾" x 4⅛" (7 x 10.5 cm). Gifts of the Girard Foundation Collection, MOIFA.

FIG. 4-129 *Market Vendors*. La Paz, Bolivia, ca. 1960. Maguey, pasta, fabric, paint. Largest: 8" x 10" (20.3 x 25.4 cm). Gifts of the Girard Foundation Collection, MOIFA.

Workshops in La Paz, Bolivia, began making sculpted figures for nativity scenes in the early twentieth century. Many portray market vendors who sell food and other products along the streets of La Paz. This occupation is dominated by cholas, who wear their distinguishing outfits of full skirts, shawls, and derby hats. The cholas in the lower photo all wear shawls made of actual fabric. The other group of figures (above) is particularly well made, with unusually fine detailing.

**CHILE**

FIG. 4-130 *Man and Woman on Horses.* Lihueimo, Colchagua, Chile, ca. 1960. Ceramic, paint. Largest: 7" x 4¾" (17.8 x 12.1 cm). Gifts of the Girard Foundation Collection, MOIFA.

FIG. 4-131 *Dancing Couple and Harp Player.* Lihueimo, Colchagua, Chile, ca. 1960. Ceramic, paint. Largest: 6" x 5" (15.2 x 12.7 cm). Gifts of the Girard Foundation Collection, MOIFA.

Sculptors working in ceramic in Lihueimo, in the Province of Colchagua of central Chile, have made colorful nativity-scene figures that portray men and women enjoying the life of that region.[68] Following a tradition introduced from Spain, couples often hold small scarves while performing folk dances, as seen here.

### ECUADOR

FIG. 4-132 José Olmos Workshop, *Market Vendors*. Pujilí, Cotopaxi, Ecuador, ca. 1950. Plaster, paint. Largest: 13½" x 7" (34.3 x 17.8 cm). Collection of Bob and Gay Sinclair.

FIG. 4-133 José Olmos Workshop, *Lion Trainer and Man Wearing Negrito Mask*. Pujilí, Cotopaxi, Ecuador, ca. 1950. Plaster, paint. Largest: 13" x 8" (33 x 20.3 cm). Collection of Bob and Gay Sinclair.

Genre figures have been made in the Pujilí region of Cotopaxi Province in the central highlands of Ecuador. Most of the pieces dating from the mid- to late-twentieth century came from the Olmos family workshop. To create the figures, they used molds to form plaster shapes in two halves that were then joined together and painted with bright colors. Since the interiors of the sculptures were hollow, a slot was often cut in the plaster so they could be used as banks. The Olmos figures portray a variety of subjects, ranging from market vendors and festival masqueraders to circus clowns and lion trainers. These figures were often given as prizes at game booths set up during festivals and fairs.[69]

FIG. 4-134 Attributed to Andrés Paucarima Workshop, *Devil Masquerader and Boxers*. Quito, Ecuador, early 20th century. Wood, paint. Largest: 12¼" x 7" (31.1 x 17.8 cm). Gifts of Peter P. Cecere, MOIFA.

IG. 4-135 Andrés Paucarima Workshop, *Female and Male Figures*. Quito, Ecuador, early 20th century. Wood, paint, cloth, metal. Largest: 12½" x 7½" (31.8 x 19.1 cm). Gifts of Peter P. Cecere, MOIFA.

FIG. 4-136 Left: *Cow*. Quito or Cuenca region, Ecuador, early-mid-20th century. Wood, paint, 9¼" x 4½" (23.5 x 11.4 cm). Right: attributed to Andrés Paucarima Workshop, *Dog*. Quito, Ecuador, early 20th century. Wood, paint. Gifts of Peter P. Cecere, MOIFA.

In the late nineteenth and early twentieth century, some sculpture workshops in Quito specialized in making secular figures for nativity scenes. One of them was run by Andrés Paucarima, who created a wide range of images portraying people seen on the streets of Quito.[70] His work was artfully sculpted in wood, and some pieces have clothing that was painted. Most of his figures were dressed in fabric garments that were carefully tailored. Animals, popular subjects for nativity scenes, were made in the Paucarima Workshop as well. Other less sophisticated sculptors also fabricated animal figures for crèches.

## COLOMBIA

FIG. 4-137 *Male and Female Figures*. Highland region, Colombia, mid-20th century. Wood, paint, cloth. Largest: 9" x 4¾" (22.9 x 12.1 cm). Gifts of Peter P. Cecere, MOIFA.

These genre figures were made in Colombia in the mid-twentieth century. They are not as well carved as the sculptures made in Quito, but they have a similar style. The two female figures in the center are wearing tailored dresses that show the fabrics and styles being worn at that time.

## VENEZUELA

FIG. 4-138 Left: Ramon Antonio Moreno, *Milkmaid*. Tabay, Mérida, Venezuela, 1993. Wood, paint. Gift of Peter P. Cecere, MOIFA. Right: Amelia de Carrero, *Musicians*. Mérida, Venezuela, ca. 2005. Wood, paint, 16½" x 10½" (41.9 x 26.7 cm). International Folk Art Foundation Collection, MOIFA.

FIG. 4-139 Left: Rosa Lina Garcia, *Man with Dog*. La Grita, Mérida, Venezuela, ca. 1985. Wood, paint, 15¾" x 7¼" (40 x 18.4 cm). International Folk Art Foundation Collection, MOIFA. Right: José Belandria, *Woman*. Mérida, Venezuela, 1993. Wood, paint. Gift of Peter P. Cecere, MOIFA.

Woodcarvers in the states of Mérida and Trujillo, in the Andean region of Venezuela, began making religious sculpture in the mid-eighteenth century, and new generations of artists continued to produce this work for the local market. In the mid-twentieth century, some began creating nonreligious figures that portrayed people from everyday life. The carvings are done in a stiff and somewhat primitive style, but they capture the character and mood of the people.[71]

# Toys

Toys are given to children at special times of the year as part of a festival celebration or other important occasion. By the twentieth century, most toys made in the Andes were based on European models available in the markets, serving as inspiration for local artists.[72]

## KINETIC TOYS

FIG. 4-140 Left: Emma Gomez Villanes, *Kinetic Toy*. Molinos, Junín, Peru, ca. 1960. Wood, paint, string. Largest: 10¼" x 4¼" (26 x 10.8 cm). Center: *Kinetic Toy*. Chile, ca. 1960. Wood, paint, wire. Right: *Kinetic Toy*. Mérida, Venezuela, ca. 1960. Wood, paint, string. Gifts of the Girard Foundation Collection, MOIFA.

Wood toys with moving parts are made in many regions of the Andes. One of the simplest forms is constructed by joining two parallel narrow wood slats with a horizontal piece at the center. An articulated wooden acrobat holds onto a string tied across the top. When the two pieces of wood are pinched together at the base, the string at the top tightens and the figure flips up and over.

## DOLLS

**FIG. 4-146** Left: Julio Urbano Rojas, *Pair of Dolls*. Huamanga, Ayacucho, Peru, 2008. Maguey, gesso, paint, glass. Largest: 12¼" x 3" (31.1 x 7.6 cm). International Folk Art Foundation Collection, MOIFA. Right: Emma Gomez Villanes, *Pair of Dolls*. Molinos, Junín, Peru, ca. 1960. Wood, paint, metal. Gifts of the Girard Foundation Collection, MOIFA.

In the Ayacucho region of Peru, children are given toys as part of the All Saints Day and All Souls Day celebrations on November 1 and 2. The girls' toys are usually dolls made in local workshops. The pair on the left is typical of those from Huamanga. They were created in 2008 by Julio Urbano Rojas, a well-known artist who specializes in making crosses and portable boxes with miniature scenes. Each year, he sets aside time to create these maguey and gesso dolls, continuing the tradition of giving them to young girls for the All Saints Day and All Souls Day celebrations. In the department of Junín, Peru, girls are given dolls at different times of the year. The pair on the right was made by Emma Gomez Villanes, an artisan who worked out of her home in Molinos during the mid- to late-twentieth century. Each figure was carved from a single piece of wood, with flat arms attached at the shoulders.

**FIG. 4-147** *Pairs of Dolls.* Left: Chucuito, Puno, Peru, ca. 1960. Wool yarn, wood. Largest: 16" x 2½" (40.6 x 6.4 cm). Right: La Paz (?), Bolivia, ca. 1960. Fabric, yarn, wood, metal, plastic. Gifts of the Girard Foundation Collection, MOIFA.

Many dolls made in the Andes portray men and women wearing traditional costumes. They are given to children and also sold to tourists and collectors. The knitted pair on the left represents a style made by women in the Chucuito Province, on the western shore of Lake Titicaca in Puno, Peru. The pair on the right portrays a man and woman wearing the traditional costume of the Tarabuco region, in the Department of Chuquisaca, Bolivia.

**FIG. 4-148** *Pairs of Dolls.* Left: Imbabura Province, Ecuador, ca. 1960. Cloth, plastic, wood. Largest: 9" x 4¾" (22.9 x 12.1 cm). Right: Mérida, Venezuela, ca. 1960. Fabric, wool yarn, paper, wood. Gifts of the Girard Foundation Collection, MOIFA.

These two pairs of dolls are wearing clothing found in different regions of the Andes. The two on the left are from the Imbabura Province in northern Ecuador, where men and women still wear traditional white-cotton garments under black-wool tunics, skirts, and shawls. The dancing couple on the right is wearing tailored, European-style clothing that was commonly seen in Mérida, Venezuela, in the mid-twentieth century.

## TOY HORSES AND HORSEBACK RIDERS

FIG. 4-149 *Toy Horse and Horseback Rider.* Huamanga, Ayacucho, Peru, ca. 1960. Wood, leather, gesso, paint, hair, paper. Largest: 9½" x 10¼" (24.1 x 26 cm). Gifts of the Girard Foundation Collection, MOIFA.

FIG. 4-150 Emma Gomez Villanes, *Men on Horseback.* Molinos, Junín, Peru, ca. 1960. Wood, paint, nails. Largest: 6" x 8" (15.2 x 20.3 cm). Gifts of the Girard Foundation Collection, MOIFA.

While the girls in Ayacucho and Junín are given dolls, the boys receive other locally-made toys that often portray horses and riders. The toys shown here are mounted on small wooden platforms with four wheels, so they can be pushed or pulled with a string. The horse and horsemen from Huamanga were made by stretching leather over an armature and then painting it. The painted-wood toy figures from Molinos were produced by Emma Gomez Villanes, who made the dolls in figure 4-146 (right).

FIG. 4-151 *Toy Horses.* Puno, Peru, ca. 1960. Left: leather, paint, batting. Right: leather, paint, fabric, wool, 10½" x 10½" (26.7 x 26.7 cm). Gifts of the Girard Foundation Collection, MOIFA.

Toy horses were made in the Puno region of southern Peru; in each, pieces of leather are stretched over an armature and sewn together. Sometimes, the painted details include a saddle and halter (see left). These accessories can also be made of other materials and then attached to the toy (see right).

FIG. 4-152 José Olmos Workshop, *Toy Horse.* Pujilí, Cotopaxi Province, Ecuador, ca. 1985. Plaster, paint, 7" x 6" (17.8 x 15.2 cm). Collection of Sue Stevens.

The Olmos family in the Pujilí region of Cotopaxi Province, Ecuador, produced toy horses and other types of figures from the mid- to late-twentieth century. They used molds to form plaster shapes in two halves that were joined together and painted with bright colors. Since the interior is hollow, a slot was cut into the saddle blanket so the toy could also be used as a bank.

## TOY VEHICLES

FIG. 4-153 *Toy Bus*. Pitalito, Huila, Colombia, ca. 1990. Ceramic, paint, metal, 6¾" x 13½" (17.1 x 34.3 cm). Gift of Lloyd E. Cotsen and the Neutrogena Corporation, MOIFA.

FIG. 4-154 *Toy Buses*. La Paz, Bolivia. Left: ca. 1990. Wood, metal, paint. International Folk Art Foundation Collection, MOIFA. Right: ca. 1960. Metal, paint, 9" x 17½" (22.9 x 44.5 cm). Gift of the Girard Foundation Collection, MOIFA.

There are many ceramic-producing towns in the Province of Huila in southern Colombia; the figural pieces made in Pitalito are particularly colorful and amusing. Among the popular subjects portrayed is the local bus, known as a *chivo*. These open-sided wooden vehicles are generally packed with people, animals, fruits, vegetables, and a variety of other things. Buses are also popular themes for folk artists working in La Paz, Bolivia; however, the examples shown here lack riders and cargo.

FIG. 4-155 Left: *Toy Helicopter*. Quinua, Ayacucho, Peru, 1980. Ceramic, pigment, 9¼" x 19" (23.5 x 48.3 cm). International Folk Art Foundation Collection, MOIFA. Right: Emma Gomez Villanes, *Toy Airplane*. Molinos, Junín, Peru, ca. 1960. Wood, paint, metal. Gift of the Girard Foundation Collection, MOIFA.

Helicopters and airplanes are always fascinating to children, particularly in the Andean communities distant from airports. The helicopter on the left was made in Quinua, a rural village in the Department of Ayacucho, Peru, known for its ceramic sculpture. In this toy the artist carefully portrayed a military-transport helicopter loaded with soldiers wearing helmets. The small airplane to the right was made by Emma Gomez Villanes, who produced some of the other toys shown earlier (see figs. 4-140, 4-146, 4-150). She depicted the type of single-engine airplane that brought passengers into the small airport in Huancayo, the capital of the Department of Junín.

FIG. 4-156 Left: *Toy Truck*. Cochabamba, Bolivia, 1974. Wood, metal, paint, 19" x 29" (48.3 x 73.7 cm). Right: *Toy Tractor*. Highland region, Ecuador, mid-20th century. Wood, metal, foam, paint. International Folk Art Foundation Collection, MOIFA.

The artists who created these toys obviously admired the actual vehicles they were modeled from. The truck from Cochabamba, Bolivia, on the left, displays all the features of a large cargo truck, complete with carefully stenciled signage. The toy tractor from Ecuador, on the right, is not quite as detailed but includes all of the essential features of the powerful vehicles that helped modernize the country in the mid-twentieth century.

## Painted Scenes of Daily Life

In late eighteenth-century Europe there was a growing interest in costumbrismo—showing the customs, dress, and daily activities of people in cities and rural communities around the world. South America was full of fascinating places and ethnic groups about which the European press eagerly published descriptive, illustrated articles. Travelers to the continent felt inspired to sketch colorful impressions of the people wearing regional clothing and carrying out everyday activities. In the post-Independence era of the nineteenth century, intellectuals in the newly-formed republics also took interest in documenting the customs of the people in their countries. Local artists began painting images of people on the streets of their cities, which were reproduced in prints that circulated throughout South America and abroad. These images were seen by mestizo and indigenous artists in different regions of the Andes; by the late nineteenth and twentieth century, some were painting scenes that depicted their own customs and activities. In the mid-twentieth century, this type of work was being patronized by a new generation of tourists and collectors who encouraged its development.

FIG. 4-157 *Chinese Copies of Paintings by Francisco "Pancho" Fierro.* Canton, China, mid-19th century. Pith paper, watercolor. Left: *Woman on Horseback in Lima, Peru.* 11½" x 8½" (29.2 x 21.6 cm). Right: *"Tapada" Woman in Lima, Peru.* Gifts of Frank and Maurine Ikle, MOIFA.

Francisco "Pancho" Fierro, a self-taught mulatto artist from Lima, became one of Peru's most famous costumbrismo painters. Fascinated with the different classes of people on the streets of Lima, he began doing quick watercolor sketches in the 1830s that he sold for very little money. A ready market of buyers led him to increase his production of watercolors and to create a lithographic series between the 1830s and 1860s. By the mid-nineteenth century, Fierro's images were being sent to Canton, China, where workshops of artists carefully copied them onto pith paper. These copies, bound with silk ribbons around the edges, were sent back to Lima and sold to tourists and seamen who wanted souvenirs to take home. Among the most popular images were those depicting upper-class Lima women with their shawls wrapped over their heads and faces, leaving only one eye visible (see right). This practice earned them the nickname *tapadas,* covered women.[73]

FIG. 4-158 Melchor María Mercado, *Señoras. Cholas.* La Paz, Bolivia, 1859. Watercolor, paper. Collection of the Archivo Nacional de Bolivia.

Melchor María Mercado was born in Sucre, Bolivia, in 1816 and graduated with a degree in law from the local university in 1845, at the age of twenty-nine. A naturalist at heart, he decided to begin a project of documenting the flora and fauna, as well as the ethnic cultures of Bolivia. Inspired by the work of Pancho Fierro and other costumbrismo artists, he learned to draw and paint with watercolors and started traveling around his country to study the different regions. The project lasted twenty-eight years; during that time he produced hundreds of watercolors depicting people from different classes and ethnic groups wearing typical clothing of the mid-nineteenth century.[74] This painting was done in the capital city of La Paz, in 1859, and portrays upper-class women (*señoras*) on the left and Aymara cholas on the right, each wearing the appropriate dress for their status in society (see also figs. 1-2, 1-3).

FIG. 4-159 *Shop Sign "Picanteria la Urubambinita."* Cuzco region, Peru, early 20th century. Galvanized metal, paint, 14½" x 22" (36.8 x 55.9 cm). Gift of Peter P. Cecere, MOIFA.

Painting workshops in Cuzco, Peru, began incorporating scenes from daily life into their religious images in the late eighteenth century. By the mid- to late-nineteenth century, indigenous artists in rural villages had become inspired to paint depictions of themselves working with their animals, while patron saints hovered beneficently overhead (see fig. 2-10). At that time, inexpensive watercolors and prints by Pancho Fierro were circulating through the region, providing further inspiration to mestizo and indigenous artists, who began painting secular scenes showing themselves enjoying life. A popular format for this was shop signs, particularly those hanging above the entrances to local bars. Known as *pinturas de picanterías* (pictures for taverns), the painted advertisements displayed the name of the establishment and usually portrayed a couple drinking, or sometimes dancing in a field outside the tavern.[75]

FIG. 4-160 Juan Villalobos, *Corpus Christi Festival Scene*. Cuzco, Peru, ca. 1975. Paint, canvas, 13¾" x 21¼" (34.9 x 54 cm). International Folk Art Foundation Collection, MOIFA.

FIG. 4-161 Pablo Julio Mendívil, *Political Rally*. Cuzco, Peru, ca. 1975. Paint, canvas, 15" x 14½" (38.1 x 36.8 cm). International Folk Art Foundation Collection, MOIFA.

By the mid-twentieth century, a few Cuzco artists and their families were producing a variety of folk sculpture and paintings. Among them was Julio Villalobos, a noted painter of costumbrismo scenes, who encouraged his daughter Luisa and son Juan to paint images that documented life in Cuzco. Juan's portrayal of the Cuzco Corpus Christi Festival can be seen here. Julio, who often painted in Hilario Mendívil's workshop in the San Blas district of Cuzco, also encouraged Hilario's son, Pablo Julio Mendívil, to try his hand at painting local scenes.[76] The image by Pablo portrays a rally with a Cuzco politician soliciting votes.

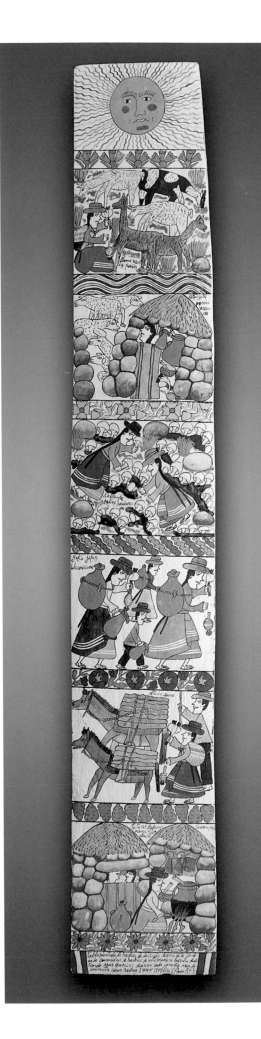

◀ FIG. 4–162 Pompeyo Berrocal Evanán, *Board with Scenes of Daily Life.* Sarhua, Ayacucho, Peru, 2009. Wood, paint, 47½" x 8" (120.7 x 20.3 cm). International Folk Art Foundation Collection, MOIFA.

FIG. 4–163 Pompeyo Berrocal Evanán, *Two Boards with Scenes of Daily Life.* Sarhua, Ayacucho, Peru, 2007. Wood, paint. Largest: 23½" x 6" (59.7 x 15.2 cm). International Folk Art Foundation Collection, MOIFA.

By the early twentieth century, artists in Sarhua, a village in the Department of Ayacucho, Peru, started portraying scenes of daily life on the main support beams being installed in the roofs of newly-built houses (see fig. 4-119). The painted beams, known as tablas, served as blessings and decoration for the families and their homes. The painting was done within horizontal sections and portrayed scenes with different members of the family engaged in activities or events they were known for. This tradition eventually died out; however, today, some artists from Sarhua, such as Pompeyo Berrocal and Primitivo Evanán, continue to paint planks of wood with costumbrismo scenes. These works follow the traditional format of dividing the boards into horizontal sections, with different subjects from Sarhua daily life depicted in each one.[77] Sometimes, there is a narrative continuity from one scene to the next, reading from the bottom up. One example is seen at left, in which a sick man is being treated by a curandero, who is using a small guinea pig (*cuy*) to read the heart of the patient and draw out the illness. In the next scene two women are killing the animal so it won't pass the disease on to anyone else.

Artists followed Fisch's advice and made wooden frames that they decorated with colorful patterns. The stretched sheepskin was then nailed across the back. At first, the artists weren't sure how to handle this new format, so they divided the space into smaller registers with different scenes portrayed in each (left). With more encouragement from Fisch and other collectors, the indigenous painters started to use the whole space to show one scene and often portrayed local festivals. By the 1980s, artists were signing their work and setting up displays in Quito parks to sell their paintings to tourists.[78]

FIG. 4-164 *Village Life*. Tigua, Cotopaxi, Ecuador, early 1970s. Sheepskin, wood, paint, 12½" x 7½" (31.8 x 19.1 cm). Private Collection.

FIG. 4-165 Juan Manuel Zoa Vega, *Festival Scene*. Tigua, Cotopaxi, Ecuador, ca. 1985. Sheepskin, wood, paint, 12" x 14¼" (30.5 x 36.2 cm). Collection of Earl and Shari Kessler.

FIG. 4-166 Francisco Ugho, *Bullfight Scene*. Tigua, Cotopaxi, Ecuador, ca. 1985. Sheepskin, wood, paint, 25½" x 28" (64.8 x 71.1 cm). Gift of Peter P. Cecere, MOIFA.

In the early twentieth century, artists in the indigenous village of Tigua, Cotopaxi Province, Ecuador, began painting the heads of their drums with festival scenes. The most popular subjects were dancers who performed in the Corpus Christi processions in late May or early June. The drum heads, made from sheepskin stretched tight over wooden rings, provided circular surfaces for the artists to paint on (see fig. 5-25). Around 1970, Olga Fisch, a Hungarian folk art collector living in Quito, visited the village and became fascinated with the painted drums. She encouraged the painters to try stretching the sheepskin over rectangular frames and expand their subject matter to include a variety of scenes from Tigua village life.

crosses, and other religious items since learning the craft from his parents in the late nineteenth century. He told the group of intellectuals about the decline in these art forms due to the drop in a rural clientele. One of the women on the trip, Alicia Bustamante, suggested they try marketing the portable altars and other items to collectors in Lima. As part of the indigenista movement, there was a growing interest in folk arts; Bustamante and her friend, Elvira Luza, were eager to help promote this work and collect it themselves. Bustamante took some of the Sanmarco shrines back to Lima to see what other collectors thought. Everyone agreed the portable altars were intriguing, but they also saw potential in broadening the subject matter portrayed in the boxes. They suggested to Joaquín López Antay, and other artists, that they depict festivals and other activities from the Ayacucho region, as well as patriotic scenes from Peruvian history. This interest in patriotism and costumbrismo had begun in the post-Independence period of the nineteenth century; the portable boxes provided an intimate setting for presenting these themes. This initiated a new folk-art tradition in Ayacucho that is still going on today. The artists continued using their traditional technique of creating the handmade or molded figures with the medium of pasta. With each workshop using a slightly different style, they also continued to paint the boxes and doors with colorful floral decoration.

Alicia Bustamante and Elvira Luza wanted to distinguish these boxes with miniature costumbrismo and patriotic scenes from the more traditional Sanmarco portable shrines. They decided to call them *retablos*, a Spanish word that means a series of paintings or carvings representing a story or event. This term was quickly adopted by the Peruvian artists and has been used ever since.[80]

FIG. 4-169 Joaquín López Antay, *Box with Virgin of Mercy*. Huamanga, Ayacucho, Peru, ca. 1955. Wood, pasta, paint. As displayed: 20" x 17" (50.8 x 43.2 cm). Gift of the Girard Foundation Collection, MOIFA.

This piece was made by López Antay, in the mid-1950s, when most of the artists were still portraying one scene per box. In this work he chose to depict a religious sculpture on the platform used to carry it through the streets of Huamanga, during certain religious feast days. The image is the Virgin of Mercy—La Merced—who became the patron saint of soldiers during Peru's battle for independence. Under her feet is the Peruvian national coat of arms flanked by two Peruvian flags. López Antay often decorated the interior of his boxes with a series of dotted paint strokes, as seen here.

FIG. 4-170 Jesús Urbano Rojas, *Box with Scene*. Huamanga, Ayacucho, Peru, ca. 1955. Wood, pasta, paint. As displayed: 15" x 18" (38.1 x 45.7 cm). Gift of the Girard Foundation Collection, MOIFA.

Jesús Urbano Rojas, and his brother Julio, were among the young artists to make the new style of boxes, or retablos. This example made by Jesús, in the mid-1950s, portrays an activity that takes place in Ayacucho and other regions of the Andes during their fiestas. The event involves tying a variety of goods at the top of a tall pole and different men try their skill at climbing up the pole to get some of the items. Depicted below this, on the right, is another popular form of festival entertainment: amateur bullfighting. Here a local man waves his poncho in front of a bull.

FIG. 4-171 Jesús Urbano Rojas, *Box with Scenes*. Huamanga, Ayacucho, Peru, 1958. Wood, pasta, paint. As displayed: 28½" x 31" (72.4 x 78.8 cm). Gift of the Girard Foundation Collection, MOIFA.

Within a few years, the artists started using larger boxes with multiple tiers where they could show a variety of different scenes. This is an early piece by Jesús Urbano Rojas in which he experimented with this idea. He created three levels, with the top and bottom divided into two sections. This gave him five separate areas in which to portray the shops in Aycacucho that sold different types of folk art, ranging from hats and textiles to ceramics and retablos.

FIG. 4-172 Nicario Jiménez and Family, *Box with Scenes*. Lima, Peru, ca. 1985. Wood, pasta, paint. As displayed: 28¼" x 31" (71.8 x 78.8 cm). Gift of Lloyd E. Cotsen and the Neutrogena Corporation, MOIFA..

Florentino Jiménez's sons and daughter assisted in his shop and became part of the next generation to carry on the creation of retablos. In 1981 the eldest son, Nicario, moved to Lima and began working directly with art galleries that wanted more and more retablos to sell to an eager group of collectors. Later, the whole family moved to Lima and helped produce hundreds of boxes with three and four tiers of crowded scenes. This example has three levels, each portraying a different step in the processing of wool and turning it into weavings. The Jiménez family workshop was known for creating all of the miniature figures by hand using the traditional pasta mixture.

FIG. 4-173 Jesús Urbano Cardenas, *Box with Scenes*. Huamanga, Ayacucho, Peru, ca. 1985. Wood, pasta, paint. As displayed: 40" x 37" (101.6 x 94 cm). Gift of Lloyd E. Cotsen and the Neutrogena Corporation, MOIFA..

Another member of the next generation to produce this type of work was Jesús Urbano Cardenas, son of Jesús Urbano Rojas. This is an example of the large-scale retablos that gallery owners in Lima were encouraging artists to make. Here we see four levels with different scenes in each. The top has a Christmas crèche that was popular with collectors. The next level down portrays an animal blessing ceremony, with the patron saints against the back wall in a similar fashion as seen in the Sanmarco portable shrines (see figs. 2-43, 2-44, 2-45). The third level shows people picking cactus fruit and the fourth has a festival scene. Some of the figures against the back walls were made in molds, while others were hand formed.

FIG. 4-174 Marino Palomino, *Box with Scenes*. Huancavelica, Peru, ca, 1985. Wood, pasta, paint. As displayed: 29¾" x 30" (75.6 x 76.2 cm). Gift of Lloyd E. Cotsen, MOIFA.

Marino Palomino, among the second generation of artists to make retablos, lived in the Department of Huancavelica, Peru. He was a perfectionist and it shows in his work. His pasta figures were carefully formed, and he used high-gloss oil paints to decorate them and to create the crisp floral ornaments on the doors and crown. He made this large box with three levels and portrayed similar scenes as those depicted in the box by Jesús Urbano Cardenas (fig. 4-173). In the top is a Christmas crèche, the center level shows a local festival, and in the bottom level people are picking cactus fruit.

FIG. 4-175 Claudio Jiménez and Vicenta Antacusi Flores, *Box with Scene*. Lima, Peru, 2007. Wood, pasta, paint. As displayed: 29" x 29" (73.7 x 73.7 cm). Gift of Connie Thrasher Jaquith, MOIFA.

Another son of Florentino Jiménez, Claudio Jiménez, and his wife Vicenta Antacusi Flores, developed their own style featuring one complex scene within a large box. Working with pasta they create elaborate sculptural pieces portraying architecture, humans, animals, floral vegetation, and other aspects of Andean life. This example, made in 2007, depicts chaos on the highway—a part of daily life on the winding roads of the Andes. In the top a bus is being loaded with animals and produce from a mountain village; the middle section shows trucks and cars trying to make their way up and down the crowded, narrow mountain road; and in the bottom, trucks are parked in a large town, where produce and other goods are being sold in the market.

At the time the Spanish arrived in the Andes, in the early sixteenth century, Indian groups throughout the highlands were carrying out festival celebrations with song and dance that told stories about their past. These performances relayed the history of their ancestors and important places and events, along with the myths and legends related to the group's identity. The performances enforced community memory and ensured that history would be passed down to future generations. The celebrations were part of a ritual cycle that observed the summer and winter solstices, the agricultural seasons, and the annual initiations of young people. Heavy consumption of chicha, a potent alcoholic beverage fermented from corn, generally accompanied the festivities. Ritual offerings of alcohol, called ch'allas, were given to the sun god Inti, to the mother goddess Pachamama, and to other important spirits and ancestors.[1]

At first the Catholic priests encouraged the Indians to perform their traditional dances and songs for Catholic feast-day observances. Some of the largest festivals took place in the new Spanish centers, including Cuzco in Peru, Quito in Ecuador, and Potosí in Bolivia. By the latter part of the sixteenth century, however, church and civic authorities were condemning the practice because of excessive drunkenness and promulgation of traditional religious beliefs. Many Spaniards took note of the subtle ways in which the Andeans were able to keep the memory of their idols and other aspects of their past alive.

In 1569 the Spanish Crown sent Francisco Toledo to the Andes to serve as the new viceroy for Peru and the surrounding region. He immediately implemented a series of ordinances aimed at resolving certain problems Spain was experiencing with the indigenous population. As part of this effort, he instituted a systematic reorganization of traditional practices and relationships to the land by forcing many groups to move and resettle in Spanish-style towns, where the Indians involuntarily served as laborers. During Catholic feast days, the indigenous people in these towns were required to participate in Spanish-derived processional dramas, in which performers acted out epics such as the Incas being defeated by Pizarro and biblical stories about good conquering evil. For the most part, the native people wore costumes and masks that impersonated the Europeans and other characters. The choreography, music, and text of the dancing and dramas were new; the overall purpose was to do away with ancient Andean identities and establish a new colonial self-image.

By the late seventeenth century, the Spanish authorities were increasingly convinced that the Andeans had converted to Christianity, and the priests became less concerned about monitoring their festival performances. Meanwhile, the Indians appropriated aspects of Christianity into their own religious beliefs and practices and figured out ways to carry on their traditional lives under the guise of orthodox Catholicism. By the early eighteenth century, ritual systems honoring the Catholic saints had become a principal means by which town- and rural-based Indian groups defined themselves. The cycle of Catholic feast days was overlaid on the Andean calendar of important celebrations. Festival activities included dancing, singing, and drinking, as well as animal sacrifices and ch'allas, or offerings, to both Christian saints and Andean gods.

This situation continued until the 1750s, when groups of laborers in some Spanish towns began staging rebellions during festivals to try and get rid of the Spaniards. The resistance escalated over the next three decades, peaking in the 1780s. Spain eventually suppressed these rebellions, only to come under attack from criollos living in Peru, Bolivia, Ecuador, and elsewhere; the criollos wanted to rid themselves of the European authorities. After gaining independence from Spain, the new governments tried to "civilize" the rural Indians by doing away with communal landownership and privatizing their holdings. In general, however, they were free to carry on their ceremonial lives in their own way. The Indians continued to practice the forms of worship, rituals, and festivals that had evolved during the colonial period, utilizing aspects of both prehispanic Andean traditions and Christianity.

During the nineteenth and early twentieth century, few elite citizens of the new republics took notice of the urban or rural Indian festivals. Beginning in the 1950s, however, groups of intellectuals in various regions of the Andes began to look at the Indian lifestyle and customs with greater interest and respect. Indigenous festivals with their lively costumes, music, and performances came to be viewed in a more positive light as folkloric pageants that celebrated the heritage of the Andean nations. The rural Indian and urban cholo status was elevated in society, and elite citizens flocked to their communities and neighborhoods to witness the pageants firsthand; in many regions this continues today.

## Festivals and Masquerade in the Cuzco Region of Peru

One of the most important Catholic celebrations introduced into the Andes in the sixteenth century was the Corpus Christi feast day honoring the Eucharist, or body of Christ. Spanish authorities felt the participation of the indigenous groups in the Corpus Christi observances symbolized a rejection of the indigenous religion and acceptance of Christianity. However, the floating date for the feast day—sometime between late May and early June—coincided with the appearance of the Pleiades in the winter sky on June 8. This constellation is known in the Andes as the Llama, and its return after thirty-seven days below the horizon heralds the June solstice and the beginning of the New Year. The Indians continued their rituals and festivities for this important event under the guise of the Corpus Christi feast day.[2]

Late sixteenth-century descriptions of this festival in Cuzco, Peru, indicate that all-male Indian groups performed pre-Columbian dances wearing traditional festival costumes. Some dressed in lion skins and others had condor wings fixed to their arms and shoulders. Costumes made of real gold and silver foil were also worn, along with masquerades displaying horrifying monsters. These intimidating beasts carried pelts of different animals they claimed to have made their victims.[3] By the late seventeenth and early eighteenth centuries, indigenous dancers participating in the Cuzco Corpus Christi processions were no longer allowed to wear prehispanic attire. It was replaced by European costumes featuring silk-brocade robes adorned with silver and gold designs and white shirts with lace ruffs at the neck and cuff. The masks depicted Spaniards with light skin, long noses, and exaggerated chins. Headgear consisted of caps with feathers, silver and gold helmets, and crowns.[4]

Indigenous dancers continued to participate in the Corpus Christi procession after the Indian rebellions of the 1780s were suppressed. An 1835 description of the Cuzco celebration specifically mentions groups wearing costumes of Contradanzas (eighteenth-century Spaniards) and Ch'unchos (Indians from the tropical forest).[5] The popularity of the Cuzco Corpus Christi festival diminished in the post-Independence period of the nineteenth century. However, indigenous groups performed masked dances in their own villages and for important feast day celebrations in other cities, towns, and pilgrimage sites in the Cuzco region.

FIG. 5-1 *Many different dance groups congregate at the shrine for Señor de Qoyllur Rit'i in Sinakara, Cuzco, Peru, during the pilgrimage festival held in his honor, 1996.* Photograph by Andrea Heckman.

FIG. 5-4 *Qhapaq Qolla dance group performs during the feast honoring Señor de Qoyllur Rit'i in the Sinakara Valley near the sacred mountain of Ausangate, Cuzco, Peru, 1996.* Photograph by Andrea Heckman.

FIG. 5-5 *Qhapaq Qolla Mask and Hat.* Cuzco, Peru. Mask: ca. 1950. Wool. Gift of Emilio Baca Putman, MOIFA. Hat: 2008. Fabric, plastic, glass, fiber, 9½" x 19" (24.1 x 48.3 cm). International Folk Art Foundation Collection, MOIFA.

The Qhapaq Qolla masqueraders portray men from Qolla, an Aymara region northwest and east of Lake Titicaca. The people of this area are primarily llama herders, but some men specialize as medicine men or healers. Up until the mid-twentieth century, they traveled throughout the central Andes selling carved-stone amulets, herbs, and other items. They also offered their services to cure the sick with herbs and rituals. The masqueraders who impersonate them wear knitted masks with white faces and flat, wide-brimmed hats that imitate those worn by men and women in the Altiplano region during the colonial period. Their name is qualified by the Quechua word *qhapaq*, meaning wealthy, and the ornate decoration on their hats reflects this status. They also wear a vicuña or alpaca skin around the neck or waist. The Qhapaq Qolla masqueraders are important participants in the celebration for Señor de Qoyllur Rit'i and in the festivities honoring the Virgin of Carmen in Paucartambo. On both occasions they perform mock battles with the Ch'unchos; in Paucartambo, the Qhapaq Qolla sing to the Virgin and accompany her statue while it is carried through the streets.[10]

FIG. 5-6 *Contradanzas wear some of the most elegant costumes in the Paucartambo festival, 2009.* Photograph by Andrea Heckman.

Contradanzas are among the most prestigious dance groups that participate in the celebration for Señor de Qoyllur Rit'i and the Paucartambo festival for the Virgin of Carmen. They portray Spaniards from the late eighteenth and early nineteenth centuries who performed European country-style dances in their salons. The masqueraders burlesque the Spaniards while carrying out line dances with complex choreography that is now associated with an agricultural ritual. The group wears matching costumes covered with embroidery, sequins, and beads; their wire-screen masks have serious expressions painted on the pink faces.[11]

FIG. 5-7 *Qhapaq Negra dancers participating in the Virgin of Carmen festival in Paucartambo, 2009. Peru.* Photograph by Andrea Heckman.

FIG. 5-8 *Qhapaq Negra Mask and Hat.* Mask: Paucartambo, Peru, 2009. Papier-mâché, plaster, paint. Collection of Andrea Heckman. Hat: Cuzco, Peru, 2006. Fabric, sequins, beads, mirror, 5½" x 15½" (14 x 38.7 cm). International Folk Art Foundation Collection, MOIFA.

Qhapaq Negra masqueraders dance in tribute to the memory of African slaves brought to the Andes during the colonial period, to work on coastal plantations and in the silver mines of Bolivia and the Paucartambo region. Different Qhapaq Negra groups participate in the pilgrimage festival for Señor de Qoyllur Rit'i. They also honor the Virgin of Carmen during her feast day celebration in Paucartambo by singing songs that tell of the slaves suffering and their adoration of the Virgin. Their costumes take on a variety of forms, but the word quapaq (wealthy) is associated with the ornate decoration on their hats and bibs. Their black masks, made from papier-mâché and plaster, often have tears painted on the cheeks. Some carry black arms with clenched fists to demonstrate solidarity and the determination to survive (see fig. 5-11, left).[12]

## Corpus Christi Festivals and Masquerade
## in the Central Highlands of Ecuador

Throughout the colonial period, Corpus Christi was a big celebration for Catholic authorities in Quito, Ecuador, as it was in Cuzco, Peru. In the late eighteenth century, Julio Ferrario, an Italian geographer, recorded his impression of the Indian dancers participating in the procession. While performing pre-Columbian dances, they wore elegantly decorated costumes, including leggings ornamented with many little bells.[18] In 1847, early in the post-Independence period, another European visitor, Gaetano Osculati, attended the Corpus Christi celebrations in Quito. He marveled at the participation of different Indian dance groups, which he could distinguish by their costumes and manner of dress. He was particularly impressed by the *danzantes* from Quito and Latacunga. Osculati explained, "[They] proceed decked out with most elegant and valuable costumes, from which hang quantities of silver coins by means of holes made directly through them. These fanatics, to show off one of these costumes, which apart from this are embroidered in gold and silver, spend in one day a year's savings, and even become slaves voluntarily for a set period of time, until the agreed is paid, and all this for the extraordinary glory of having been a danzante."[19]

The glory that motivated these dancers was actually a form of community prestige that could be attained by participating in the religious festival. Each Indian community had a hierarchical class system based on hereditary lineage and wealth. However, labor and other contributions given toward the social, political, and religious life of the village could also increase one's status. Some of these contributions came from men who belonged to religious brotherhoods that had been set up by the Spanish to help carry out religious rituals and Catholic feast day celebrations. The main sponsor, or prioste, and his assistants gained a great deal of prestige for volunteering to organize and fund the different events.[20] The dancers were among those who assisted the prioste, and they often incurred the cost of renting the costumes on behalf of their community.[21]

It is unclear when the tradition of renting costumes began, but its roots could go back to prehispanic times, when certain families provided the more elaborate ceremonial costumes worn by dancers in their villages. It is likely that the family would have gained prestige and received payment in food and other goods. After the Spanish conquest of Ecuador, the specialization of costume making evolved to meet the needs of the Catholic festival cycle, and this cottage industry was carried out by both indigenous and mestizo families. The rentable festival clothing would be refurbished and handed down through generations of the maker's family; new costumes would be made as needed. This specialized system of costume making has continued into the twentieth and twenty-first centuries.[22]

One of the groups of Indian dancers described by Osculati as paying a high price to rent their Corpus Christi costumes was from Latacunga—a city located south of Quito, in the central highlands of Ecuador, where a rich agricultural region stretches out between the snow-covered volcanoes of Cotopaxi, Tungurahua, and Chimborazo. During prehispanic times, the fertile area was shared by many Indian groups that were distinguished by different languages. In the late fifteenth century, they came under Inca rule and the whole area was converted into defined ethnic territories. Most of these groups continued to inhabit the region after the Spanish conquest of Ecuador in the early sixteenth century. Since then, the indigenous people have suffered great hardships, but many of the ethnic groups still live in this area.[23]

The Catholic priests who came into the central highlands in the sixteenth and seventeenth centuries constructed large churches in Latacunga and smaller ones in central towns of the various Indian territories. Historic documents state that each church had a large plaza in front that was used for a variety of activities, including processions, markets, and popular fiestas, especially those featuring bulls and danzantes.[24] Corpus Christi feast day processions were among the most important events, and they continued to be carried out in many towns and villages into the early twentieth century.[25] By the 1950s, however, Catholic priests did not have as much power or control over

Indian communities, and Corpus Christi dances ceased being performed in Latacunga. In the 1970s the festival in the nearby town of Pujilí converted from a religious feast day into a largely secularized event with indigenous and mestizo dance groups participating.[26] Corpus Christi celebrations are still carried out in some indigenous villages in other parts of the central highlands, including Salasaca, in the Tungurahua Province. As part of their ritual practices, dancers go to the neighboring town of Pelileo to participate in the Catholic procession there.[27]

FIG. 5-14 *Danzantes participating in the Corpus Christi procession in Pujilí, Ecuador, wearing costumes and headdresses made by Aurelio Vargas,* 1994. Photograph by Barbara Mauldin.

FIG. 5-15 *Corpus Christi Costume, Back Apron*. Cotopaxi, Ecuador, mid-20th century. Cotton, metal, fiber, 32" x 37" (81.3 x 94 cm). Gift of Tom Robinson, MOIFA.

FIG. 5-16 *Corpus Christi Costume, Headdress Panel*. Cotopaxi, Ecuador, mid-20th century. Cotton, metal, fiber, mirror, 55" x 21" (139.7 x 53.3 cm). Gift of Tom Robinson, MOIFA.

Over time, a distinctive type of Corpus Christi dance costume evolved in the central highlands region of Ecuador. Although variations can be seen, the basic style was shared by costume makers throughout the different areas. It consists of white undergarments (shirt, pantaloons, and petticoats) usually trimmed at the edges with lace or crocheting. Bibs, front aprons, and wide back aprons are worn over the undergarments; long panels hang down from the backs of the headdresses. The over-garments and panels are made from colorful fabrics, often ornamented with reflective foil. In the Cotopaxi region they also have elaborate embroidery with patterns and motifs similar to those found on church vestments. Older costumes were sometimes ornamented with hundreds of antique coins. The dancers generally carry batons or small staffs and tie strings of bells around their shins. They also wear wire-screen masks with European features made in a workshop in the Cotopaxi town of Salcedo.

FIG. 5-17 *The back of a Corpus Christi dance headdress made by José Ignacio Criollo, San Rafael, Cotopaxi, Ecuador,* 1993. Photograph by Barbara Mauldin.

The most distinctive feature of Corpus Christi costumes made in this region of Ecuador is the extremely large headdresses. They are mounted on top of felt hats that have rows of silver coins fastened around the brim. The headdresses are constructed from reeds, bent and tied to create a flat, vertical structure that extends up two to three feet above the brim of the hat. The structure is made either in the form of a simple arch or a more elaborate sunburst shape with points. Several clusters of shiny peacock feathers are tied to the back of the structure and extend up another two feet above the top. The finished headdress can be quite heavy and difficult to dance in, thus gaining prestige for the men who volunteer to wear them and perform in the celebration.[28]

FIG. 5-18 *Corpus Christi Dance Headdress.* Cotopaxi Province, Ecuador, mid-20th century. Fiber, wood, metal, plastic, glass, shell, 33⅛" x 27⁹/₁₆" (86 x 70 cm). International Folk Art Foundation Collection, MOIFA.

The front surface of the headdress is the primary focal point of the outfit worn by the danzante. It is covered with gold or silver foil and decorated with a variety of objects, creating a rich, colorful, and shiny display that reflects light as the dancers nod their heads. The front surface of the headdress also showcases the images placed within the decoration. Costume makers from different regions have developed their own local styles of ornamentation, but even within a similar style each headdress is unique.[29]

The most elaborate style has been developed by costume makers in the valley extending from Latacunga to Pujilí. A distinguishing feature is the sunburst form covered with gold foil. In older pieces, such as this one, a stylized bird symbolizing an eagle was always placed on the upper part of the center. This bird form was covered in gold foil and decorated with strings of pearls and other jewelry, along with a large reliquary framing an image of Christ or a Catholic saint. The older headdresses also had four abstracted images of sheep, decorated with foil, pearls, jewelry, and other items attached in a vertical line down the center. Additional reliquaries, jewelry, shells, metal items, and colorful plastic objects filled in the space along the sides and bottom.

FIG. 5-19 *José Ignacio Criollo with two of his Corpus Christi dance headdresses at his home in San Rafael, Cotopaxi, Ecuador,* 1994. Photograph by Barbara Mauldin.

FIG. 5-20 *A danzante participating in the Corpus Christi procession in Pujilí, Ecuador, wearing a costume and headdress made by José Ignacio Criollo,* 1994. Photograph by Barbara Mauldin.

One of the most prominent costume makers still active in the Pujilí area is José Ignacio Criollo. He is a small Indian man in his early seventies who spends most of his time at home in the small rural village of San Rafael, where he farms corn, potatoes, and other crops. He began making festival costumes in the late 1950s, following in the steps of his deceased great-grandfather. He was inspired to start this cottage industry because many of the older costume makers were dying off, and he felt it was important to carry on the tradition. He studied his great-grandfather's costumes and figured out ways to make his own versions. Gradually, he built up an inventory for a variety of Catholic festivals and dancers started coming from all over the area to rent costumes from him. Although his primary job is still farming, Criollo says he has gained a great deal of prestige within his community as a costume maker. He has a keen eye and a strong sense of the indigenous aesthetic that is reflected in his work.

FIG. 5-21 José Ignacio Criollo, *Corpus Christi Dance Headdress.* San Rafael, Cotopaxi, Ecuador, ca. 1980. Fiber, wood, rubber, metal, plastic, glass, 45¼" x 25⅝" (114.9 x 65.1 cm). International Folk Art Foundation Collection, MOIFA. *Mask.* Salcedo, Cotopaxi, Ecuador, 1992. Wire screen, metal, paint. MOIFA.

The Corpus Christi dance costumes are among Criollo's most important creations; he reveres the large headdresses almost as if they were sacred objects. Much thought goes into the ornamentation of the front surface, a process he describes as "dressing" the headdress rather than simply decorating it. At first, he copied the older headdresses by putting a reliquary or other large ornament at the top and three abstracted images of sheep down the center below. He decorated these and the rest of the surface with strings of fake pearls, reliquaries, jewelry, and other colorful objects he found in junk stores and flea markets. As time went on, it became harder to find reliquaries and jewelry, so he started using other reflective objects, including broken watchbands, old pocketknives, buttons, colored Christmas lights, metal car logos, and small metal and plastic figures of babies, soldiers, and animals. Over time, Criollo considered new ways to "dress" the headpieces to make them more aesthetically appealing and in his words "more modern." In the mid-1970s, he began using a greater variety of recycled, industrially-produced objects, many of which were larger in scale than the previous ornamentation. The overall effect is bolder, while retaining some aspects of his earlier headdress decoration.

FIG. 5-22 *Corpus Christi Dance Headdress.* Cotopaxi, Ecuador, ca. 1970. Fiber, wood, metal, plastic, glass, feathers. With trailer: 63⅜" x 16⅛" (161 x 41 cm). International Folk Art Foundation Collection, MOIFA.

Indigenous costume makers living in other rural villages around Pujilí and Saquisilí have used other, less formal styles to decorate the Corpus Christi dance headdresses. They are constructed in a simpler arch shape, with the front surface covered in gold or silver foil. Some have two stylized human forms attached to the left and right, with tiny dolls' heads on top of each. Below is an abstracted image of a sheep. The forms are all decorated with strings of fake pearls, junk jewelry, and an assortment of small, colorful plastic objects. The remaining space on the surface of the headdress is filled in with small mirrors and other shiny items. The headdress shown here was made for a young teenage boy to wear in the Corpus Christi procession.

# Carnival and Masquerade in Oruro, Bolivia

One of the most important feast days on the Catholic calendar is Easter, the commemoration of the death and resurrection of Jesus of Nazareth. To properly prepare for this day, Christians are asked to observe Lent—forty days of fasting. Twelfth-century Italians began the practice of celebrating before the beginning of Lent; by the fourteenth century, this tradition had spread to many regions of Europe. People indulged in eating meat, drinking alcohol, masquerading, and playing boisterous games before the long period of fasting. The Italian word *carnevale* (literally meaning "flesh farewell") came to be associated with this celebration; the word was translated into other languages as *carnaval* (Spanish) and *carnival* (English). In the seventeenth century, the Spanish kings Philip V and his son Charles II embraced carnival with great enthusiasm, and this spread to many cities and towns in Spain and the American colonies.[31]

By the eighteenth century, carnival was a major celebration in the silver-mining town of Potosí, Bolivia. Wealthy Europeans living there promoted the secular festival with extravagant parades, dancing, and feasting. Carnival parties and parades were also enjoyed in other mining towns in the region, including Villa de San Felipe de Asturia, now called Oruro.[32] This tradition continued into the post-Independence period of the nineteenth century. The Bolivian economy prospered in the late nineteenth and early twentieth century, when Oruro became a major tin-producing region. In the 1920s the "tin barons" of Bolivia were among the richest men in the world and the carnival in Oruro was celebrated with extravagance by the elite residents. Indian and cholo workers carried out their own carnival procession and festivities, separate from the upper-class events.

The worldwide depression of the 1930s led to the collapse of Bolivia's economy and political stability. A leftist movement began to evolve in the 1940s and the National Revolutionary Party came into power in 1952.[33] An aspect of their socialist ideology was to view the Indians and their lifestyle as a model for an idealized society. The indigenous and cholo festivals, with their masquerades and processional dance dramas, were seen as national folkloric pageants. As a result, the elite residents of Oruro began forming dance groups modeled after those of the Indians and cholos; eventually, the two carnival celebrations were combined into one big event.[34]

By the late twentieth century, Oruro's carnival had become the largest and most important festival in Bolivia. Each year it draws hundreds of thousands of people to Oruro to participate or watch from the sidelines. In 2001 UNESCO declared the celebration a "Masterpiece of Oral and Intangible Heritage of Humanity." The main processions take place on Saturday and Sunday, when hundreds of different dance groups make their way through the eight blocks of the parade route. Most of them have made a pledge to dance for the Virgen del Socavón, whose sanctuary is at the end of the route. On Saturday the dancers enter the church and crawl on their knees to the main altar to pray and ask for her blessings. Two of the most important groups that participate in the Oruro carnival are known as the *diablos* (devils) and the *morenos* (African slaves).[35]

## DEVIL MASQUERADES IN ORURO CARNIVAL

Before the Spanish arrived, the Oruro region was inhabited by different Indian groups beginning with the Uru-Uru, who were later joined by Aymara-speaking people. In the mid-fifteenth century, the Inca brought Quechua groups from Peru to colonize the area and spread their culture south. By the end of that century, silver had been discovered in the mountains and the indigenous people extracted the precious metal for use in jewelry, adornment of clothing, and ceremonial objects.[36]

The miners believed in an underground spirit called Supay, who was viewed as the god of the underworld and owner of the minerals in the mountains. This god could either help the miners locate the riches or prevent their extraction. In some instances, this could result in disastrous consequences. The miners created images of Supay that they placed in the mines and made offerings to; it was believed that the spirit's attitude depended on correct offerings and the proper respect.

As part of the Spanish conquest of Bolivia and exploitation of the mines, the Indians living around Oruro became laborers for the Europeans. As soon as the Spanish clergy became aware of

FIG. 5-28 *Miners in the Oruro region continue to make offerings to images of Supay, the Andean god of the underworld,* 1989. Photograph by Peter McFarren.

the Indians' devotion to Supay, they tried to dissuade the miners from continuing this worship. The priests told them the spirit was actually the devil and would only be an evil force in their lives. Catholic priests added horns to the Supay images to further emphasize the spirit's frightening character. The miners, however, secretly continued their devotion to Supay and came to adopt the horns as an aspect of the god's appearance (fig. 5-28).[37]

The earliest accounts of Indians participating in the Oruro carnival date to 1781; by 1783, local Spanish citizens were complaining of seeing nearly three hundred laborers dancing and singing through the streets on Monday night of carnival week. They feared this performance might escalate into a rebellion.[38] Indians and mestizos continued to participate in Oruro's carnival in subsequent years, but the ruling class was determined to remain in control of the festivities.

In 1789 a painting of the Virgen de la Candelaría appeared on the wall of a cave near one of the mine shafts, and it was reported that she had performed a miracle there. She became known as the Virgen del Socavón (Virgin of the Mineshaft), and the miners were told that she was their protector (see figs. 2-6, 2-7, 2-61, 2-65). Since her feast day, February 2, often coincided with the timing of carnival, it was decided that she would be the patron of Oruro and its pre-Lenten celebration.[39] Although the legend of the Virgen del Socavón credits the miners with these decisions, it is more likely that Spanish citizens and Catholic clergy of Oruro promoted the story of the miracle. The Virgin's patronage of the city and carnival was a way to insert a religious element into the celebration and create a less rebellious environment.

The miners feared that Supay would be jealous of the attention being paid to the Virgin, so they decided to honor him during carnival as well. In 1790 they impersonated him wearing costumes and masks that portrayed the European idea of devils. Following the colonial-pageant format, the miners performed a processional drama in which different devil characters took part. This continued into the early nineteenth century; however, in 1818, a French Catholic priest tried to introduce a biblical drama of the seven capital sins into their performance. The following year, the miners disbanded the diablo group.[40]

FIG. 5-29 *Devil masqueraders perform in the Oruro carnival parade*, 1997. Photograph by Barbara Mauldin.

FIG. 5-30 *Devil Mask.* La Paz, Bolivia, ca. 1960. Plaster, glass, paint, 19¾" x 16½" (50.2 x 41.9 cm). Gift of the Girard Foundation Collection, MOIFA.

Decades passed with no organized Indian or cholo devil groups. Then, in the early twentieth century, a new group of miners formed a carnival troupe known as "Gran Tradicional Diablada Oruro"; over time, men from other professions joined in. The devil group has performed continuously in the Oruro carnival since 1917, except when the festivities were canceled during the Chaco War in the early 1930s. Since then, many other diablo groups have joined Oruro's carnival procession. Two that started in the 1940s were comprised of men from Oruro's upper class. They initiated the tradition of wearing more elaborate costumes and masks and performing choreographed dance steps. Over time, other masked characters were added to the diablo troupes, including furry bears and condors, as well as Lucifer and St. Michael.[41]

FIG. 5-31 *Chinas diablas (female devils) enjoy carrying out their role as seductresses in Oruro's carnival,* 2000. Photograph by Barbara Mauldin.

FIG. 5-32 *China Supay Mask.* La Paz, Bolivia, ca. 1970. Plaster, paint, fake fur, 7" x 9½" (17.8 x 24 cm). Gift of David R. Thornburg, MOIFA.

A sexy, female devil character known as China Supay was introduced. (The word *china* refers to Indian or mestizo woman.) At first, she was played by men wearing feminine devil masks with large eyelashes and beauty marks and chola-style outfits with full skirts and fitted jackets. In the 1970s these roles were largely taken over by women who wore female devil masks and called themselves *chinas diablas.* They play the role of lusty devils wearing short *cholita*-style skirts and high boots..

▶ FIG. 5-33 Gonzalo Cruz, *Devil Mask*. La Paz, Bolivia, 2000. Metal, paint, glass beads, sequins, glitter, 26" x 30½" (66 x 77 cm). International Folk Art Foundation Collection, MOIFA.

▲ FIG. 5-34 Gregorio Flores, *Devil Cape*. Oruro, Bolivia, 2000. Fabric, embroidery thread, plastic, metal, sequins, 71" x 47" (180.3 x 119.4 cm). International Folk Art Foundation Collection, MOIFA.

The existence of so many devil groups in Oruro's carnival has resulted in increasing competition among dancers to wear more and more elaborate costumes and masks. Cholo families in Oruro and La Paz, known for creating masks and sumptuous embroidered garments, have been handing down these skills for three or four generations. Most dancers own their own masks and only buy a new one every few years to keep up with the changing styles. The devil's cape, chest plate, and waist panels are very expensive to purchase, so these are usually rented.[42]

FIG. 5-35 *Devil masqueraders in Oruro remove their masks and crawl up the aisle of the church of the Virgen del Socavón to pray and ask for her blessings*, 1997. Photograph by Barbara Mauldin.

The Virgen del Socavón (Virgin of the Mineshaft) is the patron of Oruro and its carnival celebration. Her sanctuary is the termination point for the carnival processions; most dancers make a vow to dance for three years in a row to receive the Virgin's blessing for good fortune in the coming year. The diablos, or devil masqueraders, participating in Oruro's carnival today are some of her most devout followers.

### AFRICAN SLAVE MASQUERADERS IN ORURO CARNIVAL

The processional dance drama of the morenos began in the early twentieth century, as part of the Indian and cholo carnival procession. The first group, Moreno Oruro, was started in 1913 by ten of the wealthiest cholo market vendors in Oruro. In 1924 other cholo market vendors established a second group called the Moreno Central. The intention behind both of these groups was to commemorate the sacrifice of African slaves who had been brought to Bolivia in the colonial period to work in the mines.[43]

FIG. 5-36 *Moreno (African slave) masqueraders wear tiered, barrel-like costumes in the Oruro carnival procession,* 1997. Photograph by Barbara Mauldin.

FIG. 5-37 *Spaniard and Moreno Masks.* La Paz, Bolivia, ca. 1970. Plaster, paint, fake fur. Left: 9" x 8" (22.9 x 20.3 cm). International Folk Art Foundation Collection, MOIFA. Right: Gift of David R. Thornburg, MOIFA.

The morenos' performances, masks, costumes, and accessories symbolize elements in the history of slavery in Bolivia. The different characters portrayed in the drama include blue-eyed Spaniards called *achachi* (at left), black slaves (at right), and slave drivers. In the early to mid-twentieth century, achachi masqueraders wore elaborately embroidered jackets and pants. Their pink-skinned masks had false whiskers, and their heads were covered with large wigs that made them look audacious and ridiculous. Men representing the slaves wore small barrel-like costumes ornamented with embroidery. Their black-plaster masks had exaggerated African facial features.

FIG. 5-38 *Female masqueraders impersonate the wives of the African slaves. They dance in one section of an Oruro moreno procession,* 2003. Photograph by Robert Jerome.

The Moreno Central group grew in size in the mid-twentieth century, as new participants from the upper and middle class joined. Today, it has between 450 and 500 members and four sections that feature new characters added to the dance drama. This includes the *doñas* (ladies), who represent the Aymara wives of the black slaves. Today, the doñas wear calf-length chola-style skirts, shawls, and derby hats, and some also wear female moreno masks.

FIG. 5-39 Left: Gonzalo Cruz, *Moreno Matraca*. La Paz, Bolivia, 2000. Metal, wood, paint, glass beads, plastic sequins, fiber. Right: Benito Cruz, *Moreno Mask*. Oruro, Bolivia, 2000. Metal, paint, glitter, fake fur, plastic, 16" x 11" (40.6 x 27.9 cm). International Folk Art Foundation Collection, MOIFA.

Over the years, the morenos' barrel-like costumes grew in size and now weigh up to sixty pounds, making movement in them difficult and slow. The dancers do a laborious side step said to represent slaves struggling to walk with chains around their ankles (see fig. 5-36). Some of the masks are now being made in metal rather than plaster, but the African features are still accentuated. Each dancer carries a *matraca* (noise maker) that makes a creaking sound when he cranks or whirls the handle. Matracas are made in different forms that symbolize themes, often referring to the name of a group or the occupation of the men who belong to it. The matraca carried by the dancers in figure 5-36, and the one at left, were made in the shape of an armadillo-like animal (*quirquincho*) that populates the hills around Oruro. This small mammal serves as the mascot for the town and for the moreno dance groups from Oruro.

## MATRACAS FROM OTHER MORENO GROUPS

FIG. 5-40 *Moreno dancer at the May 3rd celebration for the Holy Cross in Carabuco, La Paz, Bolivia. He carries a matraca (noise maker) in the shape of a truck*, 1988. Photograph by Johan Reinhard.

FIG. 5-41 *Cow Matraca*. La Paz, Bolivia, ca. 1950. Wood, paint, 5½" x 15" (14 x 38.1 cm). Gift of the Girard Foundation Collection, MOIFA.

FIG. 5-42 *Matracas.* La Paz, Bolivia, ca. 1980. Wood, paint, rubber. Left: *Grasshopper.* Private Collection. Right: *Fish.* 8" x 23½" (20.3 x 58.4 cm). Gift of Connie Thrasher Jaquith, MOIFA.

FIG. 5-43 *Matracas.* La Paz, Bolivia. Left: *Airplane Matraca,* ca. 1980. Wood, paint. Right: *Helicopter Matraca,* ca. 1990. Metal, wood, paint, 11½" x 22" (29.2 x 55.9 cm). Private Collection.

FIG. 5-44 *Toothpaste Tube Matraca.* La Paz, Bolivia, ca. 1990. Metal, wood, paint, 5" x 20" (12.7 x 50.8 cm). Private Collection.

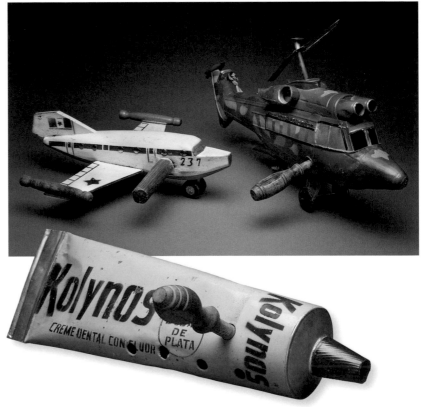

The moreno masquerade and dance drama has become popular with festival dance groups in La Paz and other cities and towns of Bolivia. Most matracas used by morenos in Oruro and elsewhere are made in small workshops in La Paz. The dance groups usually have matching costumes and noise makers. In some cases, however, each person may have his own form of matraca. The shapes relate to the occupation of the dancers, or another theme important to them. The noise makers shown here demonstrate the wide range of forms that have been made from the mid- to late-twentieth century. The cow (previous page) may have been used by a rural group of cattle herders, while the helicopter may have been carried by men involved with the Bolivian military. The toothpaste tube was probably used by a group of dentists or pharmacy workers.

# Festival Masks

Andeans have an ancient tradition of performing dances and dramas wearing masquerades. In the sixteenth century, Spanish priests introduced new forms of masked performance; by the seventeenth century, most participants were wearing costumes and masks that impersonated the Spanish. Other masks of the period portrayed a diversity of characters ranging from Inca rulers to Africans who had been brought to South America as slaves.

In the eighteenth century, the Andean people continued to perform masked dances and dramas, often combining aspects of their prehispanic customs with those introduced by the Europeans. In the post-Independence era of the nineteenth and twentieth century, Indian and cholo communities had the freedom to carry on a popular form of their religious ceremonies and festival masquerading. Following styles established in colonial times, most of the costumes and masks still impersonated Europeans. However, costume makers had a new freedom to make fun of their former oppressors in a more open manner. One of the more serious masquerades was the *negrito*, which portrayed enslaved Africans who were viewed with sympathy and respect. Devil costumes and masks and animal masquerades were also worn in some areas. Many of these masked performances still occur today, performed during feast days for local patron saints and during large celebrations, including carnival, Easter, Corpus Christi, Christmas, and the New Year.

FIG. 5-45 *Male and Female Grandparent Masks.* Department of Lima, Peru, ca. 1970. Wood, paint, wool yarn. Largest: 7¾" x 6" (19.7 x 15.2 cm). Gifts of Laura and Daniel Boeckman, International Folk Art Foundation Collection, MOIFA.

FIG. 5-46 *Spaniard Masks.* Left: Huarochiri, Lima, Peru, ca. 1970. Wood, paint, wool yarn. Right: Central highlands, Peru, ca. 1960. Wood, paint, 8" x 6" (20.3 x 15.2 cm). Gifts of Laura and Daniel Boeckman, International Folk Art Foundation Collection, MOIFA.

Masks portraying Europeans are worn in many communities throughout the central highlands and coastal regions of Peru. Those shown above were used for the dance of the *abuelitos* (grandparents). The two male masks on the left were created with funny, wide-eyed expressions. The female mask on the right is more serious; it was worn by a man who dressed in the clothing of an older woman while he humorously played out the character. The masks in figure 5-46 depict Spaniards with facial hair carved into the wood. The smaller one at left was worn in the dance of the "Three Kings" performed during the Christmas season.

FIG. 5-51 *Devil Masks.* Imbabura, Ecuador, ca. 1980. Fabric. Left: Gift of Lloyd E. Cotsen and the Neutrogena Corporation, MOIFA. Right: 30" x 18" (76.2 x 45.7 cm). International Folk Art Foundation Collection, MOIFA.

Devil masqueraders, known regionally as *diablumas*, are seen in the Imbabura Province of northern Ecuador during the festival honoring San Juan and San Pedro on June 29. Participants wear large, cloth devil masks with faces on both the front and back. The masks are made in a variety of sizes, but all have a row of cloth tubes projecting from the top of the head. Similar forms are attached to the sides to look like ears and others are sewn in the center of the two faces to portray noses. Simple embroidery is used to delineate openings for the eyes and mouth and to decorate the front and back of the masks with stylized images of flowers and animals.[48]

FIG. 5-52 Left: Huacho Family, *Tiger Mask.* Saquisilí, Cotopaxi, Ecuador, ca.1970. Wood, paint. Right: Bulti Cocha, *Wolf Mask.* Cotopaxi, Ecuador, ca.1945. Wood, paint, leather, metal, 11½" x 10" (29.2 x 25.4 cm). Gifts of Peter P. Cecere, MOIFA.

FIG. 5-53 *Dog Masks.* Cotopaxi, Ecuador. Left: ca. 1950. Wood, paint, leather. International Folk Art Foundation Collection, MOIFA. Center: ca. 1975. Wood, paint, 13" x 8" (33 x 20.3 cm). Gift of Peter P. Cecere, MOIFA. Right: ca.1950. Wood, paint, plastic. International Folk Art Foundation Collection, MOIFA.

FIG. 5-54 *Masks.* Cotopaxi, Ecuador, ca. 1970. Wood, paint. Left: *Female.* International Folk Art Foundation Collection, MOIFA. Center: *Old Man.* 13" x 7" (33 x 17.8 cm). Right: *Black Man.* Gifts of Peter P. Cecere, MOIFA.

Heavy wooden masks are worn by dancers for festivals that take place in different communities in the Cotopaxi Province, located in the central highlands of Ecuador. Some of them are made in small workshops, like the one operated by the Huacho family in Saquisilí, while others are carved by farmers during their spare time. Many of the masks represent animals, including wolves, tigers, and fierce dogs. The large heads and faces are carved from one piece of wood; the ears are made separately from wood or other materials and then attached. Each dancer within a group wears a different animal masquerade, while rowdily proceeding through the fiesta as if they were a pack of dangerous beasts. Some carvers produce masks burlesquing Anglos or negritos.[49]

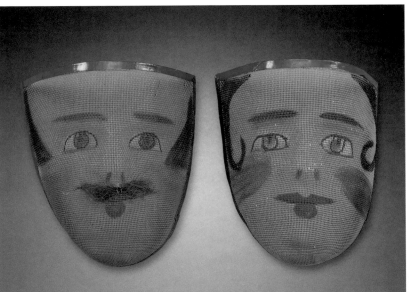

FIG. 5-55 Camac or Camerena workshop. *Male and Female Spaniard Masks*. Huancayo, Junín, Peru, 2004. Wire screen, paint, hair. Largest: 7½" x 6½" (19.1 x 16.5 cm). International Folk Art Foundation Collection, MOIFA.

FIG. 5-56 Luis Alfonso Chuiluiza Balarezo, *Male and Female Spaniard Masks*. Salcedo, Cotopaxi, Ecuador, 1992. Wire screen, paint, metal, hair. Largest: 7½" x 6½" (19.1 x 16.5 cm). International Folk Art Foundation Collection, MOIFA.

FIG. 5-57 *Male Ch'uta Masks*. La Paz, Bolivia, ca. 1960. Wire screen, paint, fabric, synthetic hair, plastic. Left: Gift of Barbara Mauldin, MOIFA. Right: 10¼" x 6" (26 x 15.2 cm). Gift of the Girard Foundation Collection, MOIFA.

The use of wire screen to produce lightweight masks was introduced into South America from central Europe sometime in the late nineteenth or early twentieth century; it is a popular form found in Peru, Ecuador, Bolivia, and elsewhere today. The wire is shaped with facial features by using plaster or ceramic molds. Usually, the masks are then painted to represent Spanish men and women from the colonial era, with pink skin, blue eyes, and light or dark hair. The pair from Huancayo, Department of Junín, Peru, in figure 5-55, are particularly well painted and actual hair was used to carefully create eyebrows, mustache, sideburns, and curls across the forehead. These masks are worn by men in the Huancayo region to perform colonial-style dances such as the Chonguino and Tunantada.

The wire-screen masks in figure 5-56 were made in a small workshop run by Luis Alfonso Chuiluiza Balarezo in Salcedo, Cotopaxi Province, Ecuador. His painting is much simpler and he occasionally adds a mustache made from dyed animal hair. The masks in figure 5-57 were made in La Paz, Bolivia. Both styles are worn by men dressed as Ch'utas (male Indians born and raised in La Paz), a popular masquerade in many areas of the Department of La Paz during the carnival season and for other festivals. These wire-screen masks are ornamented with hair, sequins, and pompoms to complement the Ch'utas' ornate costumes (see fig. 3-85).

# Festival Scenes

Folk artists in different regions of the Andes have been motivated to create sculptural work portraying important festivals that take place in their hometowns. This work relates to paintings and miniature scenes made by mestizo and indigenous artists that depict customs and activities from everyday life in their communities. By the mid-twentieth century, this folk art was being patronized by tourists and collectors who enjoyed having sculptural representations of Andean festivals as decoration in their homes.

FIG. 5-58 Javier Gonzáles Paucar, *Couple Participating in the Festival of the Cross*. Huancayo, Junín, Peru, 2003. Maguey wood, gessoed fabric, paint. Largest: 28" x 8" (71.1 x 20.3 cm). Gift of Ray and Judy Dewey, MOIFA.

The feast of the Holy Cross on May 3 is an important celebration throughout the Andes. In the southern hemisphere this date falls within the harvest season, and rural families combine the Catholic festival with their own rituals to thank Pachamama for a successful crop. These sculptures, made by Javier Gonzáles, who lives near Huancayo in the Department of Junín, Peru, portray a couple participating in the feast of the Holy Cross. The man is bringing the Tayta Mayo (May Cross) to be blessed by the Catholic priest. His wife carries their inquisitive young child, wrapped in a cloth on her back, and she holds a full offering of fresh-picked corn, wheat, and squash blossoms, as symbols of a bountiful harvest.[50]

FIG. 5-59 Pedro Abilio Gonzáles Flores, *Tree Cutting Party*. Huancayo, Junín, Peru, 1958. Maguey wood, gessoed fabric, paint, 15½" x 18" (39.4 x 45.7 cm). Gift of the Girard Foundation Collection, MOIFA.

This festival scene was made by Javier Gonzáles's grandfather, Pedro Abilio Gonzáles Flores. It portrays a Fiesta de Cortamonte (Tree Cutting Party), a popular form of entertainment during carnival and feast days for patron saints in towns throughout the Huancayo region. A designated family organizes the party with food and music, inviting other members of the community to attend. The main event is a competition to cut down a tree. Men take turns at swinging the axe and the one who finally succeeds wins a prize, and then he and his family must take on the responsibility of hosting next year's party.[51]

FIG. 5-60 Jesús La Torre Ybana, *Corpus Christi Festival*. Cuzco, Peru, 1980. Wood, ceramic, paper, foil, paint, 16" x 24" (40.6 x 61 cm). International Folk Art Foundation Collection, MOIFA.

Corpus Christi is one of the most important festivals in Cuzco, Peru. By the 1970s, it had become a popular theme many folk artists chose to portray in paintings and sculpture. This example was made by Jesús La Torre Ybana, who captured the colorful array of activities taking place in a plaza next to one of the town's churches.[52]

FIG. 5-61 *Bullfight Scenes*. Puno, Peru, ca. 1960. Leather, fabric, paint, hair. Largest: 9" x 16" (22.9 x 40.6 cm). Gifts of the Girard Foundation Collection, MOIFA.

FIG. 5-62 *Bullfight Scene*. Pujilí, Cotopaxi, Ecuador, ca. 1950. Wood, leather, paint, fabric. Bull: 4¾" x 8" (12 x 20.3 cm). Gift of Peter P. Cecere, MOIFA.

Bullfighting, a traditional spectacle of Spain, was adopted with enthusiasm in many regions of the Andes by the eighteenth century. This dangerous activity is often part of community festivals today and most towns have a *plaza del torro* (bull ring), where local men take their chances against the bulls. The bullfighting is a stimulating subject for folk artists, as can be seen in these examples from Puno, Peru, and Pujilí, Ecuador.

FIG. 5-63 Olmos Family Workshop, *Ribbon Dance*. Pujilí, Cotopaxi, Ecuador, ca. 1985. Ceramic, paint, ribbons, feathers. Group as pictured: 18½" x 21" (47 x 53.3 cm). Collection of Sue Stevens.

The Ribbon Dance, or Baile de las Cintas, was introduced by the Spaniards in the colonial period, and it continues to be a popular dance in some regions of the Andes today. Eight or more men and women usually participate, each holding the ends of different colored ribbons attached to a central pole. As the dancers move in and out while circling the pole, the ribbons intertwine creating a weav-

ing of bright colors symbolizing the union of the group. This dance is often performed during carnival celebrations and as part of the patron-saint feast-day activities. This group of figures performing the Baile de las Cintas was made by the Olmos Family in Pujilí, Ecuador, where the dance takes place in neighboring communities.[53]

FIG. 5-64 *Marching Band*. Pujilí, Cotopaxi, Ecuador, ca. 1950. Wood, paint. Largest: 10¼" x 3¾" (26 x 9.5 cm). Gift of Peter P. Cecere, MOIFA.

One aspect of many Andean festival processions are marching bands that perform with drums, cymbals, and brass wind instruments. This type of musical display was introduced from Europe, where it evolved out of military ceremony. Band musicians in cities and towns throughout the Andes are not always entirely proficient at playing the instruments, but the rousing music still entertains the crowds. In the mid-twentieth century, folk artists in Pujilí, Cotopaxi Province, Ecuador, began making sets of marching bands to sell to tourists and collectors. Initially, they were carved in wood, as seen in this example. Today, the artists use molds to create more sophisticated plaster figures.[54]

# Glossary

Quechua (Q) Aymara (A) Spanish (S) English (E)

Agave: (S and E) A succulent plant (*Furcraea andina* and *Agave americana*) that grows in various regions of the Andes. In Ecuador women extract fibers from the leaves to weave circular carrying bags (shigras) using a prehispanic looping technique.

Ahuayo: (A) A square cloth worn by women as a mantle. (Same as lliclla in Quechua).

Aksu: (Q) During Inca times, a word referring to a woman's dress. Today the term is used for a rectangular cloth made from two pieces sewn together, worn over other garments. Often called an overskirt.

Almilla: (S) A long-sleeved dress adopted by indigenous women in some regions of the Andes during the colonial era. It was based on a style worn by Spanish peasant women and was usually tailored from coarse bayeta cloth.

Altiplano: (S) The cold, dry, high plateau area of the central Andes that extends from southern Peru into southwestern Bolivia and northern Chile, ranging in height from 12,000 to 13,000 feet (3,600 to 4,000 meters).

Anaku: (Q) The term used in Ecuador for the Inca-style woman's dress. Today, the word refers to a wraparound skirt made of a rectangular piece of cloth.

Apu: (Q) A pantheon of gods worshipped by the Andean people.

Arriero: (S) A person who transports merchandise with the help of pack animals (llamas or mules).

Ayllu: (Q and A) A traditional Andean community group joined by familial lineage and territorial ties.

Aymara: (A) A native Andean ethnic group that lives in independent enclaves, primarily in the Altiplano region of northern Chile, Bolivia, and southern Peru. The Aymara inhabited this area for many centuries before becoming subjects of the Inca and later of the Spanish. This term also refers to the language they speak.

Bayeta: (S) Wool cloth woven in Spanish workshops and used to make a variety of tailored garments.

Bulto: (S) A statue, often an image of a Catholic saint.
Caja de imaginería: (S) A portable box containing an image of a Catholic saint.

Calabaza: (S) A fruit, similar to squash or pumpkin, that came to be known as mate. The dried gourds are used as drinking cups, plates, and containers.

Campesinos: (S) Indians who live in small rural communities, herding animals and growing crops, and generally considered to be at the bottom end of the social scale.

Capillita de santo: (S) A small box containing an image of a Catholic saint.

Cargo: (S) A system introduced into the Andes by the Spanish to assign community or ritual offices and responsibilities. For example, in the festival system the holder of the cargo assumes the obligation to sponsor all or part of the festival events.

Chacra: (Q and A) A carved stone amulet portraying a complete Andean household with agricultural fields and structures, flanked by domestic animals.

Ch'alla: (Q and A) A special drinking ritual to ask for fertility, good health, and prosperity from the Andean gods.

Chicha: (Q and A) A traditional prehispanic alcoholic drink (often called beer) made from fermented corn.

China: (Q) A mestiza or Indian woman.

Cholo/chola: (Q and A) Male and female Indians who moved into Spanish colonial cities and adopted aspects of the Spanish lifestyle and clothing, while retaining many of their indigenous cultural practices, including religious beliefs. They still speak their native languages along with some Spanish.

Chonta: (S) Taken from the Quecha word *chunta*. A species of palm (*Astrocaryum chonta*) that grows in the Amazon rainforest and is considered sacred by the Andean people. Its extremely hard, dark-colored wood is used to make a variety of ceremonial items.

Chullo: (Q and A) A knitted cap, made and worn primarily by men in highland Bolivia and the Cuzco region of Peru.

Ch'unchos: (Q) Indians from the tropical rain forests whom the Andeans considered to be "uncivilized," and who, in prehispanic times, habitually raided Andean settlements. As a result, Inca performances portraying Ch'unchos in mock battles with highland peoples became popular. These masquerades continued during the colonial era and are still prominent in festivals in the Cuzco region today.

Chuspa: (Q) Woven bag. Those carried by men are primarily used to hold coca leaves.

Coca: (Q and A) A plant (*Erythroxylon coca*) that grows in lowland areas near the Andes. The leaf is chewed daily by Andeans and is an important element in social and ceremonial life.

Cocha: (Q) A word derived from the Quechua *qucha*, which means pond or lake. It refers to a type of ceremonial drinking vessel—a bowl (pond) with small figures of cattle or oxen, and sometimes humans, attached in the center. Such bowls are filled with alcohol, and as the liquid is drunk the figures appear to be emerging from a pond.

Cofradía: (S) A religious brotherhood introduced during the colonial period. The group was responsible for taking care of their village church and helping to organize religious feast days.

Comparsas: (S) Dance groups that participate in religious and civic festivals.

Complementary warp: (E) A weaving technique that involves the use of two or more sets of warp yarns, usually of different colors, producing the same pattern on each side of the cloth, but with the colors reversed. Also known as double-faced weave.

Conopa: (Q and A) A ritual vessel made of stone, ceramic, silver, or wood that portrays a domesticated or wild animal found in the Andes and is distinguished by a hole in the back where offerings are placed.

Contradanza: (S) A type of prestigious dance group found in the Cuzco region of Peru. The members portray Spaniards from the late eighteenth and early nineteenth centuries who performed European country-style dances in their salons.

Costumbrismo: (S) Showing the customs, dress, and daily activities of people in cities and rural communities.

Criollo: (S) A term of the colonial era referring to men and women who descended from European parents but were born in the Americas.

Demanda: (S) A petition or request. In the Catholic religion this would be a request for help from a saint. The term is also used for portable altars with images of Catholic saints that are carried during a pilgrimage to the saints' shrines.

Diablo: (S) Devil. A type of masquerade worn by dance groups in various regions of the Andes.

Discontinuous weft: (E) A weaving technique whereby the normal interlacing of weft threads with warp threads is interrupted and instead the weft is turned back on the same warps to modify the normal texture and appearance of a fabric. This technique was used in prehispanic weaving in the Andes to create neck openings in men's tunics.

Encarnación: (S) A finishing technique used in sculptures where several layers of paint and polish are applied to create shiny, lifelike skin tones.

Estofado: (S) A painting technique used in sculpture where gold leaf is painted on the surface of the wood, and a layer of oil paint is applied then incised with very fine lines to reveal the underlying gold ground, to simulate gold thread seen in European brocade fabrics.

Ex-voto: (S) A devotional object used to fulfill a vow or promise, given by a worshipper to an image of a Catholic saint for answering a prayer.

Gesso: (E) White plaster made from gypsum or chalk used in sculpture or to coat a surface for painting.

Hapsburg double-eagle: (E) A symbol of the Hapsburg royal family that controlled Spain during the sixteenth and seventeenth centuries. The double eagle became a popular motif used in coats-of-arms and decorative arts in Spain and in its American colonies.

Herranza: (S) A festival carried out in highland regions of Peru and Bolivia for counting and marking animals owned by a family.

Hojalata: (S) Tin or tinplate. The workshops that use it and items made from tinplate are known as hojalatería.

Huaca: (Q and A) Natural stone or earth formations revered as shrines and thought to possess the spirits of sacred ancestors. (Also spelled wak'a.)

Ikat: (Malay and E) Designs created by dyeing yarn with patterns prior to weaving by wrapping sections of warp or weft threads with another yarn or plant fiber. Only warp ikat is found in the Andes.

Runa: (Q) An indigenous person.

Sanmarco: (S) A type of portable altar made in the Ayacucho region of Peru for use by rural indigenous families in Catholic/Andean religious practices. These housed multiple images of Catholic saints viewed as patrons of the people's animals. Because St. Mark was one of the saints commonly portrayed in the shrines, some scholars began using his name to refer to this style of portable altar.

Santos: (S) Catholic saints and the images portraying them.

Shigra: (Q) A traditional circular carrying bag used in Ecuador made of agave plant fibers by women using a prehispanic looping technique.

Supay: (Q and A) A name used in the mining region of the Bolivian highlands to refer to the Andean god of the underworld. Catholic priests called him the devil.

Taller: (S) A workshop or artist's studio.

Tela-encolada: (S) A European technique for dressing sculptures. Fabric is soaked in gesso and then draped around the figure. Once dried, it is painted to look like actual clothing.

Tiahuanaca: (Q and A) An important prehispanic Andean culture with an urban center in the Altiplano, just south of Lake Titicaca. The Tiahuanacans flourished from AD 500 to 1200 and built an empire that spread over much of the central Andes. After the collapse of that empire a number of independent Aymara-speaking enclaves were established in the Altiplano region.

Ttipqui: (Q) A single pin with ornamented head and thin pointed shaft traditionally worn in a horizontal position by Andean women to secure the mantle across their chests.

Tupu: (Q) One of a pair of metal pins with large flat heads and thin pointed shafts traditionally worn by Andean women to attach the fabric of a wrapped dress over their shoulders.

Urku: (A) The Ayamara name for the prehispanic woman's sleeveless, wraparound dress. In the colonial era the term referred to full, gathered skirts (taken from Spanish peasant costumes) that were made from traditional handwoven fabric rather than bayeta.

Wamani: (Q) Andean god of the mountains.

Warp and warp-faced: (E) The yarn or threads running lengthwise in the loom and crossed by the weft yarn or threads. The greater the number and the closer the spacing of warp elements in relation to weft elements, the more the warp will conceal the weft. If the warp elements hide the weft elements completely, the fabric is said to be warp-faced, a common technique used in the Andes.

# Notes

## Introduction

1.  Steward, ed., *Handbook*, 109–136, 183–330.

2.  Kubler, "The Quechua," 331–360.

3.  Ibid., 363, 375–376.

4.  The issue of ethnicity and class is much more complex than I have outlined here. For further discussion of this topic see Fiedler, "Corpus Christi," 28–44; Abercrombie, "Q'aqchas and la Plebe," 62–63; and Abercrombie, "La Fiesta del Carnaval," 286, 292–293.

5.  Abercrombie, "La Fiesta," 293–295.

6.  Kubler, "La Historia," 5.

## Religious Folk Art

1.  Spalding, *Huarochirí*, 28–34, 42–71, and Bastien, *Mountain of the Condor*, 5–10.

2.  Abercrombie, *Pathways*, 213–291.

3.  Arriaga, *The Extirpation of Idolatry*, 9–170, and Mills, *Idolatry*, 3–267.

4.  Abercrombie, *Pathways*, 275–277.

5.  Ibid., 277–304.

6.  Sallnow, *Pilgrims of the Andes*, 51–88, 177–270.

7.  Mendizábal Losack, *Del Sanmarkos*, 102–103, 157–158, and Stastny, *Las Artes*, 59–62, 101.

8.  Borea Labarthe, "Ritual Objects," 42–45, and Stastny, *Las Artes*, 59–61, 101, 104–105, 174–179.

9.  Abercrombie, *Pathways*, 293–407.

10. MacCormack, "Religion and Society," 111.

11. Leonardini and Borda, *Diccionario*, 255–285, and Vargas Ugarte, *Historia*, 1–130.

12.  Leonardini and Borda, *Diccionario*, 48.

13.  Ibid., 257–261, 273–274.

14.  Gisbert and Mesa, *La Virgen María*, 3–5, and Dean, "The Renewal of Old World Images," 175–177.

15.  Gisbert and Mesa, *La Virgen María*, 12–13.

16.  Gisbert, *Icongrafía*, 28–29, and Mendizábal Losack, *Del Sanmarkos*, 121–124, 133.

17.  Mendizábal Losack, *Del Sanmarkos*, 133–135, and Stastny, *Las Artes*, 153, 156. Author correspondence, 2010, with John Alfred Davis in Lima, Peru.

18.  Leonardini and Borda, *Diccionario*, 146–147.

19.  Mesa and Gisbert, *Historia de la Pintura Cuzqueña I*, 29–255, and Damian, *The Virgin of the Andes*, 44–91.

20.  Mesa and Gisbert, *Pintura*, 7–8.

21.  Stastny, *Las Artes*, 183–185; Mesa and Gisbert, *Pintura*, 6, 10, 13; and *Orígenes y Devociones*, 19, 58–59, 72–73.

22.  Damian, *The Virgin of the Andes*, 50–91.

23.  See other interpretations of this image in *Orígenes y Devociones*, 19, 72–73.

24.  Mesa and Gisbert, *Pintura*, 8–13.

25.  Gisbert and Mesa, *La Virgen María*, 9–10.

26.  Egan, *Relicarios*, 86–92, and Mesa and Gisbert, *Pintura*, 12–14.

27.  Gisbert and Mesa, *La Virgen María*, 10.

28.  Taboada Téllez, "Arte Popular" 215–241.

29.  Gisbert and Mesa, *La Virgen María*, 9–10.

30.  Taboada Téllez, "Arte Popular," 223, 230, 233.

31.  Stastny, *Las Artes Populares*, 187–191, and Macera, *Pintores Populares*, Figs. 1–87.

32.  Palmer, *Sculpture*, 58–149, and Escudero de Terán, *América y España*, 41–248.

33.  Palmer, *Sculpture*, 15, 111–122, and fig. 43.

34.  Ibid., 15.

35.  Arteaga, *Agrupacions Artesanales*, 67–72.

36.  Martínez Borrero, "Talla en Madera," 107–108.

37.  Juan Antonio Supliguichi, 1992, author interview, in his home.

38.  Olivas Weston, *Arte Popular*, 21–29, 178–189, 208–217.

39.  Vargas Ugarte, *Historia*, 42–44. Additional information from Santuario del Cisne, http//www.SantuariodelCisne.org.

40.  Author interview in 1992 with Patricia La Farge, who bought and sold work by Maestro Guzman for several years in the late twentieth century.

41.  Mesa and Gisbert, "La escultura en Cusco," 191–249.

42.  Leonardini and Borda, *Diccionario*, 189.

43.  Mauldin, "Images of the Christ Child," 23–24, fig. 4.

44.  *Orígenes y Devociones*, 75–89, and Mesa and Gisbert, *Escultura Virreinal*, 165–166.

45.  Mauldin, "Images of the Christ Child," 67–69, and *Orígenes y Devociones*, 25, 91.

46.  Patricia La Farge, who interviewed several people in Cuzco about these figures, in personal communication with author in 2009.

47.  Stastny, *Las Artes Populares*, 80–81, 160–162.

48.  Ibid., 162–163. Granddaughter of Hilario Mendívil, in interview with author, at family workshop in Cuzco, 2008.

49.  Mesa and Gisbert, *Escultura Virreinal*, 91, 149–150, 167.

50.  Author interview in 2006 with owner of the Charcas Family Workshop in La Paz; author's personal observations in 1996 of sales booths at the shrine to the Virgin of Copacabana.

51. Stastny, *Las Artes Populares*, 166–174.

52. John Alfredo Davis, collector and owner of the Kunta Huasi Gallery in Lima, Peru, identified the artist who made these pieces.

53. *Obras Maestras*, 50–51, and Stastny, *Las Artes Populares*, 162–163.

54. Padilla, "Connecting Cultures," 20–25, and *Obras Maestras*, 50–51.

55. Leonardini and Borda, *Diccionario*, 172–173, 219–220.

56. *Atlas de Tradiciones*, 258–259, and Aretz, *La Artesania*, 170–177.

57. *Atlas de Tradiciones*, 256–257, 260, 264–266, and Diaz, *Por Un Cielo*, 11–167.

58. Hernández and Fuentes, *Fiestas Tradicionales*, 106–108.

59. Piberm, *Novena*, 9–12; Diaz, *Por un Cielo*, 108–125; and Oettinger, *The Folk Art of Latin America*, 23–25.

60. Mendizábal Losack, *Del Sanmarkos*, 110–118.

61. Abercrombie, *Pathways*, 270.

62. Ibid., 278–279.

63. Ibid., 281–283.

64. Mendizábal Losack, *Del Sanmarkos*, 143–153.

65. Jiménez Quispe, "Santeros," 30–35.

66. Mesa and Gisbert, "La escultura en Cusco," 198–201.

67. Vargas Ugarte, *Historia del Culto de María*, 271.

68. This piece has been illustrated and discussed in several books on Andean colonial art, including: Stastny, "Plateria Colonial," 252–255; Esteras Martín, *Plateria del Peru*, 114–115; and Phipps et al., *The Colonial Andes*, 261–262.

69. Mendizábal Losack, *Del Sanmarkos*, 45–53.

70. Mesa and Gisbert, *Escultura Virreinal*, 91, 149–150, 167.

71. Information in accession records from donor, David R. Thornburg, who lived in La Paz in the early to mid-twentieth century.

72. Mesa and Gisbert, *Escultura Virreinal*, 92, 149–151, 166–169.

73. An example of an eighteenth-century baroque altar screen, from a church in Potosí, is illustrated in Mesa and Gisbert, *Escultura Virreinal*, 200.

74. Ibid., 87–89, 166–167.

75. Taboada Téllez, "Arte Popular," 230–231, 239.

76. Ibid., 215–241.

77. Mesa and Gisbert, *Escultura Virreinal*, 213–218, and Mesa and Gisbert, *Pintura*, 10–13.

78. Taboada Téllez, "Arte Popular," 219. Freddy Taboada Téllez helped identify this style of portable shrine as coming from the Cochabamba area.

79. Mendizábal Losack, *Del Sanmarkos*, 129–130.

80. Ibid., 128–133.

81. Stastny, *Las Artes Populares*, 156.

82. Solar, "Cajon Sanmarcos," 17–23.

83. Mendizábal Losack, *Del Sanmarkos*, 132–135.

84. Solar, "Cajon Sanmarcos," 24–26.

85. Mesa and Gisbert, "La escultura en Cusco," 191–249.

86. Martínez Borrero, "Talla en Madera," 107–108.

87. Juan Antonio Supliguichi, 1992, interview with author, in Gualaceo, Ecuador.

88. Leonardini and Borda, *Diccionario*, 101, 105–106.

89. Ibid., 93–108.

90. Ibid., 102–104.

91. Taboada Téllez, "Arte Popular," 219, 238.

92. Oettinger, *The Folk Art of Latin America*, 34.

93. Ibid., 36.

94. Egan, *Relicarios*, 5–29, 73–88.

95. Ibid., 86–89, and Mesa and Gisbert, *Pintura*, 13–14.

96. Ibid., 89–90.

97. Ibid., 95.

98. Ibid., 93–94, 96.

99. Ibid., 2.

100. Ibid., 100–101.

101. Egan, *Milagros*, 1–30; Francis, *Faith and Transformation,* 16–21, 36–39, 46–77; and Stastny, *Las Artes Populares*, 249–250.

102. All of the following information in the text and identification of the different styles of milagros was provided by Jonathan Williams, owner of Tesoros Trading Company, Austin, Texas. Mr. Williams has been collecting and researching the background of milagros for many years.

103. Egan, *Milagros*, 31, 34.

104. Tschopik, "The Aymara," 238–240, and Bastien, "Good Luck Fetishes," 354–356.

105. Tschopik, "The Aymara," 239.

106. More examples of this twentieth-century style can be seen in Borea Labarthe, "Ritual Objects," 42–45.

107. Bastien, "Good Luck Fetishes," 360.

108. Tschopik, "The Aymara," 239, and Borea Labarthe, "Ritual Objects," 42.

109. Tschopik, "The Aymara," 239, and Bastien, "Good Luck Fetishes," 357.

110. Ibid.

111. Tschopik, "The Aymara," 239.

112. Information on Ayachucho minature stone images of saints was provided by Jonathan Williams in 2008 interview with author. Bastien, "Good Luck Fetishes," 359, tells us that small images of saints were also being carved by Aymara men in northwestern Bolivia.

113. Author interviews with vendors of bottle amulets in Quito, Ecuador, 1992, and in La Paz, Bolivia, 2006.

114. Museo Nacional, *Cerámica*, 5.

115. Unless otherwise noted, the information in this section on conopas is from the following sources: Stastny, *Las Artes Populares*, 51, 59–62, 105–107; Mendizábal Losack, *Del Sanmarkos*, 102–103, 152; Zorn, "Textiles," 289–291; Mesa, *Platería Civil*, 16, 54; and Taullard, *Platería Sudamericana*, fig. 55.

116. Litto, *South American Folk Pottery*, 66–68.

117. Tschopik, "The Aymara," 240–261, and Heckman, *Woven Stories*, 62, 64–65.

118. Heckman, *Woven Stories*, 65–66, and Tschopik, "The Aymara," 253–261.

119. Author interviews with vendors of these items in Oruro, 2001, and in La Paz, 2006.

120. Ponce Sanginés, Tunupa y Ekako, 11–143.

121. Paredes Candia, *Las Alacitas*, 4–79, and Aramayo, *Antología del Ekeko*, 5–104.

## Textiles and Costumes

1. Much of the information in this introduction is drawn from Adelson and Tracht, *Aymara Weavings*, 21–39.

2. Recently, a few organizations have been established to help revive the old weaving technologies and materials and encourage men and women to take pride in wearing the traditional clothing. Among them is El Centro de Textiles Tradicionales del Cusco, which was established by Nilda Callañaupa. See Callañaupa Alvarez, *Weaving in the Peruvian Highlands*. Another organization is Antropologos del Sur Andino (ASUR), which works with Jalq'a and Tarabucan communities in Chuquisaca, Bolivia.

3. Adelson and Tracht, *Aymara Weavings*, 50–59; Montell, *Dress and Ornaments*, 239–244.

4. Adelson and Tracht, *Aymara Weavings*, 69; Taullard, *Tejidos y Ponchos*, 145–150, figs. 267–274.

5. Adelson and Tracht, *Aymara Weavings*, 46, 60–63, 65–69, 72–77.

6. Callañaupa Alvarez, *Weaving in the Peruvian Highlands*, 36–70, 75.

7. Adelson and Takami, *Weaving Traditions*, 45–46, 54.

8. Larsen, *The Dyer's Art*, 129–133.

9. Rowe, *Warp-Patterned Weaves*, 18–19.

10. Phipps, "Textiles As Cultural Memory," 45.

11. Larsen, *The Dyer's Art*, 133–134.

12. Adelson and Tracht, *Aymara Weavings*, 71.

13. Rowe, Miller, and Meisch, *Weaving and Dyeing*, 100–106.

14. Rowe, *Warp-Patterned Weaves*, 20–21.

15. Gisbert et al., *Textiles en los Andes*, 76–77.

16. Adelson and Takami, *Weaving Traditions*, 34.

17. Moraga, "From the Infinite Blue,"165–179, 247; Mege Rosso, *Arte Textil Mapuche*, 36–41.

18. Phipps, "Textiles As Cultural Memory," 148.

19. Adelson and Tracht, *Aymara Weavings*, 90–92.

20. Ibid., 89, 92, 94–101.

21. Gisbert et al., *Textiles en los Andes*, 212–231.

22. Adelson and Tracht, *Aymara Weavings*, 89, 100.

23. Rowe and Cohen, *Hidden Threads of Peru*, 47, 107–131.

24. Callañaupa Alvarez, *Weaving in the Peruvian Highlands*, 32, 69.

25. Ibid. 100–105.

26. Adelson and Tracht, *Aymara Weavings*, 102–112.

27. Ibid. 106–107, 112.

28. Adelson and Takami, *Weaving Traditions*, 46; Gisbert et al., *Textiles en los Andes*, 188–200.

29. Meisch, "The Living Textiles of Tarabuco," 47–50, 55–59; Meisch, "Weaving Styles in Tarabuco," 243–274; and Gisbert et al., *Textiles en los Andes*, 201–211.

30. Adelson and Tracht, *Aymara Weavings*, 116–123.

31. Author's personal observations in Bolivia, in 1997, 2000, and 2006; and in Peru, in 2006 and 2008.

32. Callañaupa Alvarez, *Weaving in the Peruvian Highlands*, 34.

33. Heckman, *Woven Stories*, 87.

34. Callañaupa Alvarez, *Weaving in the Peruvian Highlands*, 36.

35. Adelson and Tracht, *Aymara Weavings*, 134.

36. Rowe and Cohen, *Hidden Threads of Peru*, 59–61.

37. Callañaupa Alvarez, *Weaving in the Peruvian Highlands*, 36.

38. Adelson and Tracht, *Aymara Weavings*, 129.

39. Adelson and Takami, *Weaving Traditions*, 38.

40. Ibid., 50.

41. Author's observations based on an examination of the Ingavi Province coca bags in MOIFA's collection.

42. Callañaupa Alvarez, *Weaving in the Peruvian Highlands*, 38–39.

43. Heckman, *Woven Stories*, 91, 93.

44. Adelson and Tracht, *Aymara Weavings*, 126, 130–131; Rowe and Cohen, *Hidden Threads of Peru*, 56–58.

45. Rowe and Cohen, *Hidden Threads of Peru*, 63.

46. Adelson and Takami, *Weaving Traditions*, 38.

47. Bastien, *Mountain of the Condor*, 113–114.

32.  Stastny, *Las Artes Populares*, 137.

33.  Author interview, 2010, with their daughter, Bertha Medina, in Santa Fe, New Mexico.

34.  Ibid.

35.  Information on the flasks and drinking cups is drawn from Taullard, *Platería Sudamerica*, 352, 355; Stastny, *Las Artes Populares*, 25, 147–149; Mesa, *Platería Civil*, 13; and Esteras Martín, *Platería del Peru Virreinal*, 320–321.

36.  Further general reading on the subject can be found in Esteras Martin, *Platería del Peru Virreinal*; Taullard, *Platería Sudamerica*; Carcedo et al., *Plata y Plateros*; and Mesa, *Platería Civil*.

37.  Similar pieces are illustrated in Phipps et al., *The Colonial Andes*, 347–348, and Taullard, *Platería Sudamerica*, plate 102.

38.  Mesa, *Platería Civil*, 13.

39.  Taullard, *Platería Sudamerica*, plate 111.

40.  Ibid., 73–76, plates 273–287.

41.  Stastny, *Las Artes Populares*, 75–76.

42.  Rowe, *Costume and Identity*, 270–271.

43.  Stastny, *Las Artes Populares*, 249, 251.

44.  Mesa, *Platería Civil*, 15, 25, cat. no. 23, and Oettinger, *Folk Art of Spain and the Americas*, 182.

45.  Cuvi, *Crafts of Ecuador*, 103–109, and Malo, *Expresión Estética Popular de Cuenca*, 55–73.

46.  Núñez, "Maestros Desiderio Loayaza, Teófilo Araujo," 26–27.

47.  Information on the queros was drawn from Cummins, *Toasts with the Inca*. Early research on this topic was undertaken by John Howland Rowe and published in his essay "The Chronology of Inca Wooden Cups."

48.  Abercrombie, *Pathways of Memory*, 366–367.

49.  Acevedo Basurto et al., *La Loza de la Tierra*, 132–133.

50.  Mesa, *Platería Civil*, 11, 16, 18–19, and Stastny, *Las Artes Populares*, 249.

51.  Acevedo Basurto et al., *La Loza de la Tierra*, 52, 131, 134–135.

52.  Ibid., 52, 157, 164–165.

53.  Author's correspondence, 2010, from John Alfredo Davis in Lima, Peru. Also see Litto, *South American Folk Pottery*, 43–44.

54.  Much of the information on house blessing ornaments was gathered from the author's personal observations and interviews conducted in Ecuador in 1992, 1993, and 1994; and in Peru in 2006 and 2008.

55.  Guess, *Spirit of Chiapas*, 38.

56.  Malo, *Espresión Estética Popular*, 335–347.

57.  Leonardini and Borda, *Diccionario*, 100, 107–108.

58.  Oettinger, *The Folk Art of Latin America*, 34.

59.  Stastny, *Las Artes Populares*, 59–61, 101–105, 118–121.

60.  Ibid., 111–115. Further iformation on Quinua ceramic house blessing ornaments was provided in author's correspondence, 2010, from John Alfred DAvis, Lima, Peru.

61.  Information provided by Ryan Taylor, who visited this region several times and acquired these roof tiles for the museum.

62.  Stastny, *Las Artes Populares*, 191–193, and Oettinger, *The Folk Art of Latin America*, 47.

63.  For information on the evolution of the nativity scenes in Italy and Spain, see Martínez Palomero, *El Belen*.

64.  Examples of large nativity scenes set up by nuns and private citizens in the Andes can be seen in Escudero de Terán, *América y España*, figs. 131, 135–147, and in La Concepción Convent Museum, Cuenca, Ecuador, and the Casa de Murillo Museum, La Paz, Bolivia.

65.  Stastny, *Las Artes Populares*, 168–174.

66.  Ibid., 93–94, 160–163, 168. See also Mendizábal Losack, *Del Sanmarkos*, 28–34.

67.  *Obras Maestras*, 50–51, and Stastny, *Las Artes Populares*, 162–163.

68.  Berg Salvo, *Artesania Tradicional*, 30–31.

69.  Naranjo. *La Cultura Popular*, Vol. II: 164, 169–170, 175, 187–188.

70.  Information on the Andrés Paucarima Workshop was provided by Peter P. Cecere, who collected these pieces in Quito. There is a label from the shop on most of the sculptures.

71.  Aretz, *La Artesania Folklorica de Venezuela*, 167–177; *Atlas de Tradiciones Venezolanas*, 256–260, 264–266; and Diaz, *Por un Cielo de Barros y Maderas*, 11–67.

72.  Information on toys was drawn from the author's interviews in 2005 and 2007 with kinetic-toy artist Mario Calendron, in Santa Fe, New Mexico, and in Mérida, Venezuela. For toys from Molinos and Puno, Peru, information was drawn from the author's interviews and correspondence in 2008 and 2010 with John Alfredo Davis in Lima, and from Stastny, *Las Artes Populares*, 230–231, 236. For toys from Ayacucho, Peru, information was from the author's interviews with John Alfredo Davis in Lima and Julio Urbano Rojas in Ayacucho, in 2008. For toys from Pujilí, Ecuador, see Naranjo, *La Cultura Popular*, Vol. II: 164, 169–170, 175, 187–188. And, for the toy bus from Pitalito, Huila, Colombia, see Davies and Fini, *Arts & Crafts of South America*, 128, 141.

73.  Majluf, *Reproducing Nations*, 9–13, 42–56.

74.  Mercado, *Album de Paisajes*, 19–194.

75.  Mendizábal Losack, *Del Sanmarkos*, 22–28.

76.  Author's correspondence, 2010, with John Alfredo Davis, Lima, Peru.

77.  Stastny, Las Artes Populares, 191–193, and Checa, "El Lenguaje de las Tablas," 18–21.

78.  Ribadeneira de Casares, *Tigua*, 10–69, and Da Vila Vasquez, "La Pintura Popular de Tigua," 213–222.

79.  "Peruvian Children's Embroidery," 52–53; "Children of Chijnaya, Peru," 100–101; and the Chijnaya Foundation, which raises funds to support the community and is helping to market the new embroidery.

80.  Information on the history and development of Ayacucho and Huancavelica *retablos* has been drawn from the author's interviews and written correspondence with John Alfredo Davis in Lima. Further information was found in Stastny, *Las Artes Populares*, 152–157; Solar, "Cajon Sanmarcos," 22–26; Egan,"The Retablos of Nicario Jiménez, 11–13; and Mauldin, "Latin America," 231. The term retablo also means the section of an altar screen. In Mexico and New Mexico, the word has been used to refer to paintings of saints on wood boards or sheets of metal.

# Festivals and Masquerade

1.  The information in the introduction has primarily been drawn from the insightful research and publications of Thomas A. Abercrombie. See Abercrombie, *Pathways*, 179–185, 189, 214, 216–221, 223–225, 235–236, 256, 262, 271, 278, 281–284, 300–301, 304–305, 317–407; Abercrombie, "Q'aqchas and la Plebe in 'rebellion,'" 62–111; and Abercrombie, "La Fiesta del Carnival," 286, 292–295, 298–300. Good information on this topic can also be found in Estenssoro Fuchs, "Los Bailes de los Indios," 353–389.

2.  Sallnow, *Pilgrims in the Andes*, 56–58.

3.  Vega, *Royal Commentaries*, 1415–1416.

4.  Dean, "Painted Images of Cuzco's Corpus Christi," 332–335.

5.  Fielder, "Corpus Christi in Cuzco," 295–296.

6.  Sallnow, *Pilgrims in the Andes*, 177–242.

7.  Cánepa Koch, *Máscara*, 121–133, 150–153.

8.  Ibid., 258–275.

9.  Sallnow, *Pilgrims of the Andes*, 221–222.

10.  Ibid., 221; Cánepa Koch, *Máscara*, 105–106.

11.  Cánepa Koch, *Máscara*, 110–111, 135.

12.  Ibid., 106–108.

13.  Ibid., 112–113.

14.  Ibid., 266–268.

15. Ibid., 102–117.

16. Ibid., 258–259.

17. When the donor purchased the two smaller pieces in 1940, she was told they were dance costume ornaments, *chapas*, made and used in Paucartambo in the late eighteenth or early nineteenth century.

18. Ferrario, "Las Costumbres Antiquas y Modernas," 522–523.

19. Osculati, "Quito en 1874," 308–309; translated by author.

20. Kubler, "The Quechua in the Cobnial World," 341–343, 349, 404–406.

21. Naranjo, *La Cultural Popular*, Vol. II, 80–81, 107–109, 112–113.

22. Author interview, 1994, with María del Pilar Merlo de Cevallos, whose family owned a costume shop near Otavalo, Eucador, for many generations. In 1994 she was Director of Art at the Museos del Banco de Ecuador, Quito.

23. Naranjo, *La Cultura Popular*, Vol. II: 25–29, 57–58; Vol. VII: 31–54.

24. Zúñiga, *Significatión*, 186–187.

25. Moreno, *Música y Danzas*, 72–74, 77, 96–116.

26. Muratorio, *A Feast of Color*, 14.

27. Naranjo, *La Cultura Popular*, Vol. VII: 214–221.

28. Author interview, 1994, with Sr. Jaime Vizuete, Pujilí, Ecuador.

29. Mauldin, "Lightbulbs, Watchbands, and Plastic Baby Dolls," 144–151, and author's research in Ecuador, 1992 to 1994.

30. Naranjo, *La Cultura Popular*, Vol. VII: 214–221.

31. Mauldin, *Carnival in Europe and the Americas*, 3–18.

32. Abercrombie, "La Fiesta del Carnaval," 298–300.

33. Klein, *Bolivia*, 161–245.

34. Abercrombie, "La Fiesta del Carnaval," 298–300.

35. LeCount, *Dancing for the Virgin and the Devil*, 173, 180–185, 191–196.

36. Klein, *Bolivia*, 15–24, and Nash, *We Eat the Mines*, 18–20, 22–23.

37. Nash, *We Eat the Mines*, 7, 19–20, and Vargas, "El Carnaval de Oruro," 99–107.

38. Beltrán Avila, *Capítulos*, 308–309, and Cajías, "Carnaval de 1783," 5–7.

39. Vargas, "El Carnaval de Oruro," 107–108.

40. Beltrán Heredía, "Carnaval de Oruro," 69–70.

41. Cazorla Murillo, *Gran Tradicional*, 4–6, and LeCount, "Dancing for the Virgin and the Devil," 179–184.

42. LeCount, *Dancing for the Virgin and the Devil*, 189–190.

43. Ibid., 179–180, 184–185.

44. Author interview, 2008, with Javier and Pedro Gonzáles who live in the Huancayo area of Peru.

45. Domínguez Condenzo, *Danzas e Identidad Nacional*, 47–51.

46. Ibid., 79–88.

47. Ibid., 25, 38–39, 73–76.

48. Naranjo, *La Cultura Popular*, Vol. V: 165–166, 169.

49. Ibid., Vol. II: 93–96, 229, fig. 67.

50. Padilla, "Connecting Cultures," 20–21.

51. Author interview, 2003 and 2008, with Pedro and Javier Gonzáles.

52. Stastny, *Las Artes Populares*, 196.

53. Naranjo, *La Cultura Popular*, Vol. II: 93, 164, 187–190.

54. Information from Patricia La Farge, who imports newer marching bands from Pujilí, to sell in her folk art business, Que Tenga Buena Mano.

# Bibliography

Abad Rodas, Ana. "Joyería." *Artesanías de América*, no. 35 (August 1991): 65–74.

Abercrombie, Thomas A. "La Fiesta del Carnaval Postcolonial en Oruro. Clase, Etnicidad y Nacional-ismo en el Danza Folklorica." *Revista Andina* 10, no. 2 (Diciembre 1992): 279–352.

____. "Q'aqchas and la Plebe in 'Rebellion': "Carnival vs. Lent in 18th–century Potosí." *Journal of Latin American Anthropology* 2, no. 1 (1996): 62–111.

____. *Pathways of Memory and Power*. Madison: University of Wisconsin Press, 1998.

Acevedo Basurto, Sara, Fernando Torres Quiros, Universidad Ricardo Palma (Lima), and Instituto Cultural Peruano Norteamericano. *La Loza de la Tierra: Cerámica Vidriada en el Perú*. Peru: Instituto Cultural Peruano Norteamericano, and Universidad Ricardo Palma, 2003.

Acosta, Joseph de. *Historia Natural y Moral de las Indias*. Buenos Aires: Fondo de Cultura Económica, 1940.

Adelson, Laurie, and Arthur Tracht. *Aymara Weavings: Ceremonial Textiles of Colonial and 19th century Bolivia*. Washington, DC: Smithsonian Institution Press, 1983.

Adelson, Laurie, and Bruce Takami. *Weaving Traditions of Highland Bolivia*. Los Angeles: Craft and Folk Art Museum, 1978.

Aramayo, Omar. *Antología del Ekeko*. Lima: Universidad Alas Peruanas, 2004.

Aretz, Isabel. *La Artesania Folklorica de Venezuela*. Caracas: Ediciones del Cuatricentenario de Caracas, 1967.

Arriaga, Pablo Joseph de, and L. Clark Keating. *The Extirpation of Idolatry in Peru*. Lexington: University of Kentucky Press, 1968.

Arteaga, Diego. "Agrupaciones Artesanales de Cuena (Siglos XVI–XVII). *Artesanías de América*, no. 48 (December 1995): 67–88.

*Atlas de Tradiciones Venezolanas.* Caracas: Fundacion Bigott and El Nacional, 2005.

Bastien, Joseph William. *Mountain of the Condor: Metaphor and Ritual in an Andean Ayllu.* St. Paul, Minn.: West Publishing Company, 1978.

_____. "Good Luck Fetishes: Andean Amulets." In *Objects of Special Devotion: Fetishism in Popular Culture*, edited by Ray B. Browne, 352–361. Bowling Green, Ohio: Bowling Green University Popular Press, 1982.

Beltrán Avila, Marcos. *Capítulos de la Historia Colonial de Oruro.* La Paz: La República, 1925.

Beltrán Heredía, Augusto. "Carnaval de Oruro." In *Carnaval de Oruro, Tarabuco y Fiesta del Gran Poder*, edited by Hugo Boero Rojo, Augusto Beltran Heredía, Blanca Thorrez Martines, and Carlos Urquizo Sossa, 17–70. La Paz: Editorial los Amigos del Libro, 1977.

Berg Salvo, Lorenzo. *Artesania Tradicional de Chile.* Santiago, Chile: Departamento de Extensión Cultural del Ministerio de Educación, 1978.

Bernales Ballesteros, Jorge. *Escultura en el Perú.* Lima: Banco del Crédito del Perú, 1991.

Boero Rojo, Hugo. *Fiesta Boliviana.* La Paz: Editorial "Los Amigos del Libro" Werner Guttentag, 1991.

Borea Labarthe, Giuliana. "Ritual Objects from Peru and Bolivia." In *Faith and Transformation: Votive Offerings and Amulets from the Alexander Girard Collection*, edited by Doris Francis, 42–45, 145. Santa Fe: Museum of International Folk Art and Museum of New Mexico Press, 2007.

Buechler, Hans C. *The Masked Media: Aymara Fiestas and Social Interaction in the Bolivian Highlands.* The Hague, Paris, and New York: Mouton Publishers, 1980.

Cajías, Fernando. "Los Objectivos de la Revolución Indígena de 1781: el Caso de Oruro." *Revista Andina* I, no. 2 (Diciembre 1983): 407–428.

_____. "Carnaval de 1783." *Presencia*, 8 February 1997, 5–7.

Callañaupa Alvarez, Nilda. *Weaving in the Peruvian Highlands: Dreaming Patterns, Weaving Memories.* Cuzco: Center for Traditional Textiles, 2007.

Canavesi de Sahonero, Marie Lissette. *El Traje de la Chola Paceña.* La Paz: Editorial Los Amigos de Libro, 1987.

Cánepa Koch, Gisela. *Máscara: Tranformación e Identidad en los Andes.* Lima: Pontificia Universidad Católica del Perú, Fondo Editorial, 1998.

Carcedo, Paloma, Francisco Stastny, Eduardo Dargent, Luis Eduardo Wuffarden, and Felipe de Lucero. *Plata y Plateros del Perú.* Lima: Patronato Plata del Peru, 1997.

Carpio Ochoa, Kelly. "El Fruto Decorado. Mates burilados del Valle del Mantero, una aproximación a su origen." In *El Fruto Decorado: Mates burilados del Valle del Mantero (Siglos XVIII–XX)*, edited by Kelly Carpio, Maria Eugenia Yllia, and Galeria German Kruger Espantoso, 21–41. Lima: Instituto Cultural Peruano Norteamericano, 2006.

Cazorla Murillo, Fabrizio y Mauricio. *Gran Tradicional Auténtica Diablada de Oruro.* Oruro: Gran Tradicional Auténtica Diablada de Oruro, 2000.

Cerny, Charlene, and Suzanne Seriff, eds. *Recycled Re-Seen: Folk Art from the Global Scrap Heap.* New York: Harry N. Abrams, Inc., in association with the Museum of International Folk Art, 1996.

Chacon Zhapan, Juan. "La Tecnologia Artesanal del Ecuador Durante la Colonia." *Artesanías de América*, no. 34 (April 1991): 25–67.

Checa, Mariella. "El Lenguaje de las Tablas de Sarhua: Primitivo Evanán y Pompeyo Berrocal: Color y Memoria de un Pueblo." *Gaceta Cultural del Peru*, no. 30 (December 2007): 18–21.

"Children of Chijnaya, Peru." *Woman's Day*, September 1965, 76, 100–101.

Cummins, Thomas B. F. *Toasts with the Inca: Andean Abstraction and Colonial Images on Quero Vessels.* Ann Arbor: University of Michigan Press, 2002.

Cuvi, Pablo. *Crafts of Ecuador.* Quito: Dinediciones, 1994.

Damian, Carol. *The Virgin of the Andes: Art and Ritual in Colonial Cuzco.* Miami Beach: Grassfield Press, 1995.

Davies, Lucy, and Mo Fini. *Arts & Crafts of South America.* San Francisco: Chronicle Books, 1994.

Dean, Carolyn. "The Renewal of Old World Images and the Creation of Peruvian Visual Culture." In *Converging Cultures: Art and Identity in Spanish America*, edited by Diana Fane, 171–182. New York: Brooklyn Museum and Harry N. Abrams, 1996.

Dean, Carolyn Sue. "Painted Images of Cuzco's Corpus Christi: Social Conflict and Cultural Strategy in Viceregal Peru." PhD diss., University of California, Los Angeles, 1990.

Diaz, Mariano. *Por un Cielo de Barros y Maderas.* Valencia, Venezuela: Ceramica Carabobo, 1984.

Domínguez Condenzo, Víctor. *Danzas e Identidad Nacional: Huánuco – Pasco.* Huánuco: Universidad de Huánuco; Lima: Editorial San Marcos, 2003.

Egan, Martha. "The Retablos of Nicario Jiménez." *Artspace II* (summer 1987), 11–13.

_____. *Milagros: Votive Offerings from the Americas.* Santa Fe: Museum of New Mexico Press, 1991.

_____. *Relicarios: Devotional Miniatures from the Americas.* Santa Fe: Museum of New Mexico Press, 1993.

Escudero de Terán, Ximena. *América y España en la Escultura Colonial Quiteña: Historia de un Sincretismo.* Quito: Banco de los Andes, 1992.

Estenssoro Fuchs, Juan Carlos. "Los Bailes de los Indios y el Proyecto Colonial." *Revista Andina* 10, no. 2 (Diciembre 1992): 353–404.

Esteras Martín, Cristina. *Platería del Peru Virreinal 1535–1825.* Madrid: Gruppo BBV, Banco Continental, 1997.

_____. "Acculturation and Innovation in Peruvian Viceregal Silverwork." In *The Colonial Andes: Tapestries and Silverwork, 1530–1830*, edited by Elena Phipps, Johanna Hecht, and Cristina Esteras Martín, 59–71. New York: Metropolitan Museum of Art, 2004.

Fane, Diana, ed. *Converging Cultures: Art and Identity in Spanish America.* New York: Brooklyn Museum / Harry N. Abrams, 1996.

Femenias, Blenda. *Andean Aesthetics: Textiles of Peru and Bolivia.* Madison, Wis.: Elvehjem Museum of Art / The Regents of the University of Wisconsin System, 1987.

_____. "Regional Dress of the Colca Valley, Peru: A Dynamic Tradition." In *Textile Traditions of Mesoamerica and the Andes: An Anthology*, edited by Margot Blum Schevill, Janet Catherine Berlo, and Edward B. Dwyer, 179–204. New York: Garland Publishing, 1991.

Ferrario, Julio. "Las Costumbres Antiquas y Modernas de Todo los Pueblos de la América." In *Ecuador Visto pos los Extranjeros Viajeros de los Siglos XVIII y XIX*, edited by Humberto Toscano, 515–546. Puebla: Editorial J. M. Cajica, Jr. S. A., 1960.

Fiedler, Carol Ann. "Corpus Christi in Cuzco: Festival and Ethnic Identity in the Peruvian Andes." PhD diss., Tulane University, 1985.

____. "Ethnic Dress and Calcha Festivals, Bolivia." In *Textile Traditions of Mesoamerica and the Andes: An Anthology*, edited by Margot Blum Schevill, Janet Catherine Berlo, and Edward B. Dwyer, 261–279. New York: Garland Publishing, 1991.

Mege Rosso, Pedro. *Arte Textil Mapuche.* Santiago: Museo Chileno de Arte Precolombino, 1990.

Meisch, Lynn A. "Weaving Styles in Tarabuco, Bolivia." In *The Junius B. Bird Conference on Andean Textiles, April 7 and 8, 1984*, edited by Ann Pollard Rowe, 243–274. Washington, DC: The Textile Museum, 1986.

____. *Otavalo: Weaving, Costume and the Market.* Quito: Ediciones Libri Mundi, 1987.

____. "The Living Textiles of Tarabuco, Bolivia." In *Andean Aesthetics: Textiles of Peru and Bolivia*, edited by Blenda Femenias, 46–69. Madison, Wis.: Elvehjem Museum of Art / The Regents of the University of Wisconsin System, 1987.

____. "We Are Sons of Atahualpa and We Will Win: Traditional Dress in Otavalo and Saraguro, Ecuador." In *Textile Traditions of Mesoamerica and the Andes: An Anthology*, edited by Margot Blum Schevill, Janet Catherine Berlo, and Edward B. Dwyer, 145–177. New York: Garland Publishing, 1991.

Meisch, Lynn A., ed. *Traditional Textiles of the Andes: Life and Cloth in the Highlands.* New York: Thames and Hudson, 1997.

Mendizábal Losack, Emilio. *Del Sanmarkos al Retablo Ayacuchano.* Lima: Universidad Ricardo Palma; Instituto Cultural Peruano Norteamericano; Instituto de Investigaciones Museológicas Artísticas, 2003.

Mendoza, Zoila S. *Shaping Society Through Dance: Mestizo Ritual Performance in the Peruvian Andes.* Chicago: University of Chicago Press, 2000.

____. *Creating Our Own: Folklore, Performance, and Identity in Cuzco, Peru.* Durham, NC: Duke University Press, 2008.

Mercado, Melchor María. *Album de Paisajes, Tipos Humanos y Costumbres de Bolivia (1841–1869).* La Paz: Banco Central de Bolivia, Archivo Nacional de Bolivia y Biblioteca Nacional de Bolivia, 1991.

Mesa, Jóse de. *Platería Civil.* La Paz: Producciones "CIMA," 1992.

Mesa, José de, and Teresa Gisbert. "La escultura en Cusco." In *Escultura en el Perú*, edited by Jorge Bernales Ballesteros, 191–249. Lima: Banco del Crédito del Perú, 1991.

____. *Pintura en Lata Siglo XIX.* La Paz: Instituto Boliviano de Cultura, 1990.

____. *Historia de la Pintura Cuzqueña, Vols. I, II.* Lima: Banco Wiese, 1982.

____. *Escultura Virreinal en Bolivia.* La Paz: Academia Nacional de Ciencias de Bolivia, 1972.

Miller, Laura Martin. "The Ikat Shawl Traditions of Northern Peru and Southern Ecuador." In *Textile Traditions of Mesoamerica and the Andes: An Anthology*, edited by Margot Blum Schevill, Janet Catherine Berlo, and Edward B. Dwyer, 337–358. New York: Garland Publishing, 1991.

Mills, Kenneth. *Idolatry and Its Enemies: Colonial Andean Religion and Extirpation, 1640–1750.* Princeton: Princeton University Press, 1997.

Montell, Gösta. *Dress and Ornaments in Ancient Peru.* Göteborg, Sweden: Elanders Boktyckeri Aktiebolag, 1929.

Moraga, Vanessa and Andrés. "From the Infinite Blue: Mapuche Textiles from Southern Chile." *The 1994 Hali Annual*, no. 1 (1994): 164–179, 247.

Moreno Aguilar, Joaquin. "Paños con Técnica de Ikat." *Artesanías de América*, no. 35 (August 1991): 85–98.

Moreno, Segundo Luis. *Música y Danzas Autóctaonas del Ecuador/ Indigenous Music and Dances of Ecuador*, trans. Jorge Luis Pérez and C. W. Ireson. Quito: Editorial Fray Jodoco Ricke, 1949.

Muratorio, Ricardo. *A Feast of Color: Corpus Christi Dance Costumes of Ecuador*. Washington, DC: Smithsonian Institution Press, 1989.

Museo Chileno de Arte Precolombino. *Plateria Araucana*. Santiago de Chile: El Museo, 1983.

Museo Nacional de Etnografía y Folklore. *Cerámica Continuidad, Cambio y Persistencia*. La Paz: MUSEF and Funcacíon Cultural del Banco Central de Bolivia, 2006.

Naranjo, Marcelo. *La Cultura Popular en el Ecuador*. Vol. 2, *Cotopaxi*. Cuenca, Ecuador: Centro Interamericano de Artesanías y Artes Populares, 1984.

____. *La Cultura Popular en el Ecuado*. Vol. 4, *Imbabura*. Cuenca, Ecuador: Centro Interamericano de Artesanías y Artes Populares, 1989.

____. *La Cultura Popular en el Ecuador*. Vol. 7, *Tungurahua*. Cuenca, Ecuador: Centro Interamericano de Artesanías y Artes Populares, 1992.

Nash, June. *We Eat the Mines and the Mines Eat Us: Dependency and Exploitation in Bolivian Tin Mines*. New York: Columbia University Press, 1993.

Núñez, Evelyn. "Maestros Desiderio Loayaza, Teófilo Araujo: Reyes de la Hojalata." *Gaceta Cultural del Peru*, no. 30 (December 2007): 26–27.

*Obras Maestras en las Colecciones del Museo Nacional de la Cultura Peruana*. Lima: Instituto Nacional de Cultura, 2008.

Oettinger, Marion Jr. *The Folk Art of Latin America: Visiones del Pueblo*. New York: Dutton Studio Books, 1992.

Oettinger, Marion Jr., ed. *Folk Art of Spain and the Americas: El Alma del Pueblo*. New York: Abbeville Press Publishers, 1997.

Olivas Weston, Marcela. *Arte Popular de Cajamarca*. Lima: Antares, Artes y Letras, 2003.

*Origenes y Devociones Virreinales de la Imagineria Popular*. Lima: Universidad Ricardo Palma; Instituto Cultural Peruano Norteamericano, 2008.

Osculati, Cayetano. "Quito en 1847." In *El Ecuador Visto pos los Extranjeros Viajeros de los Siglos XVIII y XIX*, edited by Humberto Toscano, 297–310. Puebla: Editorial J. M. Cajica, Jr., S. A., 1960.

Otero, Gustavo Adolfo. *La Vida Social en el Coloniaje (Esquema de la Historia del Alto Perú hoy Bolivia, de los siglos XVI, XVII y XVIII)*. La Paz: Editorial Juventud, 1958.

Padilla, Carmella. "Connecting Cultures, Changing Lives." *El Palacio* 110, no. 2 (summer 2005): 20–22.

Palmer, Gabrielle G. *Sculpture in the Kingdom of Quito*. Albuquerque: University of New Mexico Press, 1987.

Paredes Candia, Antonio. *Las Alacitas, Fiesta y Feria Popular de la Ciudad de La Paz*. La Paz: Libreria Editorial Popular, 1982.

____. *La Chola Boliviana*. La Paz: Ediciones ISLA, 1992.

Penley, Dennis. *Paños de Gualaceo*. Cuenca: Centro Interamericano de Artesanías y Artes Populares, 1988.

*Campesinos* (rural Indians), 16–17, 32–33, 46, 58–59, 274
Cañar Province, Ecuador, 118–19, *155*, 157
Candleholders, *182*, 189–90
Capes, *144*, *258*
Caps, 18, 134–36, 239
Cardenas, Jesús Urbano, 232–33
Carnival (Oruro, Bolivia), 254–62
Carrero, Amelia de, *214*
Carrying Cloths, *110*
Casa de la Moneda museum, 52
Catholic: artwork, 16–18, 24, 33, 38, 44; ban of amulets, 80; brotherhoods, 24, 69, 189, *240*, 246, 265; iconography, 27, 33; imagery, 42, **46**, *66*; religion, 13, 16–18, 23–24, 42, 46
Catholic priests, 23–24, 33, 39–40, 93, **189**, 237–38, 240, 246–47, 254–55, 263. *See also* Missionaries
Catholic saints, 18, 24–25, 28, 32–33, 43, **46**, 85, 238. *See also* individual names
Center for Traditional Textiles (Cuzco, Peru), 107
Centro Poblado de Chijnaya (Puno, Peru), *228*
Ceramics, 17, 168, 191, *195*, 197–99, 202–05, *207*, *211*, 220–21
Ceremonies: accessories for, 110–11, *153*, *156*; for Illpa, 27; objects for, 23, 25, 80–81, *84*, 87–88, 110, 134, 161–62; portrayals of, 23–22, *90*, *232*; types of, 46, 80
*Chacras*, 25, *81*, 274
Chalán Guamán family, *130*
*Ch'allas*, 237–38, 274
Charazani, La Paz, Bolivia, *106*, *111*, *116*, *150*
Chapels, 46, 199
Charcas Family Workshop, *41*
Checca Pupuja, Puno, Peru, *197*, *202*
*Chicha*, 86, *171*, 191, 194, 197–98, 204, **237**, 274
Chinchero, Cuzco, Peru, 28, *107*, *124*
Child Jesus (Niño Dios), *39*, 265
Chile, 31, 98, 101, *103*, 144, 158–60, *164*, **173**, *180*, *211*, *215*
Chimborazo Province, Ecuador, *101*, *125*, *157*, *186*
*Cholas / Cholos*: depictions of, *17*, *31*, *210*, *223*; and festivals, 238, 254, 256, 258–60; history of, 17–18; and jewelry, 149, 152; traditional clothing of, 129–31
Chordeleg, Azuay, Ecuador, 168, *171*
Christianity, 23–24, 40, 237–38
Chucuito province, Puno, Peru, 47–49, *218*
*Ch'unchos*, *29*, 192, 239, 241–42, *245*, 274
Chuquisaca, Bolivia, *100*, *109*, *128*
Churches, 25, 40, 55, 149, 163, 168, 180, 206, 246
Clothing, ceremonial, 18, *99*, *105*, *108*, *117*, *124*, *145*, *150*
Clothing, European style, 16–18, 108, 123–25, *218*
Clothing, festival, *96*, 111, *118*, *123*, *130*, *132*, 134–37, *139*, 142–44, 152. *See also* Festival costumes
Clothing, traditional, 16–18, 97–98, 104, **107**–09, *117*, 123, 126–31, 141–42, 144, *150*, *154*, *209*, 222–23
Coca leaves, 46, 80, 86, 90–91, 110, 115, **137**, 187, *192*, 274
Cocha, Bulti, *266*
Cochabamba, Bolivia, *17*, 55, *89*, *106*, *108*, 111, *117*, *221*
*Cochas*, 194–96, 274
Cochas Chica, Junín, Peru, 174–76
Colombia, *70*, *164*, *179*, *214*, *220*
Colonial period, 13, 16–18, 23–25, 31, 50, 55–56, 60, 62, 69, 80, 134
*Conopas*, 25, 86–89, *198*, *202*, 275
Contradanzas, 239, *242*, 244, 275
Copacabana, Bolivia, 25, 47, 69
Corpus Christi festivals, *225*, *227*, 238–40, 246–53, 263, *270*

*Costumbrismo*, 18, 28, 32, 149, 173, 222–23, 225–26, 229–30
Cotopaxi, Ecuador: and clothing, *130*; and Corpus Christi, 247–51, *253*; and festival masks, 266–68; and fiber bags, *140*; and figures, 45, *212*, 271–72; and paintings, *227*; and roof ornaments, *200*; and staffs, *161*; and toys, *219*
Criollo, José Ignacio, 249–51
*Criollos* (creoles), 16–17, 24, 33, 98, 126, 157, 238, 275
Crosses, 90; and festivals, 269; for homes, 63–67; iron / metal, 199–202; in jewelry, 156, 158; large, outdoor, *62*; of maguey, *66*; of natural branches, *68*; for processions / pilgrimmages, 67–68; on roof tops, 199–202; on staffs, *161*; of tinplate, 189–90; of wood, 63–65, 67–68
Crucifixes, *55*, 62, 66–67, *153*
Cruz, Gonzalo, *258*, *261*
Cuenca region, Azuay, Ecuador: and ceramics, 168; and clothing, *143*; and crosses, *67*; and *milagros*, *79*; and portable altars, 61; and roof ornaments, 199; and sculpture, 35; tinwork of, 189–90
Cups, 172, 178–81, 191–93, *196*, *198*, 241
*Curanderos* (healers), 91–92, *226*, 242
Curi, Elias, *206*
Cuzco, Peru, 13, *120*; and amulets, *85*; ceremonial drinking vessels, 191–93, 197–98; and clothing, 136–37; and *conopas*, 87–89; and costumes, 126–27, *142*; and crosses, *62*; festivals in, 237–45, *270*; genre figures, *208*; jewelry, 150–53; leather/silver coca bags, 187; and majolica, 168–70; and paintings, 27–29, 33, 60, 224–25; Religious practitioners in, *90*; roof ornaments, *202*; sculpture workshops in, 38–39; textiles, *100*, *102*, 106–07, 110, *114*, *124*; workshops in, 32–33

Dances, 24, 99, 237–48, 252–54, 256–65, 268, 272
*Danzantes*, 246–47, 249–50, 252–53
Deities, 23–25, 80, 86, 89–93, 110, *145*, 191, 196, 199, 204, 237–38. *See also* individual names
*Diablos / diablas* (devils), *213*, *245*, 254–58, 263, *266*, 275
Dolls, 218–19
Dresses, 108–09, *123*, 132, *150*, 158, *214*, *223*
Dress and manta pins, *148*, 150–52, 157–58
Drinking vessels, ceremonial, 191–98
Drums, *253*

Ekeko cult / figures, *93*
El Señor del Arbol, 68
Embroidery: on animal ornaments, *121*; on clothing, 18, 123–25, 131–32, 142–43; on festival costumes, 142–44, 246, *248*, 258–60, *266*; on hats, 127–28; on scapulars / badges, 71–72; of scenes from daily life, *228*
*Encarnación* technique, 34, 36–38, 50, *66*, 275
*Estofado* technique, 34–35, 275
Evanán, Pompeyo Berrocal, *226*
Evanán, Primitivo, 226
*Ex-votos*, 73, 275

Feast days: celebrations for, 237–38, 240–41, 246; history of, 162, 237–38; for the Holy Cross, 62, *201*, *269;* and indigenous traditions, 24; and masked dances, 263–64; for the Virgin, 25, 36, 47, 93, 133, 255. *See also* Corpus Christi; individual saints
Featherwork, *145*
Ferrario, Julio, 246
Festival costumes: for carnival, 134–35, 254–61; *chola*-style, *257*, *260*; for dances, *111*, 238–61; European style, 238–39, 263; makers of, 246, 248–51, 263; ornaments for, *245*; for pre-Columbian

dances, 238, 246; renting of, 246, 250, 258; traditional, 98, 238. *See also* Masks
Festivals: history / meaning of, 24, 162, 237–38, 246–47; of the Holy Cross, 62, *65, 67, 269*; portrayals of, *65, 135, 217, 225, 227,* 230–33, *245, 253,* 269–72; post-independence, 239, 246, 254; for Señor de Qoyllur Rit'i, 239–42; for Virgen de Carmen, *240,* 242–45.. *See also* Corpus Christi
Fierro, Francisco "Pancho", 222–24
Fiesta de Herranza, 46, 58, *120,* 275
Figures: ceramic, 18, 25, *207, 211, 272*; of festival participants, *245, 253,* 269–72; genre, 149, 206–14, *220*; maguey, 208–10, *245, 270*; *pasta, 208,* 229–33; plaster, *212, 253, 272*; stone, 25, *206*; wood, 213–14, 269–72
Fisch, Olga, 227
Flasks, 178–79
Flores, Gregorio, *258*
Flores, Pedro Abilio Gonzáles, *43, 209, 270*
Flores, Vicenta Antacusi, *233*
Flores Vilcacoto, Francisca Medina de, *175*

Garcia, Rosa Lina, *214*
Gods. *See* Deities
Gonzáles, Felipe, *63, 209*
González de la Casa, Hernan, 46
Gourds, carved, 18, 172–77, 180
Gualaceo, Azuay, Ecuador, *35, 61, 67, 133*

Hapsburg double-eagle motif, *121,145,* 166–67, *245,* 275
Hats, *123,* 126–30, *142,* 222–23, *231,* 242–44, *249*
Headbands, *116, 148, 150*
Headdresses, *145, 245,* 247–52
Hernández, José Gregorio, *45*
Holy Spirit, *63, 68*
Horse gear, 158, *164,* 180, 184–86
House beams, 163, 199, *205, 226*
*Huaca,* 23–24, *31,* 54
Huacho Family, *266* 67
Huamanga, Ayacucho, Peru, 33, 42, 56–59, 63–65, *70,* 166–67, 189, *218*
Huancavelica, Peru, *139, 233*
Huancayo region, Junín, Peru, *43, 63, 130, 132,* 143–44, 174–77, *209,* 215–16, 218–19, *221,* 264, 269–70.
Huánuco, Huánuco, Peru, 264–65

Idols / idolatry, 24, 59, 86, *237,* 254–55
*Ikat* weavings, 101–03, *133,* 275
*Illas,* 25, *80,* 276
Imbabura, Ecuador, *125, 154, 156,* 218, *266*
Inca period, 13, 16, 23, 25, 86–87, 118, 191–92, 241, 246, 264, 276
*Indigenista* movement, 229–30, *238, 254*
Ironwork, *188,* 199–201

Jesus Christ, 62–68, *71, 189,* 199, 201, 206, 238, 240, 254
Jesús de Machaca, La Paz, Bolivia, 40, 50
Jewelry: brooches, *159*; devotional, 69–70; earrings, *152,* 156–57, *160*; headbands, *160*; on headdresses, *249, 251*; history / styles of, 18, 149–50, 152–53, 158; neckbands / collars, 159–60; necklaces, 153–56, *160*; pectorals, *159*; pins, 150–52, 157–58; of silver, 150–53, 157–60, 254
Jiménez, Claudio, *65, 233*
Jiménez, Florentino, *229,* 232–33
Jiménez, Gregoria, 229
Jiménez, Nicario, *65, 232*
Junín, Peru: and clothing, *118,* 129–30, *132,* 143–44; and crosses, *63*; and figures, *209,* 269–70; and gourds, 174–77; and masks, 264, 268; and sculp-

ture, 43; and toys, 215–16, 218–19, *221*

Knitting / knitted items, 18, 97, 134–38, *218, 242*

La Paz, Bolivia: and amulets, *85*; clothing, *99, 129, 131, 136,* 137–38, *144, 150*; and crucifixes, *66*; and Ekeko cult, *93*; and festival masks, 256–58, 260–61, *268*; genre figures, *210*; and jewelry, *152*; and *matracas,* 261–62; and portable altars, 50–51, 53; and ritual offerings, 91–92; roof ornaments, *205*; and sculpture, 40–41; silverwork, 161–62, 180; staffs, *162*; textiles, *104, 106, 111, 113,* 115–17, *124*; toys, 218, *220*
Lake Titicaca, 13, 40–41, 46–50, 69, 117, 136, 145, 150–53, 228
Lambayeque, Peru, *141*
Latacunga, Cotopaxi, Ecuador, *200,* 246–47
Leatherwork, 18, 166–67, 186–87, *219, 264, 271*
Leggings, 134, *139,* 246
Lima, Peru: and ceramics, 168; and *costumbrismo,* 222; and crosses, *65*; and dance masks, 263; markets in, 190; and *milagros,* 73; and portable boxes with genre scenes , 229–30, 232–33; and religious badges, *71*; saints of, 43; and silverwork, 180; workshops in, 27, 33
Loayza, Desiderio, *190*
Loja Province, Ecuador, 36–37, *72,* 133, 155, *157, 187*
Luza, Elvira, 230

Maestro Aquino, 74–75
Maestro de Arani, *30*
Maestro Guzman, *37*
Majolica, 168–71, 197, *276*
Mantaro River Valley, Peru, 173–77, *179, 264*
Mantles, 18, 97, 104–07, 110, 131–32, *134,* 150–52
Maps, 14–15
Mapuche Indians, 98, *103,* 158 60, 276
Marching bands, *272*
Markets / fairs, 93, 130, 133, 139 41, 143, 174, 190, 202, *206,* 208–10, *212,* 229, *231, 233*
Masks, 238–39, 241–44, 248, 252, 255–61, 263–68
Masquerades, 240; *ch'utas, 144, 268*; *Chuto, 264*; and Corpus Christi, 238; *diablos, 213, 245,* 254–58, 263, 266; history of, 18, 263–64; Mestiza Qullacha, *244*; *morenos,* 254, 259–62; *negrito, 212, 245, 265, 267,* 263; in Oruro, Bolivia, 254–62; portrayals of, 28–29, *60, 227, 245, 253*; Qhapaq Qolla, *242*; Qhapaq Negra, *243, 245. See also* Ch'unchos; Contradanzas
*Matracas* (noise makers), *259,* 261–62
Medals, *153*
Medicine men, 80, 242
Medina, Bertha, 176–77
Medina, Evaristo, 175–76
Mendívil, Hilario, *39, 208,* 225
Mendívil, Pablo Julio, *60, 225*
Mendoza, Don Filiberto, 54
Mercado, Melchor María, *16, 17, 223*
Mérida, Venezuela, 44–45, 214–15, 217–18
*Mesas,* 25, *80,* 87, 110, 196
*Mestizos / Mestizas:* 276, artists, 27–28, 31, 33, 52, 56, 222, 224, 269; and carnival, 255; ceramics for, 168; and clothing, 16–17; and costume making, 246; dance groups, 247, 265; garments of, 98; history of, 16–17; jewelry worn by, 18, 149, 157; and roof ornaments, 200; and silverwork, 180; and Virgin of Carmen, 240; workshops, 18, 24, 149, 206, 208
Metalwork, *88,* 201–02
*Milagros,* 73–79, *85,* 276
Miner's lamps, *188*
Mining, *16,* 33, 43, 52, 55, *188,* 254

Missionaries, 24, 40, 46–47, 50, 55, 60, 62, 106, 180
Moreno, Ramon Antonio, *44, 214*
*Morenos* (African slaves), 254, 259–62, *276*
Mother-of-pearl (*nacar*), 69
Mummy bundles, 24

Nativity scenes, *39, 43, 149,* 206, 208–11, *213,* 232–33
Nuestra Señora de Dolores, *38*
Nuestra Señora de la Merced, *69. See also* Virgin of Mercy
Nuestra Señora de los Amparos, *30*
Nuns, 31, 69, 71, 206

Ocaña, Diego de, *26*
Offerings for dieties: 24–25, 46, *53,* 80–86, 88–93, 191, 196, 204, 237–38, 254–55
Olmos Family Workshop, *253, 272*
Olmos, José, *212, 219*
Oruro, Bolivia, *30,* 46, *72,* 91, *99,* 120, *138,* 254–62
Osculati, Gaetano, 246
Otuzco, Peru, *76*
Our Lady of Carmen, *71. See also* Virgen de Carmen
Overskirts, 108–09, *132*

Pachamama, 25, 28, 110, *138,* 194, 237, *269, 277*
Paintings: of daily life, 18, *149,* 222–28, *269;* religious, 18, 27–33, 54–55, 69–70, 224, 229
Palomino, Marino, *233*
*Pasta* technique, *39, 43,* 54, 56, *208,* 229–33
Paucar, Javier Gonzáles, *269*
Paucarima, Andrés, *213*
Paucartambo, Cuzco, Peru, *152,* 240–45.
Pilgrimmages, 23–25, 36, *41,* 46–47, 68–69, 239–41
Pitchers, 191, *197, 204*
Plates, *168, 170,* 173–75
Pomasqui, Pichincha, Ecuador, *68*
Ponchos, 18, 22–23, 91, 97–103, *277*
Portable boxes, with genre scenes, 229–33
Post-independence era, 17–18, 31, 70, 80, *149,* 263
Potosí, Bolivia: and carnival, 254; ceramics, *197;* and clothing, *103, 129, 132,* 134–35, *139;* and crucifixes, *66;* festivals in, 237, 254; and portable altars, 46, 52–55; and *relicarios,* 31, *69;* and scapulars / badges, 71–72; silverwork, 180; textiles, *123;* workshops in, 27, *31,* 33
Prado, Antonio, *201*
Prehispanic culture / traditions, 13, 23–24, 27, 62, 93, 238, 263
*Priostes,* 162, 240, 246, *277*
Processions: for Corpus Christi, 246–47, 250–52; for feast days, 71; for Oruro carnival, 254–56, 259; and portable shrines, 46; for Virgin of Carmen in Paucartambo, 240–45
Pucará, Puno, Peru, 168–70, *202*
Pujilí, Cotopaxi, Ecuador, *45, 212, 219, 247,* 249–50, *253,* 271–72
Puno region, Peru: and bull fighting scenes, *271,* and ceramics, 168–70, *197;* and clothing, *105,* 126–27, *129;* and *conopas, 87, 89;* dolls, 218–19; and jewelry, 150; and portable altars, 47–49; and roof ornaments, 201–02; and silverwork, 180; and textiles, *115. See also* Taquile Island

Qolla and Qollahuaya people, *16,* 80, *277*
Qoyllur Rit'i, Señor de, 239–43
Quechua people, 13, 18, 104, 106, 108, 111, 114–15, 118, 134, *277*
*Queros,* 191–92, 241, *277*
Quinua, Ayacucho, Peru, *198,* 203–04, *207, 221.*
Quispe, Lidelia Callañaupa, *107*
Quito, Ecuador, 27, 33–35, *85, 165, 213,* 227, 237, 246

Ramos, Bernabe Garcia, *132*
Rangel, Angel Jesús, *45*
Rangel, Mariano, *45*
Rangel, Patrocino, *44*
*Relicarios, 31,* 69–70, *249, 251, 277*
Religious: freedom, 24–25, 46, 86, 263; practices, 23–24, 46, 58, 60, 238; practitioners, 23, 25, 86, 90–91, 110, 191, 196; prints, *71,* 189
*Repoussé* technique, 73, *78,* 150–51, *182*
Republican era, 25, 28, 30, 46, 173, 238
*Retablos,* 230–33, *277*
Ritual objects. *See* specific types
Rituals, 16–18, 24–25, 90–91, 191–97, 229, 237–38, 246–47
Rococo style, *34*
Rojas, Jesús Urbano, 63–65, 231–32
Rojas, Julio Urbano, *218,* 231
Rojas, Santiago, 208, *245*
Roof ornaments, 198–205

Sacred Heart, *71, 73, 189*
Salasaca, Tunguarahua, Ecuador, *155,* 246–47, *252*
Salcedo, Cotopaxi, Ecuador, 248, *268*
San Antonio, *34, 42, 44, 53, 55, 57. See also* St. Anthony
San Benito, *44, 217*
San Francisco Cathedral, Sucre, 25–26, 31, 54
San Francisco Church, Cuzco, *62*
San Jacinto, *34*
San José, *70*
San Juan Bautista, *43, 53, 217, 266*
San Juan de Dios, *38*
San Lucas, *35*
San Marco. *See* St. Mark
San Martín de Porras, *43, 71*
San Martín, José de, 98, 144
San Pedro, 266
San Ramon, *61*
San Ysidro, 27, *35, 39, 44,* 60–61
Sanabria, Catalina, *174*
Sánchez, Mamerto, *198, 203–04, 207*
Sandoval, Don Benigno, 54
Sanmarco shrines, 58–59, 229–30, 232
Santa Catalina Convent, Cuzco, Peru, *71*
Santa Inez, 27, *85*
Santa María de Guadalupe, 26. *See also* Virgen de Guadalupe
Santa Rosa de Lima, *21, 43, 71*
Santa Teresa, 70
*Santeros, 35, 61*
Santiago (St. James), 27, *32, 41,* 46, 51–52, 55–56, *61, 70, 72*
*Santos,* 24, 46, *53, 278*
Sapallanga, Junín, Peru, festival, 144
Saquisilí, Cotopaxi, Ecudaor, *67, 130, 251, 266*
Saraguro, Loja, Ecuador, *130, 155, 157, 187,*
Sarhua, Ayacucho, Peru, *163, 205, 226*
Scapulars, 71
Sculpture, of daily life: 18, *149,* 206–13; of festival figures, 269–72
Sculpture, Catholic religious: 24; of European influence, 33, 40; of gesso, 52–53, 56; of maguey, 38–41, *43;* miniature, *85;* in *pasta,* 54, 56; in plaster, *45;* of popular, folk style, 33, *35, 40, 44,* 50, *53;* and prehispanic methods, 33, 38–39; in relief, 47; in stone, *42;* in wood, 34–38, 44. *See also* Altars, portable
Sequil, Sixto, *174*
Shawls, 131–33, *157,* 209–10, *222*
Shrines, 23–24, 27, 46, 189, 229–30, 239–40. *See also* Altars, portable; *Cajas de imaginero;* Sanmarco shrines